The Limits of Law Enforcement

Hans Zeisel

The Limits of Law Enforcement

With a Foreword by
Edward H. Levi

The University of Chicago Press
Chicago and London

Hans Zeisel is professor emeritus at the University of Chicago Law School. He is the author of *Say It with Figures,* and coauthor of *Marienthal: A Sociological Study of Unemployment, Delay in the Court,* and *The American Jury,* which is published by the University of Chicago Press.

The University of Chicago Press, Chicago 60637
The University of Chicago Press, Ltd., London

Printed in the United States of America
89 88 87 86 85 84 83 82   5 4 3 2 1

Portions of Chapters 2 and 3 were originally published in the American Bar Foundation *Research Journal,* no. 2 (Spring 1981); portions of Chapter 5 were originally published in the ABF *Research Journal,* no. 4 (Fall 1979). Reprinted here with permission.

Library of Congress Cataloging in Publication Data

Zeisel, Hans.
The limits of law enforcement.

Includes index.
1. Criminal Justice, Administration of—New York (N.Y.)
I. Title.
KFX2093.Z44 1982   345.747′105   82-8644
ISBN 0-226-97901-6   347.471055   AACR2

For
Evan and Kristen
the future

Contents

List of Figures

Foreword

Reduction in serious crime, through improvements in criminal law enforcement, consistent with security and fairness, is an important, intriguing, and elusive goal. The importance for the United States is emphasized by the destructive effects of the fear of violent crime on American cities, highlighted by the striking difference in their homicide rates and that of many comparable foreign cities. The quest is intriguing because of the assumption that better law enforcement practices by the police, proscecutors, or the courts could dramatically reduce the amount of crime, particularly, when, as at present, out of any number of serious crimes committed, so few in comparison result through the criminal law process in any formal punishment. Witness to the elusiveness of the goal is one of Professor Zeisel's conclusions in his model essay, namely, "[T]he truth is that law enforcement, important and essential as it is, cannot by itself significantly reduce crime."

Professor Zeisel is a leader in an important contemporary movement to bring to the study of the institutions of the legal system an approach which combines, in a way suitable to the subject, modern techniques of measurement with qualitative insights; that is to say, measured factual relationships combined with disciplined intuition. *The American Jury,* which Professor Zeisel authored with Professor Harry Kalven, Jr., in 1964, was, as it is acknowledged to be, a brilliant demonstration of the method and a major contribution to our knowledge of the jury. *The*

Limits of Law Enforcement is a similar incisive demonstration of the method, and a major contribution to our knowledge of the contours of what Professor Zeisel aptly calls the "almost invisible part of the law enforcement process." Through the study of two different kinds of data on the disposition of felony cases in New York City, the essay searches out the key relationships which result in and characterize the disposition of such criminal cases without a trial. The essay carefully separates the "reflective argument" of the author from the data which are presented. The study reveals some steps which could be taken which would likely decrease somewhat the disparity between the number of arrests and the number of offenders punished, and at least one significant way in which different sentencing practices might reduce the actual crime rate. The study also reveals ways in which justice as fairness of these dispositions would be improved.

The essay emphasizes the limits of law enforcement. This probably is the touchstone to wisdom in this troubled area. It would be a most unnatural relationship between law and a democratic society if it were not so. The study should help clear the way for other investigations which with similar methods will go beyond our present knowledge of where the causes of crime thrive to a better understanding of what these causes are. If progress is made on this line, the directions and indeed the limits of law enforcement may change.

This is an important, significant, and welcome essay.

Edward H. Levi

Introduction

Origin and History

In 1964 *The American Jury* appeared. It has since become the standard work on that institution which forms the final stage in the law enforcement process.[1] Only a small fraction of all felony prosecutions, however, ever reach the trial stage, normally not more than 10 percent. The far greater number end long before, in a chain of decisions about which we know little.

The two spheres of disposition, with trial and without, are very different. In the trial sphere, the process is governed by strict rules that invest the defendant with the presumption of innocence until such time as jury or judge convict. In the other, earlier sphere, discretion reigns supreme, and the presumption of innocence has little force. Indeed, the defendant is expected to be guilty and eventually to plead so.[2] This almost invisible part of the law enforcement process, which disposes of the vast majority of cases, is the subject of this book. *The Limits of Law Enforcement* is thus a companion volume to *The American Jury*. It illuminates the twilight zone in which criminal cases are disposed of without trial.

The data for this book come from New York City. New York has always been suspected of being different from other American cities, but its law enforcement system, it turns out, is not different. Thus, this study allows us to

1. Harry Kalven, Jr., and Hans Zeisel, *The American Jury* (Boston: Little, Brown & Co. 1964). In 1971 the University of Chicago Press published a paperback edition with a new foreword.

2. See Herbert L. Packer, *The Limits of the Criminal Sanction* (Stanford, Calif.: Stanford University Press, 1968), chap. 8.

learn something about our law enforcement process in general. And by looking at the context in which law enforcement operates, the study allows us also to see how well or how poorly it works.

In its own terms, law enforcement, although flawed in many respects, works reasonably well. The public firmly believes that the control of lawbreaking is the responsibility of law enforcement. And so it is. But its power to control crime is unexpectedly small; law enforcement is unable to reduce significantly our high rate of crime.

This book is addressed above all to the concerned citizen and to those engaged in law enforcement and crime control. While I hope that my academic colleagues too will find the book interesting, I trust they will forgive me for having bypassed even the more elementary forms of mathematical analysis. With few exceptions, I have avoided even statistical tables because tables make difficult reading. In their place are sixty-three figures which convey the statistical evidence without pain and perhaps even with pleasure.

The structure of the book requires a word of explanation. Chapters 2 through 5 report the data and the primary findings. I have kept these chapters deliberately lean, free from critical comment. Comments, reflections, and evaluations, usually the conclusion of a book, form Chapter 1; they precede the detailed data and illuminate their relevance. This first chapter gives an overview of the main findings and discusses their implications for both law enforcement and crime control.

Chapter 2 reports the data around the starting point of the disposition process: the structure of crime in New York City and the demographic profiles of the persons arrested for these crimes.

Chapter 3 reports the main dimensions of the disposition process: the rates at which arrests result in prosecutions and the way these prosecutions are channeled into bargained guilty pleas and trials. Five sections discuss the mechanisms which guide these dispositions.

Chapter 4 presents close-ups of some of the major crime categories and their individual disposition patterns.

Chapter 5 deals with special problem areas in the law enforcement system, primarily the activities of the police and the operation of the bail system.

The Afterword shows that the court disposition pattern as I found it in 1973, despite numerous changes of law and procedure enacted in the intervening years, has not substantially changed. Hence our basic conclusions remain intact.

The separation of reflective argument and data grew out of a desire to keep the description of how the world is apart from what we think it ought to be. The separation has the advantage of allowing the critical reader to appreciate the value of the findings even if he or she disagrees with my reflections. That option should remain open since I have arrived at the disturbing conclusion that law enforcement by itself is relatively powerless to control crime.

The study was conceived in the spring of 1972 after New York's police commissioner, Patrick V. Murphy, in an address before the bar of the City of New York, had taken the criminal courts to task.[3] While acknowledging that crime is a complex social problem and that many institutions share in the failure to solve it, he asked the courts to accept "the giant share of the blame for the criminal rise in crime." The courts, he said, overly concerned with processing a heavy caseload, are neglecting to punish the guilty offenders.

The charges themselves were not new; it was the accompanying statistics that gave them special interest. The Police Department had begun to collect disposition data for selected major crimes. It had sampled, for instance, 156 arrests for criminal possession of handguns, 136 of which involved felony charges. Not one of these 136 defendants was convicted of the original felony charge; 53 defendants were imprisoned for an average of one month each. "No wonder," the commissioner concluded, "so many people with criminal intent carry handguns in New York City."

3. Patrick V. Murphy, *The Police, the Lawyers, and the Courts* (Record of the Association of the Bar of the City of New York, 1972), 27:23.

The commissioner's speech attracted considerable attention, but there was no agreement about his conclusions. It occurred to me that a study of the felony disposition process in New York City could shed light on the general problems he had raised. Herbert Sturz, then the director of the Vera Institute of Justice,[4] with which I was then associated, liked the idea and secured funds for such a study from the Division of Criminal Justice Services of New York State, the funding branch of the Law Enforcement and Assistance Administration of the United States Department of Justice. Then we set to work.[5]

The endeavor builds on a history of prior efforts. More than a half century ago, during an earlier period of alarming crime rates, Roscoe Pound and Felix Frankfurter published the first disposition data—they called them "mortality statistics"—in their pioneering study, *Criminal Justice in Cleveland*.[6] Later, the Wickersham National Commission on Law Observance and Enforcement, of which Pound was a member, extended these searching investigations to other cities. Its fourteen published volumes are a neglected treasure chest of criminological research.[7]

Further insights into the discretionary processes were afforded by the monumental five-volume study of the American Bar Foundation under the directorship of Frank

4. Now chairman of the Planning Commission of the City of New York.

5. Much later, after all the data were collected and I had begun to write the report, differences of opinion developed between me and Vera concerning the scope of the study. These differences were most amicably settled by the agreement that Vera would first publish its report and later I would publish mine. Vera's report was published in 1977 as a Vera Institute of Justice monograph: *Felony Arrests: Their Prosecution and Disposition in New York City's Courts*.

6. Roscoe Pound and Felix Frankfurter, *Criminal Justice in Cleveland* (Cleveland: Cleveland Foundation, 1922).

7. The Wickersham Commission (National Commission on Law Observance and Enforcement) published a series of reports that set new standards for the analysis of law enforcement. Published first by the U.S. Government Printing Office in 1931, the reports were republished in 1968 by Patterson Smith in Montclair, N.J.

J. Remington.[8] That study and Remington's later essays provided a clear view of the many types of decisions which compose the phases of the law enforcement process. Each phase, however, was presented separately; their interconnection and the magnitudes of their relative importance remained unexplored. This book attempts to make this last step by presenting the law enforcement in its systematic entirety, combining qualitative insights with measurements at each stage of the disposition process.[9]

The Study Design

The first goal of the investigation was to generate a broad body of disposition data, similar to those developed by the police commissioner but covering all felony arrests. Moreover, by collecting data on each defendant, on his bail status, and on the stage at which his case was disposed of, we hoped to learn more about the important qualitative details that affect the disposition process.

8. Frank J. Remington, ed., *Survey of the Administration of Criminal Justice in the United States,* 5 vols. (Boston: Little, Brown & Co., 1965–69): Wayne R. LaFave, *Arrest: The Decision to Take a Suspect into Custody,* vol. 1 (1965); Donald W. Newman, *Conviction: The Determination of Guilt or Innocence without Trial,* vol. 2 (1966); Lawrence P. Tiffany, Donald M. McIntyre, and Daniel Rotenberg, *Detection of Crime: Stopping and Questioning; Search and Seizure; Encouragement and Entrapment,* vol. 3 (1967); Frank W. Miller, *Prosecution: The Decision to Charge a Suspect with a Crime,* vol. 4 (1969); and Robert O. Dawson, *Sentencing: The Decision as to Type, Length, and Conditions of Sentence,* vol. 5 (1969).

9. The design of this study aimed at removing a dichotomy that continues to plague much of social science research. In 1932 I wrote, "American sociography has not achieved a synthesis between statistics and full description of concrete observations. In works of impressive conceptualization . . . statistics is completely missing; . . . statistical surveys are often of a regrettable routine nature. The task of integration lies still ahead" ("Toward a History of Sociography," Afterword to M. Jahoda, P. F. Lazarsfeld, and H. Zeisel, *Marienthal: The Sociography of an Unemployed Community* [Chicago: Aldine-Atherton, 1971], p. 125; originally published in Leipzig, 1933).

The second goal was to illuminate these data. Disposition data by themselves do not explain the process. We not only wanted to see the results of the process, we also wanted to understand them. Traditionally, the police will blame prosecutors and courts for the gross disparities between arrest charge and final disposition, while prosecutors and courts will blame the police for the quality of the arrests and the accompanying evidence. To find out what factors shape the steps that lead to the final disposition, it was necessary to interview the persons who made the decisions.

Accordingly, this study is based on two sets of data, as shown in figure 1. The first is a probability sample of 1888 (the aim was 2000)[10] felony arrests representing the roughly 102,000 felony arrests made in 1971 by the police in four of New York City's five boroughs—New York County (Manhattan), the Bronx, Brooklyn, and Queens. Richmond County (Staten Island), the small, fifth borough, was not sampled since it generates only 2 percent of the city's felony arrests and would have increased the cost of the study out of proportion.

The cases were randomly selected from the arrest register, a monthly compilation of arrests maintained by the Police Department. The development of the selected cases was traced from arrest to disposition.[11] Our sources were the court papers, the Judicial Conference 500-forms which report disposition, and the criminal history record from the New York State Identification and Intelligence System (NYSIIS).[12]

10. The difference was due to our inability to locate some of the files.

11. Each arrest represents one defendant's case, which may consist of multiple complaints. If, for instance, a defendant was initially charged with robbery and subsequently drugs were found on his person, police would record the arrests as separate events, but we treated them as one case.

12. The Judicial Conference is the state agency charged with the administration of the judiciary. The 500-form is filled out by court clerks and transmitted to NYSIIS, now the Division of Criminal Justice Services, which is responsible for collecting criminal history data for the courts and other law enforcement agencies.

Fig. 1
The Two Samples of This Study

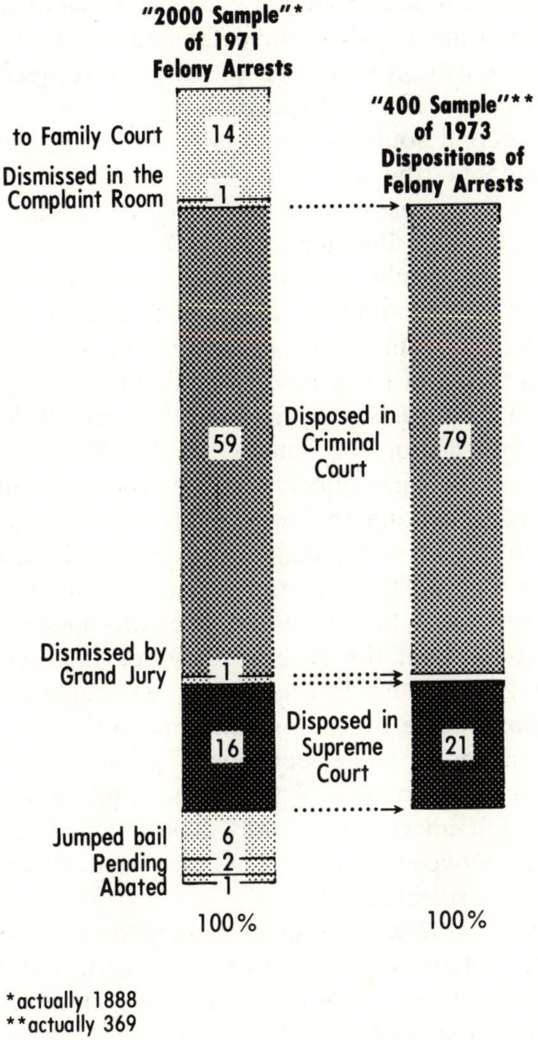

Information was also collected on the defendant's age, ethnic background, sex, criminal history, bail status, type of counsel, the time elapsed between arrest and disposition, the type of crime for which the defendant was arrested, the eventual disposition of the case, and, where needed, the reasons for the lack of a disposition.

The second source of data is a probability sample of 369 defendants (the aim was 400), arraigned on felony charges, whose cases were disposed of during the ten-month period from January through October 1973.[13] These cases were randomly selected from court calendars after disposition in the Criminal and Supreme Courts, about 100 from each of the four major counties.[14] The arrest dates for these cases ranged from 1966 through 1973, but the great majority of the arrests were made in 1972 and 1973.

The information we sought for the 400-case sample went beyond the data collected for the 2000-case sample. In addition to collecting the basic disposition data, we attempted to interview the major participants in the disposition of each case—the arresting officer, the defense counsel, the prosecutor, and the judge. They provided us with as many details about the case as they remembered or for which they had notes. In this fashion we learned not only the decisions made by each participant in the process but also the reasons for those decisions. The "400 sample" thus provides a close-up view of the decision process, the outlines of which emerged from the "2000 sample." There are differences between the groups of cases from which the two samples were selected.

As figure 1 shows, not all felony arrests are represented in the 400 sample, only those disposed of in the criminal court system, that is, the Criminal Court or the Supreme Court. Only the 2000 sample contains the felony arrests

13. All but three cases stem from felony arrests; in these three cases an original misdemeanor arrest was later elevated to a felony charge.

14. An additional forty or so cases were selected from the Central Narcotics Court, but they are not used in the present study since the narcotics dispositions were covered by a special study (see n. 53, Chap. 1).

routed out of the system into the Family Court, arrests disposed of in the Complaint Room, cases dismissed by the grand jury, and arrests not disposed of because the defendant jumped bail or died. Also, there is a time lag between the two samples: the cases represented by the 2000 sample were disposed of for the most part in 1971 and 1972, the 400 sample represented dispositions made in 1973. The time lag is of importance because a new judicial administration came into office.[15]

The data collection extended over a period of one-and-a-half years and encountered many obstacles. The main difficulty was that criminal justice records are kept in many different places. Each court and the district attorney's office in each county has its own record-keeping system. The only centralized data sources, apart from the police arrest register, were the Office of Court Administration in New York City and NYSIIS in Albany.

Also freshness of recollection was often a problem. Interviewing did not begin until a case was disposed of; the cases, it will be recalled, were sampled from the calendar of disposed cases. We did not interview earlier because such interviewing could have affected the disposition of the cases. Although interviewing began within a few days of disposition, not all participants could easily recollect the case, which may have been one of fifty handled that day. When a participant's memory was insufficient, he was asked to consult his file notes. In the few cases where these too were unavailable, we asked how he would ordinarily handle this type of case. The then prevailing practice of assigning prosecutors to courtrooms rather than to cases contributed to the difficulties of tracing the details of the disposition process.

Another interviewing problem was bias. It is in the nature of the adversary system that each participant sees

15. A new judicial administration was established when Judge David Ross became the administrative judge for the criminal court of the City of New York. Priority was given to procedures aimed at clearing up the backlog, making court calendars current, and reducing the number of defendants in jail. Also, sentencing practices may have changed.

the disposition process from a different perspective and tries to justify it. Police officers tend to emphasize the strength of the evidence, prosecutors are inclined to blame reductions or dismissals on shortcomings of the evidence. Defense counsel, depending on whether his client received a good deal from the prosecutor or accepted a bad one, will emphasize either the shakiness of the evidence or the necessity of pleading guilty in the face of alleged irrationality of juries and near impossibility of obtaining acquittal. Judges will explain lenient dispositions and sentences by pointing to the minor nature of the crime or the defendant's rehabilitation potential rather than to pressure from an inordinately large case load. In some instances, interviewees were reluctant to answer, partly out of bureaucratic reticence, partly out of disdain for researchers whom they equated with reporters. Outright refusals, however, were rare.

Finally, there are general methodological limits to the usefulness of such interviewing. Reason analysis, as the approach is called, asks the decision maker why he acted the way he did, for his views of the facts, his values, the outside influences to which he was subject, and the way these factors eventually combined. The response is inevitably shaped by psychological factors which the interviewee cannot articulate because he is unaware of them.[16] Still, in most cases we were able to reconstruct the history of the disposition and thereby bring to life the dry statistical categories. Thus, in spite of these many obstacles, some overcome and some not, the anatomy of the law enforcement process emerged with sufficient clarity, sufficient at least for this first effort to present it comprehensively.

16. Cf. chaps. 10 and 11 on reason analysis in Hans Zeisel, *Say It with Figures,* 5th ed. (New York: Harper & Row, 1967).

One / Summary and Reflections

The Dimensions of the Problem

Characteristically, law enforcement begins to function when it has failed. The process begins, as a rule, after a crime has been reported to the police.

Compared with other large cities in the United States, the number of crimes reported to the New York City police, adjusted for the size of its population, is not extraordinary. Its rate of violent crimes is lower than that of Miami, Atlanta, and Baltimore. As to the rate of nonviolent property crimes, New York ranks about seventh among the larger cities. Otherwise, New York has a greater volume of crime only because it is America's largest city.[1]

Compared with cities on other continents, however, the rate of violent crime in New York and other American cities is high. Figure 2 shows the number of homicides and robberies for New York, London, and Tokyo, cities of comparable size. The contrast is staggering.

Whenever we are reminded of our high crime rate by some new atrocity, our thoughts instinctively turn to the law and its enforcement agencies in the expectation that they can do something to curb the outrage. The truth is that law enforcement, important and essential as it is, cannot by itself significantly reduce crime. If we are serious in our concern over crime, we must look elsewhere for relief. This

1. See fig. 21, Chap. 2.

Fig. 2
Number of Homicides and Robberies in London, Tokyo, and New York City

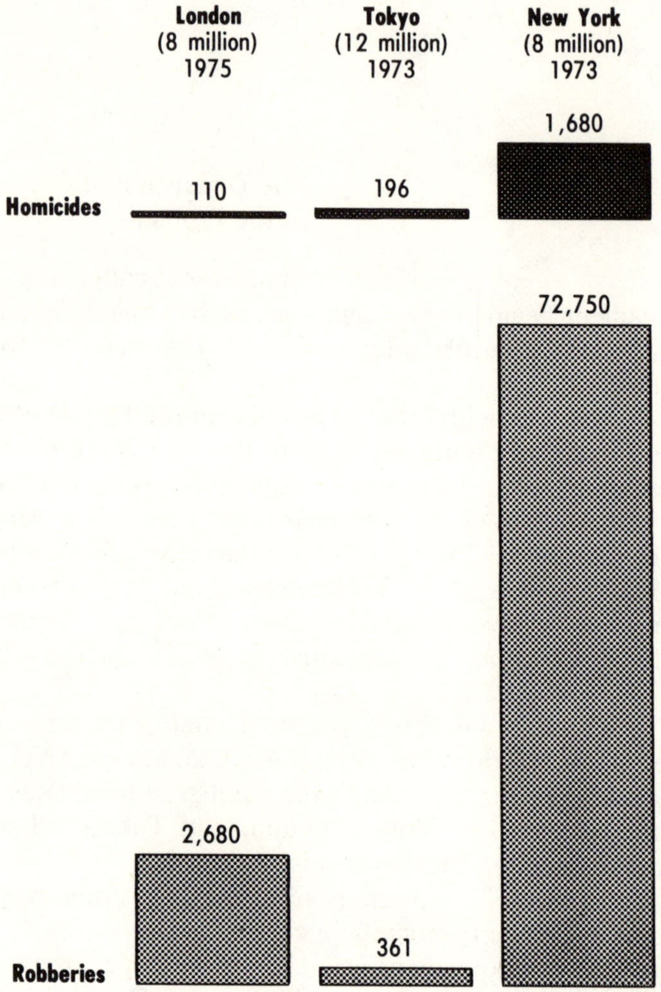

Sources: 1975 Annual Abstract of Greater London Statistics, 1977; Japan Statistical Yearbook, 1977; FBI, Uniform Crime Report, 1976.

conclusion will become clear as we explore the law enforcement process in some detail.

A good point to start from is the overview of the basic dimensions of the enforcement process in New York City provided in figure 3. Of every 1000 committed "index felonies"[2]—homicide, rape, aggravated assault, robbery, burglary, auto theft, and other grand larceny—on the average only 540 are reported to the police, 65 result in an arrest, 36 end in a conviction, 17 obtain a custody sentence, and 3 result in a prison sentence of over one year. We began the countdown with 1000 committed index felonies.

In one respect these figures exaggerate the apparent inefficiency of the enforcement process. The first two columns refer to *events,* the crimes committed and reported; the remaining four columns refer to *persons,* the suspected and accused offenders. Some arrested offenders will have committed more than one crime, and if the police are able to identify them, this fact will raise the so-called clearance rate, the proportion of crimes for which the offender is eventually arrested, or at least identified. The numbers in figure 3, however, are not affected by such changes in the clearance rates.

2. So-called because their partial or total sum is suggested as an index of the level of crime for any given time period for any part, or the total, of the United States. The categories in fig. 3 differ slightly from the FBI definition of Index Crimes because the New York State definition of "felony" is somewhat, but not significantly, narrower. Critics have wondered why so-called white-collar crimes are not part of the index crimes. To the extent to which they are fraud, one form of what the law calls larceny, they are included. Other white-collar crimes, although they may involve great sums, are excluded, not because they are unimportant but because it is difficult to determine their frequency with any degree of reliability; this was also the reason for excluding arson from the Index Crimes. Against expert advice, the Congress has now ordered that arson be included in the count of the FBI's Uniform Crime Reports.

For a description of the index crime categories, see U.S. Department of Justice, Federal Bureau of Investigation, *Uniform Crime Reports for the United States, 1977* (Washington, D.C.: Government Printing Office, 1978), pp. 1–5, 304–5; or, more briefly, U.S. Department of Justice, Law Enforcement Assistance Administration, National Criminal Justice Information and Statistics Service, *Sourcebook of Criminal Justice Statistics, 1978* (Washington, D.C.: Government Printing Office, 1979), pp. 750–53.

Fig. 3
Attrition of Law Enforcement:
1,000 Committed Index Felonies

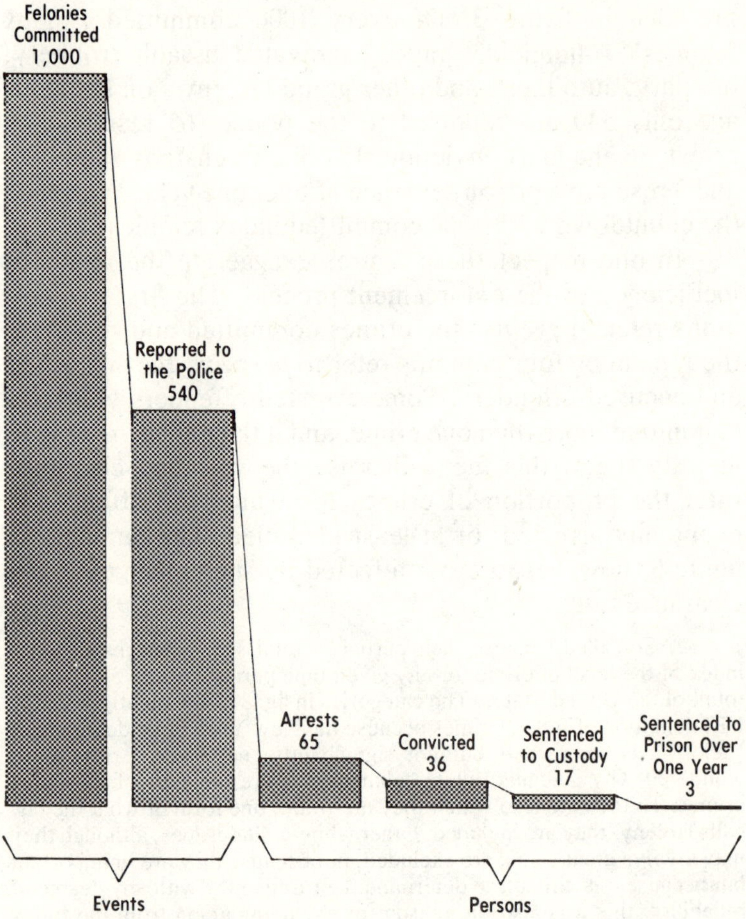

Sources: 2000 Sample and LEAA Victimization Survey

These are the stark dimensions of the law enforcement process. As it turns out, with one exception, these dimensions are fairly rigid and cannot be changed easily. The exception is the level of sentencing; but a change there, as we shall see, promises at best only moderate leverage toward reducing crime.

Figure 4 is a close-up of the last four bars of figure 3, the disposition as to guilt and sentence in the criminal court system of New York City. Dismissals of the case form 44 percent of all dispositions; 54 percent of the defendants pleaded guilty. Only 2 percent of all cases were disposed of through trial. The (54 + 1 =) 55 percent of the defendants who were convicted obtained the sentences shown in the second bar of figure 4. Roughly half of them, 28 percent, obtained what in court parlance is called a "walk," a fine, a discharge under a condition (e.g., not to visit a certain place), or probation. The other 27 percent of the defendants obtained custody sentences.

The third bar of figure 4 shows the length of the custodial sentences: 22 percent, the overwhelming majority of these defendants, received jail sentences up to one year; 5 percent of all defendants arrested for a felony end up with a prison sentence of more than a year.

The High Rate of Dismissals

Of all the numbers in the disposition statistics, the one most puzzling at first glance is the high proportion of arrested defendants whose case is dismissed.

Some such loss should be expected. But by dismissing almost half of all defendants who were arrested on a felony charge, the law enforcement system of New York City appears to be woefully inefficient. One's first impulse is to remark, "Well, that is New York, the city that has never been typical of the country as a whole."

It thus comes as something of a surprise to find that the New York pattern is by no means unique but is in fact

Fig. 4
Disposition of Felony Arrests in the Criminal Court System

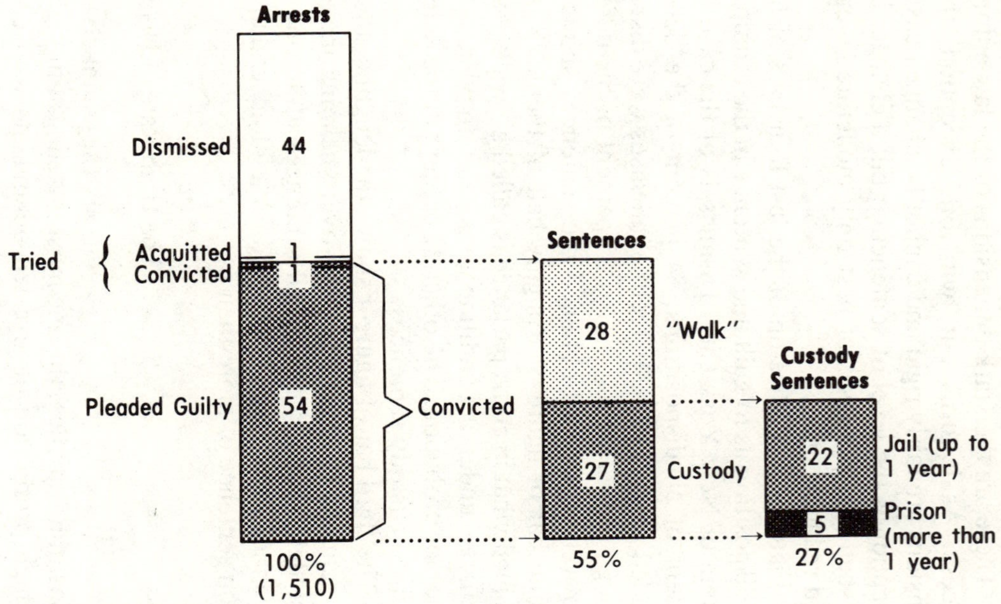

Source: 2000 Sample

typical, as shown by figure 5 where New York City is compared with other American jurisdictions. The nonconviction rate after felony arrest for the State of California was 60 percent; for Portland, Oregon, 40 percent; in Washington, D.C., it was 51 percent, and in New Orleans 63 percent.[3]

It turns out, moreover, that the high nonconviction rate is not a recent development. In 1928, Felix Frankfurter and Roscoe Pound recorded disposition figures for felony arrests in Cleveland, and in 1936 the Wickersham Commission developed such figures for New York City. These figures, presented in figure 6, do not look too different.

The consistency of these high nonconviction rates in different places and at different times tempts one to expand the charge of inefficiency to the entire American law enforcement system. Prosecutors are wont to blame it on the elaborate network of exclusionary rules and other procedural safeguards of the defendant's rights. It is, therefore, with considerable interest that one turns to the disposition statistics of countries whose criminal procedures differ radically from ours.

Figure 7 compares the nonconviction rates for the crime of robbery in New York City with the corresponding rates in Austria and Germany.[4] The criminal procedures in these two countries differ in many respects from ours. There, the prosecutor is a member of a special branch of the civil service which, as a rule, he never leaves; in his preparation of a case, if he considers it desirable, he can command additional help from the police; in Austria, the evidence for serious crimes is sifted by an investigating magistrate. At trial, the prosecutor does not face formal rules of

3. These data represent all the reliable data on nonconviction rates I could find at the time; they were not selected from a larger group of cities.

4. The selection of the two European countries is due to the simple access I had to these data. In Germany, I am indebted to Dr. Doerman of the Bundeskriminalamt, in Austria to Dr. Sepp Rieder of the Ministry of Justice. The comparison is made for the crime of robbery because this happened to be the crime for which the Austrian Ministry of Justice had collected disposition data.

Fig. 5
Conviction Rates after Felony Arrests:
New York Compared to Other Jurisdictions

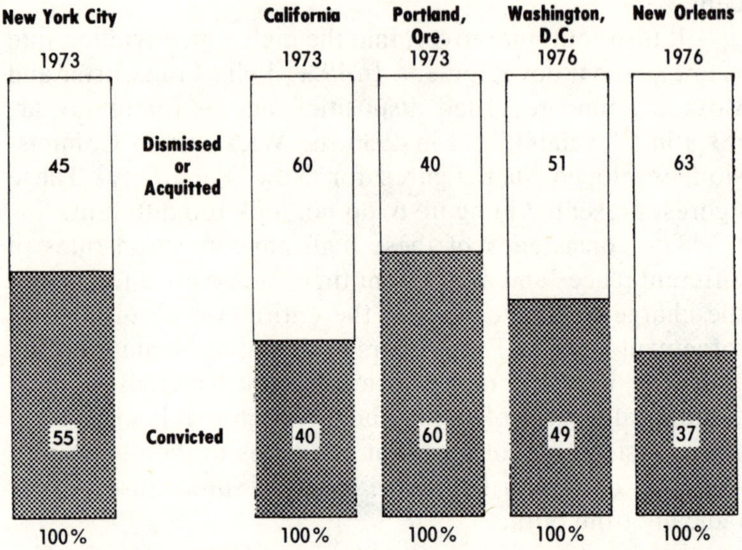

Sources: NYC, 2000 Sample
Calif, Peter W. Greenwood with Marvin Lavin, The Disposition of Felony Arrests: Prosecution and Sentencing Policies in California and Their Effects on Crime. RAND Publ. WN-10061-1-DOJ-1977 (mimeogr.), p. 14 (California).
Washington, New Orleans, Portland: PROMIS data, Institute for Law and Social Research (Washington, D.C. and New Orleans, La.).

Fig. 6
Conviction Rates over Time:
1973, 1926, 1919

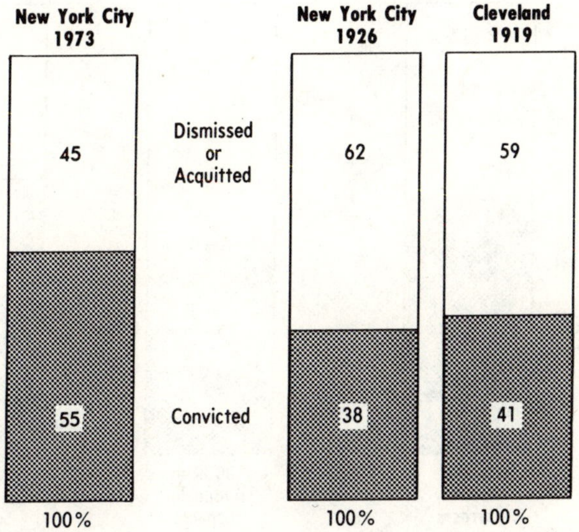

Sources: 1973, 2000 Sample.
1926, National Commission on Crime and Law Enforcement, Public Report #4 on Prosecution, A. Bettman, Criminal Justice Survey Analysis, p. 55, Gov't Prt'g. Off. 1931.
1919, F. Frankfurter and R. Pound, *Justice in Cleveland*, p. 95.

Fig. 7
Prosecution Rate for Robbery in New York
Compared to Germany and Austria

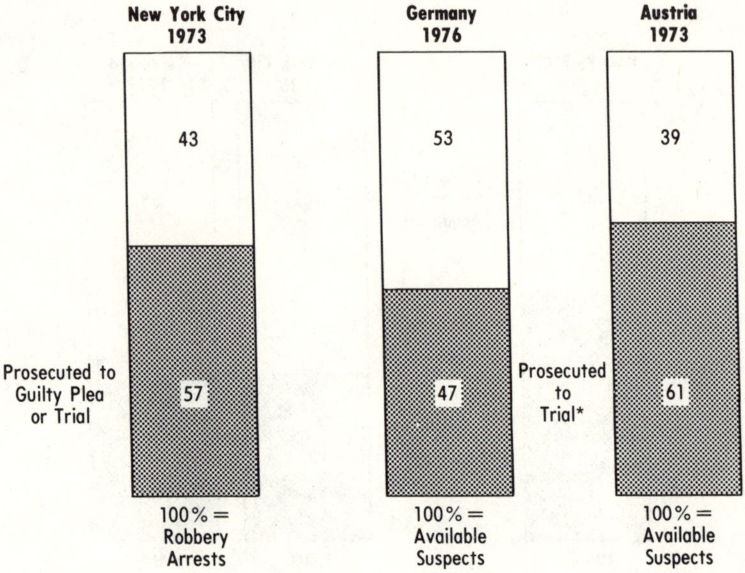

*There is no "guilty plea."

Sources: Germany, communication from the Bundeskriminalamt; Austria, Special Report (mimeographed) prepared by the Ministry of Justice; New York, 2000 sample.

evidence and hardly any exclusionary rules; there is no plea bargaining; in Germany there is no jury; and both there and in Austria no conviction can be obtained without trial.

The comparison limps in one respect: in the continental systems the arrest is not the crucial step it is in the United States; the figure that comes closest to being comparable is the number of known suspects whom the police could pick up. Despite this limitation, the data clearly indicate that the loss rates in all three legal systems are of similar magnitude.

The comparison of the inefficiency rate of New York City, first with other American cities and then with systems on the European continent, suggests that the loss between locating a suspect and convicting him are neither peculiar to New York City nor to the American criminal law enforcement system. However much the details of criminal procedure may vary from country to country, the loss between arrest and conviction appears to be the unavoidable result of the judicial safeguards built into all Western law enforcement systems, requiring probable cause for arrest and proof beyond reasonable doubt for conviction. Like the steam engine in the course of transforming heat into motion, civilized law enforcement must allow a large part of its energy to go to waste.[5]

Reducing the Dismissal Rate

The ubiquity of the high proportion of arrests that fail to end in conviction does not settle the question of whether there are ways of reducing the dismissal rate.

The chief cause of dismissals, as we shall see,[6] is lack of sufficient evidence, either from the outset or because the

5. Some scholars consider the German and Austrian criminal procedures, which are typical of Central Europe, to be superior to ours and believe that reforming our laws in their direction would make them more efficient. The numbers in fig. 7 suggest that one may easily overestimate the effect of procedural differences.

6. See section on Reasons for Dismissal in Chap. 3.

expected evidence did not become available. The first question to ask, therefore, is whether some of the evidence the prosecutor considers deficient could not have been strengthened, thus enabling him to increase the conviction rate. Prosecutors remark with some regularity that the police routine often stops short of buttressing the victim's complaint through more than one witness, through fingerprints, or other forms of corroborating evidence. The police, we are told, do not sufficiently realize that uncorroborated testimony of the complaining witness does not always suffice. The point has been made repeatedly in earlier studies and reflects the organizational separation in American law enforcement of police and prosecutor and their somewhat divergent goals. If incentives could be developed to improve their cooperation, more efficient evidence gathering might reduce the dismissal rate somewhat.[7]

The primary reason, however, for the deterioration of the evidence is the frequent loss of the principal prosecution witness, the victim of the alleged crime. Every so often, after having lodged the complaint and prompted the arrest, the victim for one reason or other withdraws from the prosecution process. Theoretically, the prosecutor can force the victim to testify, but it is difficult to win a case with a reluctant or hostile victim. Such withdrawal is particularly likely to occur when victim and offender had a close prior relationship or at least had known one another. Such cases may pose an additional dilemma: the continuation of the relationship may be more important than prosecuting the offense which disrupted it. Already the arrest-

7. E.g., D. M. McIntyre, "Impediments to Effective Police Procedure Relationships," *American Criminal Law Review* 12 (1975): 201. The complaint is echoed by Patrick Murphy, New York's former police commissioner: "Most departments fall short of providing documentary key evidence a prosecutor needs to obtain conviction" (P. V. Murphy and T. Platt, *Commissioner: A View from the Top of American Law Enforcement* [New York: Simon & Schuster, 1977], pp. 183 ff., chap. 7). See also Peter Greenwood's study, n. 13 below.

Very recently New York City police and prosecutors have begun a special joint effort to improve evidence gathering against particularly dangerous offenders.

ing officer is aware of the problem when he decides whether to make an arrest or leave it at mediating the conflict. Recently a number of cities have made efforts to bring such arrests before a mediation board. It is too early to say whether this is a promising route. The evidence goes both ways.[8]

A more perplexing version of the problem arises when the withdrawal is brought about through intervention, not always of a friendly character, by the defendant or his intermediaries.

The situation is different if the complaining witness withdraws because the burden of further cooperation exceeds his ebbing anger, or his sense of civic duty, or his tolerance of the treatment he received in court. He (I apologize here, once and for all, for using the traditional "he" instead of the correct but unbearably cumbersome "he or she") may live far from the courthouse, and his presence is required on a great many occasions along the enforcement route—when he files the complaint, at the preliminary hearing, before the grand jury, and finally at trial. While not all cases travel the whole route, some of these occasions require repeated appearances because of unforeseen adjournments and other managerial obstacles. There is room for alleviating the burden on the witness and thereby insuring that he stays with the case. A beginning has been made by the Vera Institute of Justice by developing what is now the Victim Services Agency of New York City.

The commanding role of the complaining witness derives not solely from his evidentiary position. Undertones in the district attorney's language suggest that he often considers the complaining witness the prime mover of the prosecution. This works in both directions: a persistent complaining witness may sustain the prosecutor's efforts. A disinterested complaining witness may move an overburdened

8. See for New York City, "Mediation and Arbitration as Alternatives to Prosecution in Felony Arrest Cases," Vera Institute of Justice in cooperation with N.Y.C. Victim Services Agency, April 1980 (mimeographed).

prosecutor to ask himself: If the victim does not care, why should I?—echoing ancient days when the criminal process was a private dispute. Significantly, the very term "complaining witness" has no counterpart, for instance, in Austrian or German law; in fact, there is not even a word for it.[9]

Finally, there are concomitant nonevidentiary reasons that at times contribute to the prosecutor's decision to dismiss a case. By themselves they hardly ever suffice, but when the evidence is at the balance point, the minor character of the offense or the defendant's lack of criminal record may tip the scales. First offenders and those arrested for one of the lesser felonies have a better chance of escaping.[10]

The question is whether such considerations ought to affect the decision to dismiss rather than be taken up by the sentencing judge after conviction. If we were to conclude that the prosecutor ought to consider such nonevidentiary circumstances, the second question arises: whether these considerations should remain in his unfettered discretion or be controlled at least by internal guidelines. For the time being, the New York courts have left little doubt that the prosecutor's discretion is wide.[11]

Thus, there is some leeway for more vigorous prosecution, although the costs of obtaining convictions in these cases are likely to exceed those of the average case.

The decision whether to dismiss or to pursue borderline cases is bound to be affected by the capacity limits of the system, that is, of the prosecutor's staff and the size of the court. If the system operates close to those limits as it now does, there will be pressure to abandon borderline prosecutions.

9. For an overview of the American situation, see D. J. Hall, "The Role of the Victim in the Prosecution and Disposition of a Criminal Case," *Vanderbilt Law Review* 28 (1975): 931.

10. See text at fig. 29 below.

11. See Kenneth C. Davis, *Discretionary Justice* (Baton Rouge: Louisiana State University Press, 1969), pp. 188 ff.; but see particularly James Vorenberg, "Decent Restraint of Prosecutorial Discretion," *Harvard Law Review* 94 (1981): 1521 ff.

Can We Increase the Number of Arrests?

There appears to be another possible avenue for bringing more criminals to justice: have the police arrest more of them.

Traditionally we view the police as the first line of defense against crime. And so it is in many ways. We expect them to arrest criminals promptly and thereby, by their feared omnipresence, to deter other would-be criminals. Since our crime rates are high and our arrest rates low, we wonder whether the police could not narrow the gap by arresting more offenders. The truthful answer to this question is no. Barring radical changes in the size and structure of the police force, it cannot do much better than it now does.

The police arrests, their frequency and quality, form in a real sense the foundation of all law enforcement. Unless the police can deliver a suspect, nothing can happen; and unless they can provide good evidence against the arrested suspect, not much can happen. Our data provide some insights into the limitations of both the quantity and the quality of the police arrests.

Figure 8 provides an overview of the level of arrests. The arrest rates for violent crimes is relatively high: 47 percent for homicide, rape, and assault, and 20 percent for robbery. Arrest rates for the nonviolent property crimes, burglary and larceny, are considerably lower—8 percent—because there usually is no witness to those crimes. The average arrest rate for all index crimes is 12 percent.

If one adds the nonindex crimes and computes the combined arrest rate for all reported crimes, the arrest rate rises from 12 to 20 percent. That figure however must not be taken as a measure of arrest efficiency, because the arrest rate for nonindex crimes is not only much higher (90 percent) but also different in kind. That group of crimes comprises violations of the narcotics laws, of the weapon laws, of embezzlement, fraud, arson and gambling. The arrest rate for these crimes is that high because it is as a rule only

Fig. 8
Arrest Rates by Type of Felony

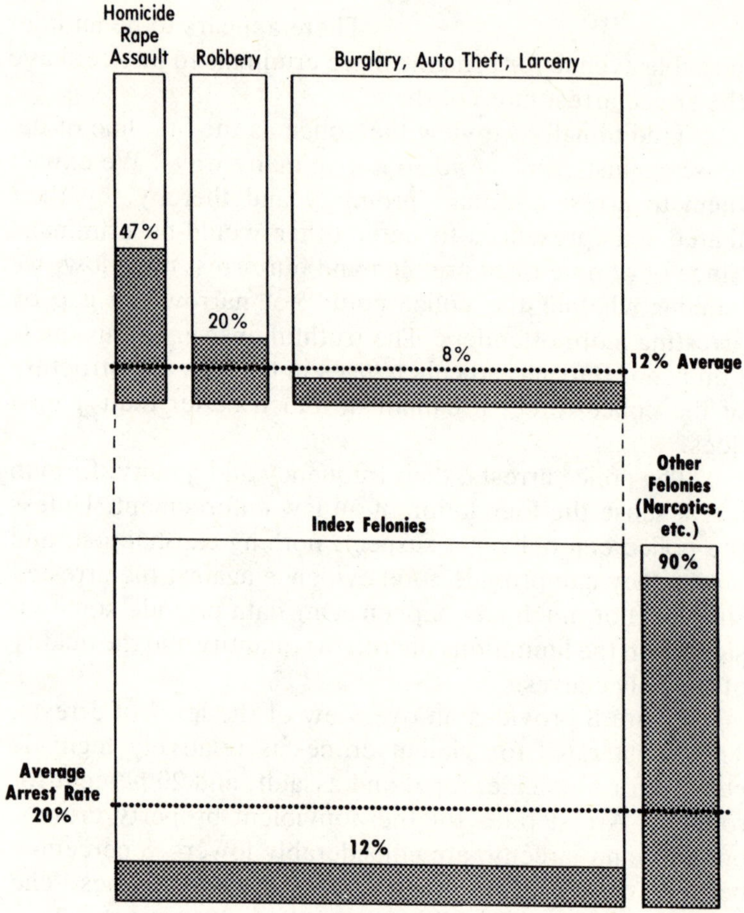

Source: N.Y. Police Statistics

the arrest that causes the crime to be entered as "known to the police." Such arrest rates, therefore, are meaningless as a measure of police efficiency.

All the arrest rates in figure 8 are, of course, based on the crimes reported to the police. Since many crimes remain unreported, the ratio of arrests to the number of *committed* crimes is considerably lower.

The question is whether these arrest rates can be significantly increased. Figure 9, which shows how felony arrests for index crimes come about, suggests why it is so difficult to increase the rate of arrests. The great majority of them are the result of calls made to the police in the hope that they will rush to the scene of the crime. If the call is made promptly and the police are fast, skilled, and lucky, they will find the offender at or near the scene of the crime. Once he has escaped from there, the offender is for all practical purposes lost, unless his identity is known.

Efforts to increase the number of arrests either by reducing the time interval between report to the police and their arrival at the scene of crime or by other means have on the whole failed to increase the arrest rates.[12] And to find an escaped, unidentified offender through detective work is a costly, largely unsuccessful, and therefore extremely rare effort. Detective work, even in the loosest sense of the term, is involved in a little more than 10 percent of all arrests. This is not a new discovery. A distinguished study by the Rand Corporation found that "investigating efforts have only a marginal effect on the rate at which arrests are made. Our primary finding was the crimes are solved by the

12. As a member of the Evaluation Advisory Group of the Police Foundation (of which Joseph L. Lewis, the foundation's former research director, was then its chairman), I had the opportunity of studying in detail well-financed efforts—and their failure. Here are the main ones, all published or to be published by the Police Foundation in Washington, D.C.: George L. Kelling, *Kansas City, Preventive Patrol Experiment* (1974); John E. Boydstun, *San Diego Community Profile* (1975); Tony Pate, *Police Response Time, Its Determinants and Effects* (1976); and Mary A. Wycoff's report on the Birmingham, Alabama, effort (in preparation). All these reports confirmed the cumulative experience that police departments are unable to increase their arrest rates substantially.

Fig. 9
How Police Arrests Come About

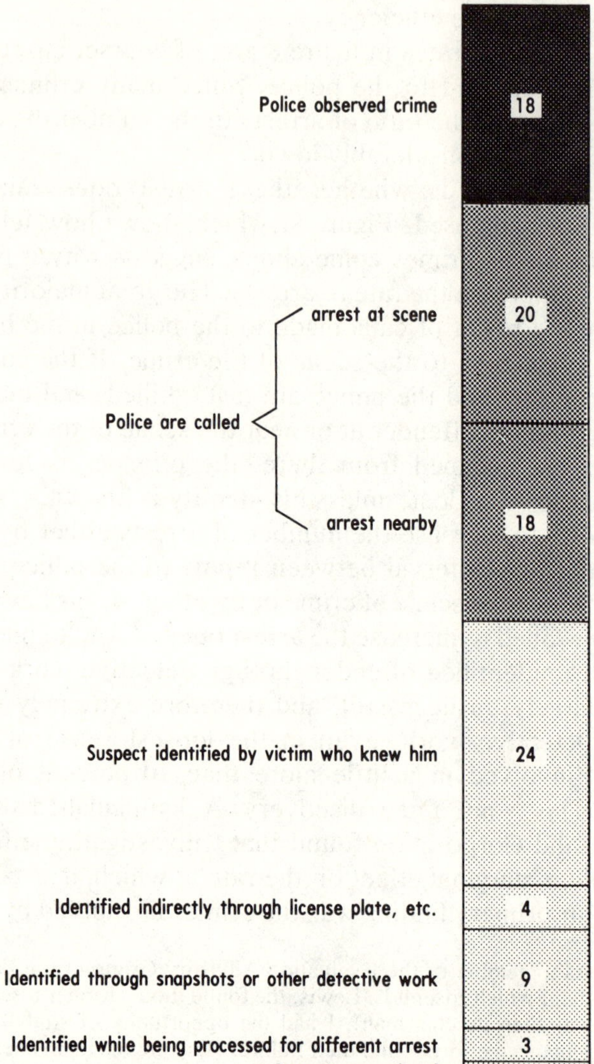

Source: 400 Sample

patrolmen who respond to the scene or the witnesses they talk to, not by the painstaking sifting of evidence or clever deduction."[13] And Patrick Murphy, the former police commissioner of New York City, one of the country's experienced police chiefs, in his memoirs has taken great pains to expose what he calls the detective mystique: "Detectives tended to make an . . . insignificant contribution to the control of crime."[14]

But are there not some ways by which the police could increase arrests? Among the index crimes there is only one that would allow a substantial increase in arrests. The police could increase the number of arrests for aggravated assault (particularly in domestic fights) where up to now they have been satisfied with calming down the assaulting parties. But these would be poor arrests; too many of the victims, after the first flush of anger, would withdraw from the prosecution, and the prosecutor, faced with the prospect of a reluctant witness, is likely to abandon the case. An increase of such arrests would increase arrest rates and add to the court's caseload but would have only a minimal effect on the number of convictions.

The question remains whether other felony arrest rates could not be increased by a reallocation of police manpower or by an increase of police. Efforts to do this have by and large failed.[15] Armchair efforts to prove by however sophisticated mathematical analyses that the police nevertheless could significantly increase arrest rates bear a heavy burden of proof.[16]

13. Peter Greenwood, *Insights from a Police Investigation Study: A Potential Adversary Role for the Police*, RAND Paper Series no. 5722, Santa Monica, Calif., 1976, p. 17.

14. P.V. Murphy, in Murphy and Platt, p. 188 (see n. 7 above).

15. See, e.g., John E. Eck, *Managing Case Assignments* (Washington, D.C.: Police Executive Research Forum, 1979). The Law Enforcement and Assistance Administration, before going out of business in 1980, made several new grants to police departments which are now making another effort in this direction. See, however, fig. 24 below.

16. Thomas Pogue, "Effect of Police Expenditures on Crime Rates: Some Evidence," *Public Finance Quarterly* (1975), pp. 14, 15; James Q. Wilson and Barbara Boland, "The Effect of Police on Crime,"

Barring police expansion on a scale that is politically and financially improbable, the arrest basis on which our law enforcement effort builds is not likely to grow by much. Of course, our refusal to expand the police force radically might be seen as confirmation of the theory of Emile Durkheim, the nineteenth-century French sociologist, that all societies have informal ways of insuring that the tolerable limit of criminal prosecutions not be overstepped.

Inducements to Plead Guilty: Charge Reduction

In New York City, close to 98 percent of all convictions after a felony arrest, as we saw in figure 4, were the result of a guilty plea. That plea, as a rule, is preceded by some bargaining with the prosecutor. A defendant who sees some chance of being acquitted at trial will need an inducement if he is to give up that chance and plead guilty. In the New York courts, as a rule, two such inducements are offered: a reduction of the charge, and a reduction of the sentence. We will look first at the less important of the two, the charge reduction.

Prosecutors in most court systems allow some modifications of the charge in exchange for a guilty plea. Often, these reductions are limited to dropping collateral charges or multiple counts of the principal charge. Routine reductions of the principal charge itself, as practiced in New York City, is widely spread but not the general rule.

Charges, of course, are reduced everywhere if the evidence requires it. Our data allowed us to separate these evidentiary charge reductions from the ones made as re-

---

Law & Society Review 12 (1978): 367. A subsequent discussion in that journal between Wilson and Boland and two authors who challenged their findings—Herbert Jacob and Michael J. Rich—confirmed the low analytical power of the Wilson-Boland analysis (15 [1981]: 109; and 16 [1982]: 222). Recently, Professor Wilson appears to have reduced his expectations as to what realistically can be expected from the police (J. Q. Wilson and G. L. Kelling, "Broken Windows," *Atlantic Monthly* [March 1982], p. 29).

ward for pleading guilty. The detailed interviews with the police officer, the assistant district attorney, the defense counsel, and the judge in each case of the 400-sample allowed us to make that distinction. Figure 10 presents its results.

In 60 percent of the cases—the wider bar on the left—there were some evidentiary problems; in 40 percent of the cases—the narrower bar on the right—the evidence did not deteriorate between arrest and disposition. In the former group the discrepancy between the charges at arrest and the charges to which the defendant pleaded guilty was on the average 2.8 crime classes. The term refers to the grading of crimes by the New York Penal Law, which groups, in descending order of gravity, all crimes into nine classes: five felony classes (A through E), two misdemeanor classes (A and B), and violations or infractions.[17] In the group without evidentiary problems the average charge reduction was 1.6 crime classes. This figure is the best estimate of the average reward for pleading guilty. The estimate may be slightly on the high side since one cannot exclude the possibility that our inquiry missed some evidentiary weaknesses known to the prosecutor.

In response to our inquiry as to the reasons for these routine reductions, two rationales were offered. The first was that these charge reductions were considered insignificant concessions which allowed defense counsel to report a nominal victory to his client. The other rationale was connected with the interesting observation that hardly any of these charge reductions were necessary to accommodate the reduced sentence offered as part of the bargain. Except for the rare conviction for a class A crime, which mandates a sentence of not less than fifteen years, New York sentences at the time of this study had practically no lower boundaries. In the vast majority of cases the court

17. The purpose of this classification is to define the severity of the crime and to delineate its sentence frame, primarily its upper limit, the maximum sentence that can be imposed upon conviction for that crime (see table 4, p. 128).

Fig. 10
Average Amount of Charge Reduction
at Guilty Plea:
Cases with and without Deteriorated Evidence

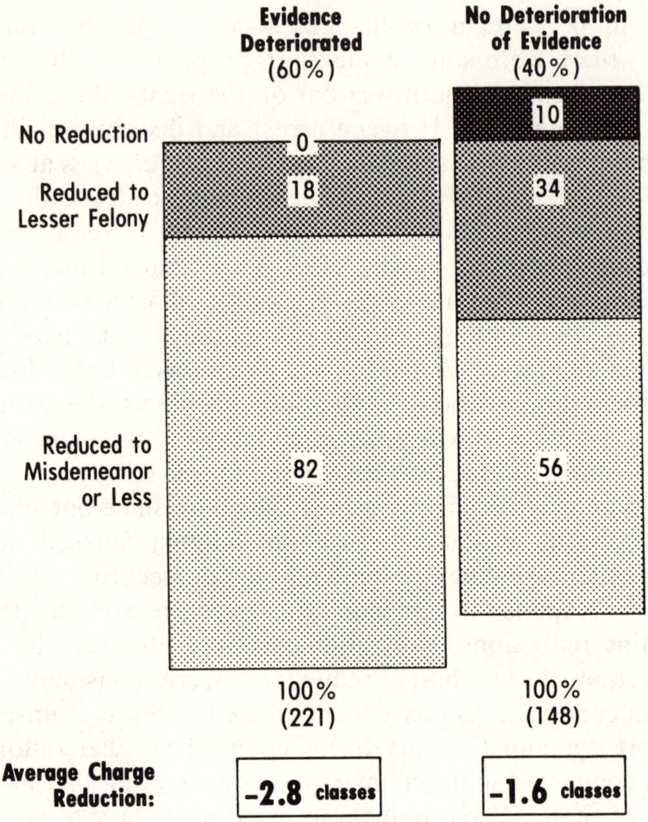

Source: 400 sample

could have imposed its sentence even if the charge had not been reduced. The charge reduction, we were told, makes it easier for the judge to go along with the negotiated sentence reduction. Sending a defendant to jail for a few months for a crime punishable with a prison sentence of up to ten years might not look good. Reducing the felony to a misdemeanor comfortably narrows the distance between the maximum sentence and the one the judge imposed.

Figure 11 shows that the New York pattern of charge reductions is not a recent innovation. It compares the downgrading of felony arrests in the New York courts in 1973 with the comparable figures found and criticized by the Wickersham Commission almost a half-century earlier. The change is imperceptible.[18]

Charge reductions that do not reflect the evidence have undesirable consequences. They falsify the true criminal record of the defendant. This is particularly serious where a felony charge is reduced to a misdemeanor, because the law considers a felony by a magnitude more serious than a misdemeanor. Only a prior felony conviction, for instance, can make a defendant a "habitual offender." Charge reductions, moreover, that do not reflect reality destroy the value of the statistics of which they eventually become a part. Finally, the falsification of the individual's record has the effect of making criminal records no longer accepted at face value.[19]

Sentence Reduction

The second inducement to plead guilty—the promise of a reduced sentence—is by far the more important ingredient of the bargain offered to the defendant. Giving the defendant who pleads guilty a lower

18. For a historical perspective on plea bargaining, see Albert W. Alschuler, "Plea Bargaining and Its History," *Columbia Law Review* 79, no. 4 (1979): 1; and the more recent "The Changing Plea Bargaining Debate," *California Law Review* 69 (1981): 652. These are two of several important papers on plea bargaining by that careful and concerned chronicler and analyst of that uniquely American institution.

19. See Problems of the Criminal Record, this chapter.

Fig. 11
Charge Reduction in New York City:
1973 and 1926

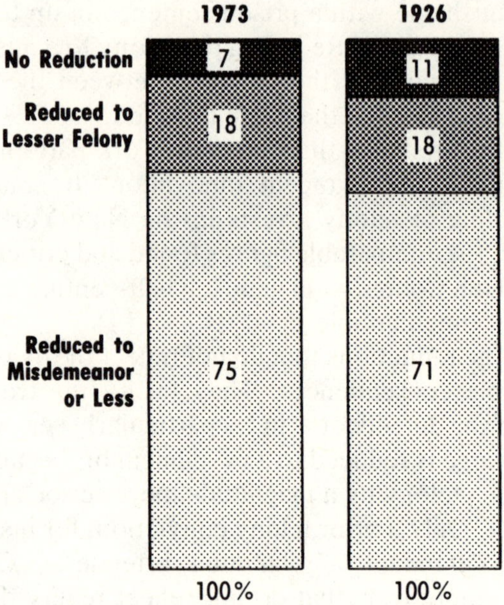

Sources: 2000 Sample
See source to Fig. 6 above

sentence than the one he would receive if he were found guilty at trial is a widely accepted practice. In nearly all legal systems, confession mitigates the sentence, albeit normally with emphasis on contrition instead of on the formal act of confession. Under American law the motive matters not; the defendant may even accompany his guilty plea by a protestation of innocence, the so-called Alford plea, named after the case in which the U.S. Supreme Court sanctioned it.[20]

In cases involving homicide and other serious crimes, especially when they had received wide publicity, the prosecution will at times insist on the maximum penalty and offer no concessions for a guilty plea. Occasionally one hears of judges who do not allow their sentence to be affected by whether the defendant is convicted after a guilty plea or after trial. Some of these judges will abandon this principle if, in their view, the defendant lied during his trial on the witness stand. The prosecutor's gain from a guilty plea is twofold: he avoids a time-consuming trial, and he makes sure that the defendant does not totally escape conviction, an ever-present possibility if he goes to trial. The defense, too, has cost considerations. Since the defendant is as a rule indigent, these considerations evolve to the institution that defends him, the Legal Aid Society, which must allocate its limited manpower reasonably.[21]

The trouble with concessions made to obtain a guilty plea is that they have, by definition, a disturbing counterpart: defendants who refuse to plead guilty and are convicted after trial receive a higher sentence for that reason alone. Such a penalty for going to trial has a potentially chilling effect on the defendant's right to a fair trial. The sentence differential, thus, raises troublesome questions.

Since the prospect of being acquitted is seldom a clear

20. Provided the state shows a strong factual basis for the guilty plea: North Carolina v. Alford, 400 U.S. 25, 91 S. Ct. 160, 27 L. Ed. 2d 162 (1970).

21. See also David M. Crowe, "Costs and the Plea Bargaining Process: Reducing the Price of Justice to the Nonindigent Defendant," *Yale Law Journal* 89 (1979): 333.

yes-or-no issue but one of varying degree of likelihood, increasing the sentence differential will increase the proportion of defendants who, had they gone to trial, would have been acquitted or convicted of a lesser offense. There will be defendants who feel that their trial should, or at least might, end that way but nevertheless plead guilty because the size of the sentence differential is too frightening. In some jurisdictions, in North Carolina for instance, the threat of such a differential is effectively enhanced by the prosecutor's power to assign cases of hesitating defendants for trial to a particular judge, if necessary to a notoriously severe judge. Efforts to estimate the number of such defendants improperly frightened away from going to trial have not been successful so far. Whatever that number, it must be affected by the size of the sentence differential or, rather, by its perceived size, the one suggested to the defendant by his counsel.

The size of the differential, one suspects, is determined less by principles of justice than by case-load pressure and the resulting desire to avoid time-consuming trials. Both prosecutor and defense lawyer are intensely aware of the relationship between case load and the quality of the bargain. An assistant district attorney told us: "Word came down from . . . to work out deals and good sentences and start moving the cases faster. Every case was preconferred in my office, and the lawyer received my bottom offer for sentence and plea. We needed one of the most lenient judges who would ignore the [probation] report and go along for a disposition." And, from the other side, an attorney from the Legal Aid Society: "Great offers were being made at the time in that court in order to speed up dispositions."

One tactic in the game played between prosecutor and defendant involves a permanently open courtroom that enables the prosecutor to say with credibility: "Either you accept the offer or we go to trial—now." The prosecutor, of course, hopes that this added threat will increase the likelihood that the plea offer is accepted and that the courtroom will remain permanently open for the next case. In prosecutions for misdemeanors, that bargaining balance was reversed for several years because the prosecutors had a hard time finding a trial judge and courtroom.[22]

It is not so much the fact of the sentence differential that causes problems but its size. Consider the case of a defendant charged with a capital crime who was offered a sentence of life in prison in exchange for a guilty plea, refused the offer, and was convicted after trial and sentenced to die.[23] The differential thus can reach terrifying proportions.

A negligible concession may prove ineffective; above a certain level the difference may threaten the legality of the guilty plea, which, the law prescribes, must be given intelligently and voluntarily.[24] A large and only vaguely known differential between the sentence offered for a plea and the sentence expected after conviction at trial impairs both these requirements. It is difficult to see how a plea can be given intelligently unless the defendant knows the size of the differential; and if that differential is large, it can threaten also the voluntariness of the plea. Narrowly interpreted, only physical harm or mental coercion "overbearing the will of the defendant" render the plea involuntary.[25] A distinguished federal judge takes for granted that the defendant is aware of the sentence differential: "His [the judge's] awesome power to impose a substantially longer ... sentence in excess of that proposed (in exchange for the plea) is present whether referred to or

22. Recently, efforts have been made to ameliorate the situation.

23. E.g., the cases of Sammie Felder, Jr. (564 S.W.2d 776; Tex. Crim. App. 1978), and Billy Joe Woods (569 S.W.2d 901, Tex. Crim. App. 1978). Both these cases were researched in detail by Kenneth Schubb, Esq., of Austin, Tex.

24. Santobello v. New York, 404 U.S. 257, 260 (1971).

25. See U.S. v. Brady, 397 U.S. 742 (1970) at 751 ff., which held that even a guilty plea motivated by fear of the death penalty is not necessarily involuntary.

not . . . . [A] defendant needs no reminder that if he rejects the proposal, stands upon his right to trial and is convicted, he faces a significantly longer sentence."[26]

It would seem to me, however, that there are additional issues: namely, whether in fact there will be, or would be, a sentence differential, whether the differential is correctly perceived, and whether its size is proper.

The first question that arises is how big that sentence differential is. The present study, for the first time, has measured its size with some precision by comparing the sentence actually imposed after conviction at trial with the sentence offered and refused during the negotiations for a guilty plea. Figure 12 shows the differences albeit only for the seven such cases in our sample. If both the offered and the imposed sentence were prison sentences, the average sentence increase was +42 percent. If the cases are added in which the offered sentence was probation and the imposed sentence prison, the sentence increase, as measured by the point scale used by the Administrative Office of the U.S. courts, is +123 percent.

This picture, however, is incomplete. To see all comparisons, we would have to know what sentences *would* have been imposed after trial on the many more defendants who pleaded guilty.

In any event, the average sentence differential in the New York courts must be large enough, because it has been extraordinarily effective. During the year of our study, over 98 percent of the convictions after a felony arrest were obtained through a guilty plea and that percentage has remained fairly constant.

The obvious next question is: Should there be such a differential, and, if so, how large should it be?[27] Should it vary with the individual circumstances of the case or should it be a fairly constant margin, such as one-fourth off for

26. Judge Edward Weinfeld in U.S. ex rel. Elksins v. Gilligan, 256 F. Supp. 244 (1966) at 254.

27. Under our laws there seems to be no limit to the differential. In Bordenkircher v. Hayes, 434 U.S. 357 (1978), the U.S. Supreme Court held that it was not a violation of due process for the prosecutor to charge

Fig. 12
Sentence Offered (and Refused) for Guilty Plea
Compared to Sentence after Trial

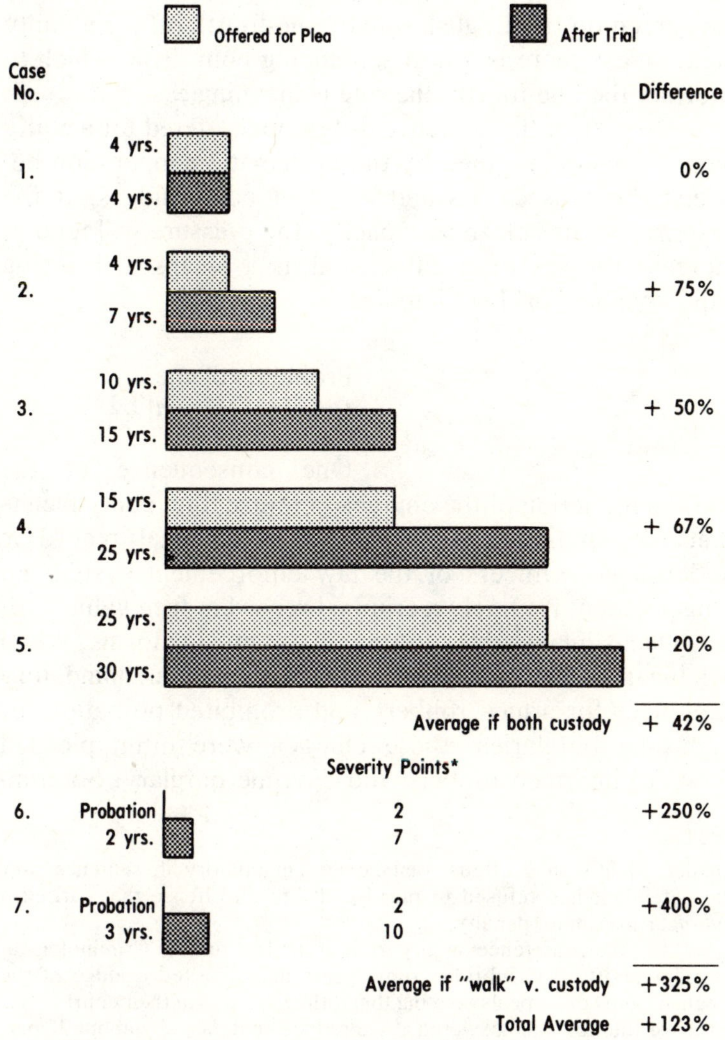

*Scale used by the Administrative Office of the U.S. Courts.
Source: 400 Sample

pleading guilty, as is apparently the practice in England.[28] The latter policy, however, can be effective only in a sentencing structure with relatively firm guidelines. Suppose we agreed on the English rule of one-fourth off for a guilty plea; unless there is a firm sentencing point from which to subtract the one-fourth, the rule is meaningless.

The size of the sentence differential offered for a guilty plea is thus determined by the systematic cooperation between the prosecutors and the sentencing judges. If the system operates close to capacity, the pressure will tend to increase the sentence differential as a means of bringing capacity and workload into line.

Problems of the Criminal Record

One consequence of the routine reduction of the charges in return for a guilty plea is that the credibility of the reported criminal record is undermined. Officers of the law enforcement system no longer accept routinely a criminal record at face value.

Occasionally, this attitude takes amusing forms. When Michigan in the 1950s prescribed substantial mandatory sentences for armed robbery and prohibited probation for nighttime burglaries, these charges were often pleaded down to unarmed robbery and daytime burglary. So com-

---

the defendant with an offense that carries a mandatory life sentence after the defendant had refused to plead guilty to an offense that carried a five-year maximum penalty.

28. At a conference on jury trials at the Institute for Criminology at the University of Cambridge some years ago, I asked a judge of the English Court of Appeals how big that difference was in their courts. "As a rule of thumb," he answered, "we reduce sentences by about 25 percent." Plea bargaining, incidentally, is not part of the English court system, notwithstanding the claim made in John Baldwin and Michael McConville, *Negotiated Justice: Pressures on Defendants to Plead Guilty,* Law in Society Series (London: Martin Robertson & Co., 1977). If a sentence differential of predetermined magnitude is known to exist, there is sentencing practice (see the illuminating standard work by David A. Thomas, *Principles of Sentencing* [London: Heinemann, 1970, 1982]).

mon was the practice that the parole board would start the interview of a convicted robber by asking: "I see you were convicted of unarmed robbery; what caliber gun did you use?" and expected the convict to name it.[29]

Arrest charges are often considered more accurate indicators of the committed crime than the recorded conviction.[30] From there it is but one treacherous step to giving weight to arrests that fail to result in convictions. The St. Louis, Missouri, prosecutor, for instance, defined his prime target, the career criminal, as a person with "either two felony convictions or five felony arrests,"[31] and there is evidence that prior arrests affect also the sentencing decision. The tendency to give weight to arrest records is strengthened by the fact that criminal records are often incomplete; at times, they report arrests without noting their disposition.

Since even arrests for serious crimes occasionally turn out to have no foundation whatsoever, it is not easy to reconcile such interpretation of an arrest with the law's cherished tenet that a man is innocent until proven guilty, however difficult it may be to maintain this position in practice. It has been persuasively argued that arrests which do not end in convictions should altogether disappear from the criminal record.[32] Moreover, since we have a legitimate interest in knowing who the dangerous offenders are, on

29. Frank Remington, "Fair and Certain Punishment," a review of E. v. d. Haag, *Punishing Criminals* and J. Q. Wilson, *Thinking about Crime*, in *Vanderbilt Law Review* 29 (1976): 1309–15.

30. At times, even scholarly crime analysis will prefer such reading. "We used original charge at arrest rather than conviction offense for the following reasons: first, charge at arrest is probably a more accurate reflection of the actual crime committed than is the offense for which the offender is eventually convicted . . . as many as 95 percent [of the cases] in some jurisdictions . . . are adjudicated by guilty pleas . . . in return for a reduced charge" (C. E. Pope, *Sentencing of California Felony Offenders* [Washington, Department of Justice, 1975], p. 13, n. 9).

31. *Time*, January 30, 1978, p. 62. On the difficulties of expunging such records, see Tom Ballinger, *Clean Slate: A State-by-State Guide to Expunging an Arrest Record* (New York: Harmony Books, 1979).

32. The New Court of Appeals has sanctioned this rule in Tatum v. Rogers. But, as so often, the trial courts have been slow in implementing the new policy.

balance we might be better off if a man's conviction record reported his crimes truthfully and if we disregarded arrests that did not end in conviction. This is the rule, for instance, in Austria, the country in which I received my first legal education. Criminal records there differ also in another interesting respect from ours. Austria has an automatically administered statute of expunction. It allows removals of conviction records after a specified time period, provided the offender has not committed another crime in the interim; the time period varies with the severity of the crime for which the defendant had been convicted. These expunctions of the record are effected by the recording office through a computer program.

Misgivings about the Bail System

The constitutional promise of bail that is not excessive may once have evoked visions of law enforcement without substantial pretrial detention. Today's reality is that about one-third of all persons arrested on a felony charge are kept in pretrial detention—a few because they are held without bail, most of them because they could not make bail.

The bail system has been under attack for a long time.[33] Most generally, it has been criticized for discriminating against the indigent defendant who cannot make bail. The system has also been blamed for detaining in jail too many defendants who would appear in court anyway, many of

33. The first critical analysis of the bail problem can be found again in that first seminal study of the justice system by Roscoe Pound and Felix Frankfurter, *Criminal Justice in Cleveland* (Cleveland: Cleveland Foundation, 1922), pp. 290 ff. Next came Arthur Beeley, *The Bail System in Chicago* (Chicago: University of Chicago Press, 1927; reprinted 1966). The honor of the first comprehensive discussion of the bail problem with empirical data goes to Caleb Foote for his "Compelling Appearances in Court: Administration of Bail in Philadelphia," *University of Pennsylvania Law Review* 102 (1954): 685; and his "Coming Constitutional Crisis in Bail," *University of Pennsylvania Law Review* 113, no. 4 (1965): 959.

whom subsequently are not even convicted. This point was powerfully demonstrated by a famous experiment conducted in the early sixties by the Vera Institute of Justice.[34] The Vera findings sparked a nationwide reform movement that gave bail judges more information and encouraged them to release more defendants without bail. Since the bail-jumping rate remained unchanged, everybody except the bail bondsmen profited from the reform.

The same Vera experiment brought to light yet another dysfunction of the bail system, perhaps the most disturbing one. It showed that the very fact of pretrial detention affected the defendant's chances of being acquitted and, if convicted, his chances of avoiding a custody sentence. These points have since been urged upon the courts, albeit without success, by carefully assembled evidence of that discriminatory effect.[35] The present study reconfirms that discrimination and reveals part of the mechanism that brings it about.

The effect of pretrial detention on the *sentence* is easily understood. If a defendant pleads guilty after having spent some time in jail, the judge will be tempted to impose a custody sentence equal to the time spent in detention, thereby legitimizing the past detention without adding to it. Reported the Legal Aid attorney in one case: "If he had been in jail, they might have tried for 'time served,' because then, they knew, he's in a bind. The fact that he was out, changed the plea to a misdemeanor with probation."

Why pretrial detention should increase the likelihood of *conviction* is more difficult to understand. It has been suggested that this effect is due to the jailed defendant's diminished ability to prepare his defense. The present study

34. Charles E. Ares, Anne Rankin, and Herbert Sturz, "The Manhattan Bail Project: An Interim Report on the Use of Pre-Trial Parole," *New York University Law Review* 38 (1963): 67; Patricia Wald, "Pretrial Detention and Ultimate Freedom: A Statistical Study," *New York University Law Review* 39 (1964): 631. Anne Rankin, "The Effect of Pretrial Detention," *New York University Law Review* 39 (1964): 641.

35. Cf. Roballo v. Judges of N.Y. City, U.S. District Court for the N. District of N.Y., 74 Civ. 2113-MEL.

shows that there is also a more direct connection. Many times a defendant in pretrial detention is told by his counsel at some point that, if he agrees to plead guilty, the court would impose a sentence of "time served" or at least one that would not exceed by much the time served in pretrial detention; pleading guilty would thus mean immediate or early release. Often the detained defendant will accept such an offer. Against the defendant free on bail the prosecutor has no comparable leverage; all he can do, if the defendant refuses to plead guilty, is go to trial.

This leverage is the primary cause of the differential conviction ratés of otherwise equivalent defendants in jail and defendants on bail.

The discriminatory effect of pretrial detention cannot be doubted any longer. But how can it be eliminated? In theory, speedy disposition of the cases in jail could reduce the differential. But the "time served" cases which account for the bulk of this type of discrimination are found in the lower ranges of crime where sentences are measured in weeks or months. And since "speedy trial" normally means within three months after arrest, this is not speedy enough; three months for pretrial detention often provide a sufficient basis for the promise of a "time served" sentence.

Since the discrimination arises from a shift in the bargaining power of the prosecutor, it can be reduced only by reducing that discretionary power. The only way to eliminate this effect of pretrial detention would be an early, *unchangeable* decision by the prosecutor to go to trial if the defendant fails to plead guilty to the charged crime, irrespective of whether or not he is in pretrial detention.[36] Under our practices this solution is not feasible.

36. The problem cannot easily arise under continental European law because there the guilty plea is unknown; no conviction can be obtained without trial. In that trial, however, after the charge has been read to the defendant the presiding judge, as the first step in the proceedings, asks the defendant whether he acknowledges the charge to be correct. If he does that, the evidentiary proceedings are greatly reduced.

It is, incidentally, not immediately clear in which direction one should eliminate the discriminatory effect. Should the conviction rates of the detained defendants be reduced, or should the conviction rates of the defendants on bail be increased?

Our data illuminate still another problematic facet of the bail system, one affecting primarily the lower end of the crime scale. In contrast to earlier experience, now some 9 percent of all defendants released after felony arrest, or about 6 percent of all defendants, whether released or not, jump bail and thereby bring the law enforcement process to a halt. This is no longer a negligible proportion. One might compare it, for instance, to the 5 percent of all arrested defendants who receive a prison sentence of over one year.

This looks like evidence that the system errs in the direction of releasing too many defendants before trial. Our data suggest that this would be a poor answer. Unless one could pinpoint the future bail jumpers in advance, which one cannot, increasing pretrial detentions would substantially increase the number of unnecessary incarcerations; for every foiled bail jumper one would have to jail ten defendants who would have appeared in court anyway. This follows from the finding that in all groups at risk the average bail-jumping rate is approximately 9 percent, about one out of every eleven defendants. And since some of these new detainees will not even be convicted, jailing more defendants cannot be the right answer.

The data suggest a better remedy. Most bail jumpers, it turns out, face only modest charges and have either no record or only a minor one; they therefore have relatively little to fear from the law.[37] The worst they face is a minor jail sentence. This suggests that bail jumping is not so much a decision to disappear because the consequences of the pending prosecution are too threatening but rather because the consequences of bail jumping are negligible. A more thorough follow-up by the police of the court-issued

37. See fig. 57, Chap. 5.

warrants for the arrest of these defendants, perhaps also a more rigorous collection of forfeited bonds, should bring many of these defendants back into court.

Our bail system suffers also from more fundamental difficulties. It is predicated on the legal fiction that its sole purpose is to insure the defendant's appearance on his appointed day in court. In fact, another purpose often has greater weight with the judge. Since he is likely to be blamed if a defendant whose release he made possible commits another serious crime, he may set bail at an amount he is sure the defendant cannot make. In other cases the judge will set bail at a nominal amount, expecting, perhaps even hoping, that the defendant will make bail. Generally, however, the judge will follow the prosecutor's recommendation or set bail at a routine amount without knowing, possibly also without caring, whether or not the defendant will make bail.[38]

We should explore the bail judge's thoughts on whether the defendant will make bail, whether if released he will continue his criminal activities, on the likelihood of his reappearance in court, and on the likelihood that he will be convicted.

European countries, including England, handle pretrial detention more directly. They allow it if the court believes one of three dangers obtains: of flight, of continuing the crime, and—a ground hardly known to American law—the danger of collusion with witnesses and of other tampering with the evidence. Under continental law, release on bond is permissible only if the danger of flight is the sole ground for detention.

Since the realities of our pretrial detention are not so different from those in systems that attack the problem more directly, we might consider rethinking, within the con-

38. On the prosecutor's role and the judge's thoughts, see E. B. Ebbessen and V. J. Konecni, "Decision Making and Information Integration in the Courts: The Setting of Bail," *Journal of Personality and Social Psychology* 32 (1975): 805.

stitutional restraints, not only the modalities of our present bail system but also that institution itself.[39]

Reform in Perspective

The present study affords a close-up view of the law enforcement process of the country's largest metropolis and brings to light what at first appears as major shortcomings of the system. On second look, the system offers few opportunities for radical change. Dismissal rates probably can be tightened by more circumspect collection of evidence by the police, by lightening the burden on the complaining witness, and by diminishing his dominant position in the prosecution process. Charge reductions that are not warranted by evidentiary deficiencies could be offered on a more moderate scale, and the differential between the sentence offered as part of the guilty plea and the sentence that would be imposed after trial could be narrowed. These moves, however, would increase the number of cases that will have to be tried and therefore would require an increase in the prosecutor's staff and in the available trial parts. Bench warrants for the arrests of bail jumpers could be followed up more diligently. That move too would require much new money, and it would have the disadvantage of increasing the efficiency of the system at the level of lesser crimes. In general, the law enforcement system could be strengthened by increasing its capacity to cope with an oversized case load.

If these reforms were implemented, dismissal rates could be cut perhaps by some ten percentage points; bail jumping might be reduced by two or three percentage

39. A recent study of the bail system concludes: "A cautious conclusion then is that the often-expressed fears, that further experimentation or reform of the bail system will result in rampant crime and uncontrollable levels of bail forfeiture are unfounded" (Samuel L. Myers, Jr., "The Economics of Bail Jumping," *Journal of Legal Studies* 10 [1981]: 381 ff.; see also William M. Landes, "An Economic Analysis of the Courts," *Journal of Law and Economics* 14 [1971]: 61).

points. Both changes would increase the eventual rate of convictions. On the other hand, narrowing the differential between sentence after guilty plea and sentence after trial would lead to fewer guilty pleas and more trials, hence to fewer convictions and a greater work load.

Whatever their tangible effects, these reforms should be carried out. They would bring the system closer to both the meaning and the letter of the law. And they would raise both the system's self-respect and the respect in which it is held by the community, an important goal for the institutional symbol of an orderly society. But whether these improvements of the enforcement system would have a significant impact on our high level of crime is a very different question. Since it is unlikely that the police can substantially increase the number of arrests for index crimes, it is unlikely that the attrition of the law enforcement process as recorded in figure 2 would noticeably change. One thousand committed crimes would be followed by, say, forty-six convictions instead of the present thirty-six.[40]

If there is little room for increasing our arrest and conviction rates, there remains one point at which we can substantially alter the law enforcement process. We can and now do increase the sentences of convicted offenders. This is a new development, and we will now consider its likely effectiveness.

Since most of the more severe sentences now imposed are well below the legal maximum, judges have as a rule ample leeway to increase their sentences under existing laws. If they should hesitate, the legislatures can and do raise minimum sentences.[41]

40. These rates understate the risk of arrest the criminal faces because they pertain to the aftermath of *one* criminal act. If an offender, as many do, commits more than one crime, his chances of being arrested increase. There may be, however, a countervailing factor: increased criminal activity might be accompanied by knowledge of how to avoid arrest. None of these considerations alters the conclusion that enforcement reforms, however necessary, will not significantly increase crime control.

41. The New York legislature has raised sentences for drug crimes. California and other states have legislated sentence increases on a more general basis.

Increasing Sentences: Incapacitation

Increasing the duration of prison sentences would clearly reduce crime by the amount of crime these offenders would have committed had they been out on the street instead of in prison.

Efforts have been made to estimate the size of this incapacitation effect.[42] The most recent and most complete estimate comes from a group of scholars at the Rand Corporation.[43] They computed the impact of the incapacitation effect on some of the major crime categories for the State of California. By carefully interviewing a probability sample of prison inmates, they determined the frequency with which these convicts had been committing crimes prior to their latest arrest. Appropriate analysis yielded the following estimate of the number of crimes prevented by their imprisonment (table 1).

Armed robberies are reduced considerably, partly because once apprehended the offenders are invariably sent to

Table 1
Estimated Incapacitation Effect through Imprisonment of Felons

	Approximate Number of Actually Committed Crimes (1)	Crimes Prevented through Incapacitation (2)	Percent (2) of (1) (3)
Armed robbery	60,000	16,000	27
Burglary	940,000	60,000	6
Auto theft	200,000	11,000	6

42. See Alfred Blumstein, ed., *Panel on Research on Deterrent and Incapacitative Effects* (Washington, D.C.: National Academy of Science, 1978).

43. P. W. Greenwood, J. Chaiken, J. Petersilia, and M. Paterson, *The Rand Habitual Offender Project,* RAND Paper Series no. 5957, Santa Monica, Calif., no. 1978, p. 22.

prison and kept there for a long time. The reduction for burglary and auto theft is relatively small.

The question that concerns us here is by how much this incapacitation effect could be increased if, let us say, the sentences of these prison inmates were to be doubled, that is, if they were kept in prison twice as long as they are kept now.

At first, one might conclude that by such doubling of sentences one would reduce the number of armed robberies by another 27 percent, the number of burglaries and auto thefts by another 6 percent, and so forth. But this conclusion would overstate the effect in two respects. To begin with, every year added to the sentence would make the offenders one year older, and we know that crime sharply declines with age.[44] More important, a considerable proportion of the convicts released from prison return anyway, because they commit another crime, are rearrested, reconvicted, and resentenced, as a rule to longer sentences than before.

Allowing one-third of the "full" doubling effect to be discounted by this return to prison, and another one-sixth for the aging effect, we estimate the incapacitation effect through doubling of the sentences to be about one-half of the original number of "prevented" crimes ($1-\frac{1}{3}-\frac{1}{6}=\frac{1}{2}$). We thus estimate that a doubling of sentences would reduce, as shown in figure 13, armed robberies by 13.5 percent, and burglary and auto theft by 3 percent, one-half of the values in table 1.

Making prison sentences twice as long must be distinguished from doubling the number of offenders sent to prison. The incapacitation effect of such doubling is likely to be even smaller than that of doubling the prison sentences. The above estimates of the incapacitation effect are based on the frequency with which the convicts now in prison had been engaged in criminal activity. That frequency is likely to be higher than that of those offenders

44. See fig. 19, this chapter.

Fig. 13
Estimated Crime Reduction through Incapacitation
If All Custody Sentences Were Doubled

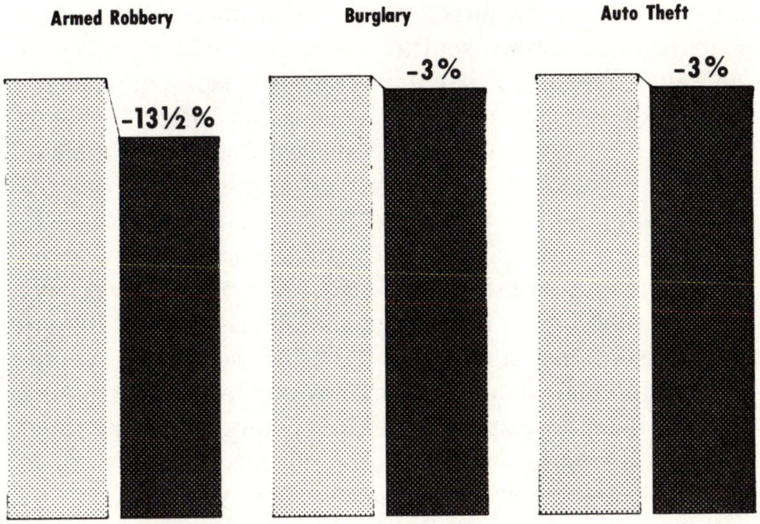

Source: See accompanying text

who after their conviction had not received a prison sentence.

All these computations concern the State of California. But the sentencing level there is not unlike that of New York City. In both jurisdictions, for instance, the crucial proportion of persons sent to prison after a felony arrest is the same, namely, 5 percent. Since we lack the data required for computing the incapacitation effect for New York City, it is not improper to suggest that the outcome of such a computation would not differ radically from the California estimates.

Whatever the amount of crime reduction achieved through increased prison sentences, the measure will have its costs, initially by crowding existing prisons, resulting in more prison tension and more crime in the prison; eventually by having to spend more money on new prisons.[45] And we will incur also another, less obvious cost: the effect which doubling of the sentences will have on the spirit in which these prisoners will return to society.

It remains to be seen whether sentences are increased generally or only selectively for offenders who committed a violent crime and for the habitual offender. The latter has long been the focus of prosecutorial attention, and the states have great leeway in defining him. The main basis for his identification is a record of repeated convictions, especially if the crimes were similar in character. As an extreme, one will recall the decision of the U.S. Supreme Court that upheld a Texas law that had imposed a life sentence on a defendant who had committed three larcenies in the total amount of $229.[46]

Two difficulties surround the habitual defender problem. One is the question of what to do with habitual offenders who commit minor crimes. The other difficulty concerns the scope of the identification. Ostensibly, the offender is

45. See Lee H. Bowker, *Prison Victimization* (New York: Elsevier, 1980); see also Edith E. Flynn, Jan Schreiber, and Richard Knudten, "Victimizations in State Prisons" (unpublished, on file with the U.S. Department of Justice, Washington, D.C.)

46. Rummel v. Estelle, 445 U.S. 263 (1980).

punished for having been a habitual offender. But the barely hidden expectation is that, by drastically increasing the prison sentences for the habitual criminal, one can eliminate the relatively small fraction of offenders who are responsible for a relatively large share of the committed crimes.

The search for the means of identifying the habitual criminal has been going on for some two-hundred years and has been stepped up during recent decades. Yet whenever the efficiency of these identification efforts was examined, it was found wanting.[47]

Deterrence

What do we know about the law's deterrent effect which is so foremost in our minds when we think about the power of the criminal law? We are intuitively certain that the criminal law has the power to deter, and there is good empirical proof. We have, for instance, no difficulty imagining that, if every would-be criminal had a policeman at his elbow all the time, few crimes except those of passion would be committed. We know that we ourselves are more likely to observe the speed limit when squad cars are around; and we know that after a well-publicized conviction for tax evasion the number of amended tax returns rises spectacularly, particularly in the occupation of the convicted offender. More dramatically, a revealing involuntary experiment occurred in 1944, when the entire Danish police force was arrested by the German invaders. At that time, the number of robberies in Copenhagen, normally around ten per month in that law-abiding country, quickly rose to over one hundred per month and kept rising.[48]

47. See Sir Leon Radzinowic and Roger Hood, "Incapacitating the Habitual Criminal: The English Experience," *Michigan Law Review* 78 (1980): 1305–89. On the American experience, see John Monahan, "The Clinical Prediction of Violent Behavior" (Washington, D.C.: Government Printing Office, 1980).

48. Jorgen Troble, *Seven Months without Police* (Copenhagen, 1948; in Swedish; cited in Andenaes, n. 49 below).

More generally, we know that the power of deterrence varies with the immediacy of the threat, with the type of crime, and with the type of criminal.[49] The question before us, however, is not whether the general threat of arrest, conviction, and sentence deters crime, which it clearly does, but whether a substantial increase of the now prevailing sentences for serious crimes will significantly increase their deterrent power.

We know that such increases are effective at the lower end of the crime spectrum. Increasing, for instance, penalties for parking violations,[50] and establishing mandatory prison sentences for drunken driving,[51] have clearly reduced the incidence of these transgressions.

We cannot, however, automatically extrapolate from these experiences to the more serious crimes. Before turning our attention to actual efforts to deter major crimes by increasing the penalty, it will be useful to see with the help of the diagram in figure 14 the precise nature of the question. For any crime, the population may be seen as falling into three groups:

> Group 1. Those who do not commit the crime but whose abstinence has nothing to do with law enforcement; they are simply not interested.
>
> Group 2. Those who are interested in committing the crime but abstain because of the threat of law enforcement.
>
> Group 3. Those who commit the crime in disregard of

49. Most of what we know about deterrence can be found in two important books: in the systematic and comprehensive *Deterrence* by Franklin E. Zimring and Gordon J. Hawkins (Chicago: University of Chicago Press, 1973); and in *Punishment and Deterrence* by the Norwegian criminologist Johannes Andenaes (Ann Arbor: University of Michigan Press, 1974). See also Ph. J. Cook, "Punishment and Crime: A Critique of Current Findings Concerning the Preventive Effects of Punishment," *Law and Contemporary Problems* (Winter 1977), pp. 165 ff.

50. See W. Underhill Moore and Charles C. Callahan, "Law and Learning Theory: A Study in Legal Control," *Yale Law Journal* 53 (1943): 1.

51. See H. Lawrence Ross, "Law, Science and Accidents: The British Road Safety Act of 1967," *Journal of Legal Studies*, vol. 2 (1973); also Andenaes, pp. 95–104 (n. 49 above).

Fig. 14
How Increased Deterrence Is Supposed to Work

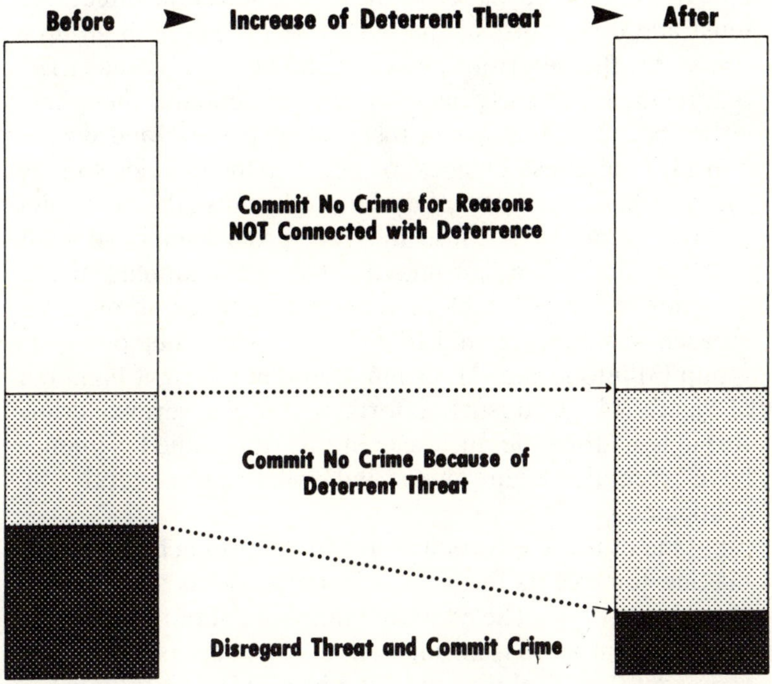

the threat of law enforcement and those who lack the mental capacity to connect that threat with their crime.

If we want to increase the law's deterrent effect, we must aim our efforts at the would-be offenders in group 3 for whom the deterrent power of the present threat of law enforcement is clearly insufficient. They commit the crime, either because they act in the heat of passion and do not consider the consequences, or because they decide to take the risk, be it in a spirit of daring, or because they consider the risk small, or because they are professional criminals who see the risk as an unavoidable occupational hazard. The hoped-for effect of increased deterrence through increased sentences would be a shift of some persons from group (3) into group (2), as illustrated in the right hand bar of figure 14. Two such efforts to reduce serious crime through a dramatic increase of the threatened sentence have recently been made and were subsequently investigated.

One of these efforts was aimed at curbing homicide by making some of its forms a capital offense, as many of our states have done. The overwhelming weight of the evidence suggests that there is no such effect. The curves in figure 15 represent the development of the homicide rate (number of homicides per 100,000 population) for the years 1960 through 1969 in states with and without executions. Figure 16 shows the homocide rates for the years 1970 through 1980 for three groups of states: those that had the death penalty continuously during those years, those states that had it intermittently (interrupted by court decisions), and those that did not have the death penalty at any time. These curves show with great clarity, first, that the homicide rate fluctuates dramatically over the course of the years; second, that these fluctuations are startlingly similar in all groups of states and therefore obviously independent of the availability of the death penalty. As if to underscore that independence, the latest surge in the homicide rate begins about the time we began executing again after a decade during which the death penalty was in limbo.

Fig. 15
Homicide Rates 1960–69 in
States with and without Executions

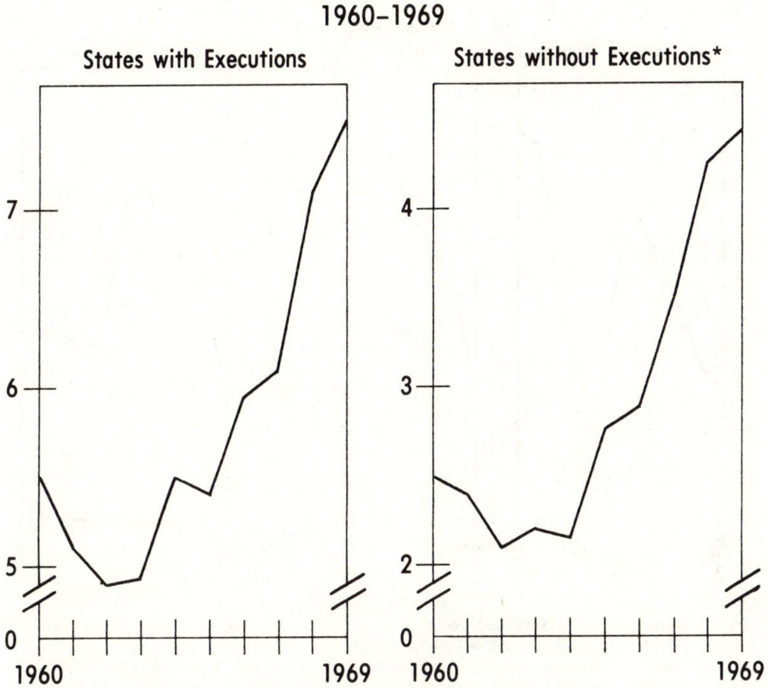

*Abolition states and 6 states with no executions since 1948.
Source: FBI Uniform Crime Reports

Fig. 16
Homicide Rates 1970–80 in
States with and without the Death Penalty

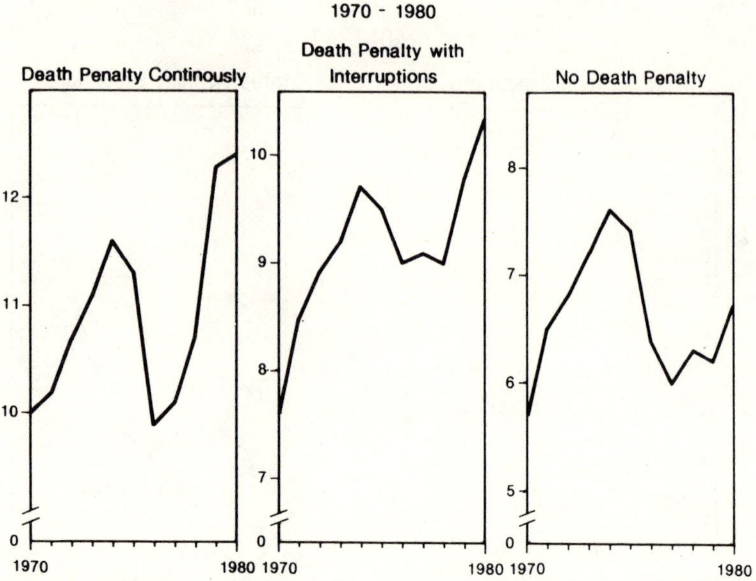

Source: FBI, Uniform Code Reports 1970–80.

Note: States that had the death penalty continuously: Arizona, Arkansas, Connecticut, Florida, Georgia, Montana, Nebraska, Nevada, Oklahoma, Texas, Utah, Virginia. States without the death penalty: Alaska, Hawaii, Iowa, Maine, Michigan, Minnesota, New Jersey, North Dakota, West Virginia, Wisconsin, Washington, D.C. The remainder of the states had the death penalty with interruptions.

Thus, this most dramatic shift to a more severe sentence failed to deter.[52]

The second important and well-investigated instance of a drastic sentence increase that was expected to reduce crime but failed were the so-called Rockefeller laws which established in 1973 draconian minimum sentences of fifteen

52. All the many efforts but one, to learn whether the death penalty reduces the murder rate, failed to show such an effect. The exception was a study by Isaac Ehrlich, "The Deterrent Effect of Capital Punishment: A Question of Life and Death" (*American Economic Review* 65 [1975]: 397). It received nationwide attention when the solicitor general of the United States, in the course of litigating the death penalty before the U.S. Supreme Court, put that study into his brief to show, as he explained to me, that there was respectable opinion also on the other side of the fence.

Because of its arrogant claim that every execution saved eight persons' lives by deterring their murder, Ehrlich's study came under the close technical scrutiny of a number of scholarly investigations, and here are their conclusions: W. J. Bowers and G. L. Pierce ("The Illusion of Deterrence: A Critique of Isaac Ehrlich's Research on Capital Punishment," *Yale Law Journal* 85[1975]: 187): "We conclude that he [Ehrlich] failed to provide any reliable evidence that the death penalty deters murder. His data are inadequate for the purposes of his analysis and he misapplies the highly sophisticated statistical techniques he employs."

P. Passell ("The Deterrent Effect of the Death Penalty: A Statistical Test," *Stanford Law Review* 28 [1975]: 61, 80): "We know of no reasonable way of interpreting the [Ehrlich] cross-section data that would lend support to the deterrence hypothesis."

Lawrence R. Klein, Brian Forst, and Victor Flatov ("The Deterrent Effect of Capital Punishment: An Assessment of the Estimates," in *Deterrence and Incapacitation* [Washington, D.C.: National Academy of Sciences, 1976], pp. 336, 358): "In short, we see too may plausible explanations for his finding . . . other than the theory that capital punishment deters murder . . . Ehrlich's results cannot be used at this time . . . to pass judgment on the use of the death penalty."

Kenneth L. Avio ("Capital Punishment in Canada: A Time Series Analysis of the Deterrent Hypothesis," *Canadian Journal of Economics*[1979], p. 647): "The major finding is that the probability of execution is found to be statistically insignificant[ly related to the frequency of homicides] under a wide variety of empirical formulations."

S. S. Brier and S. E. Fienberg ("Recent Econometric Modelling of Crime and Punishment: Support for the Deterrence Hypothesis?" in *Indicators of Crime and Criminal Justice: Quantitative Studies,* NCJ-62349 [Washington, D.C.: Dept. of Justice, Government Printing Office, 1980]): "Ehrlich's affirmative conclusions regarding the deterrent effect of punishment on crime in general, and of capital punishment on murder in particular, do not stand up to careful scrutiny."

and twenty-five years in prison for possessing more than two ounces or for selling one ounce or more of heroin. The stated purpose of these laws was to "frighten drug users out of their habits and drug dealers out of their trade." The report that evaluated the effects of these drastic sentence increases, written by a joint committee of the Drug Abuse Council and the bar of the City of New York, arrived at the following conclusions:[53]

1. Neither heroin use nor drug-related crime declined in New York State.

2. The new law may have temporarily deterred heroin use; there is, however, no evidence of a sustained reduction of heroin use after 1973.

3. Serious property crime of the sort often associated with heroin users increased sharply between 1973 and 1975; the rise in New York was similar to increases in nearby states.

A third piece of evidence on the dubious deterrent power of increased sentences for serious crimes comes from a daring controlled experiment conducted in 1954 by the Prison Authority of the State of California on the power of what is called individual deterrence, that is, not of the threat but of the actual sentence experience.

A group of 800 prisoners was divided randomly, that is, by lot, into two groups. In the one group, the prisoners were released nine months before their assigned time; in the other group, the prisoners had to serve their full assigned time. The purpose of the experiment was to find out whether the prisoners who got off with a nine-month lighter sentence than normal would have a greater propensity to return to crime. The opportunity for the experiment was offered by the sentencing procedures then in force in California. Convicted defendants were sentenced to an indeterminate sentence, the court merely stating the range

53. *The Nation's Toughest Drug Law: Evaluating the New York Experience,* Final Report of the Joint Committee on New York Drug Evaluation and the Association of the Bar of the City of New York (New York: Drug Abuse Council, 1977), pp. 7 ff., 11. I wrote the original plan for that study but had nothing to do with its execution.

provided for the particular crime in the criminal code, for example, "from 1 to 5 years." The Prison Authority then decided where between the extremes the actual sentence was to fall. The sentence was determined in a preliminary way fairly early, depending on the circumstances of the crime and the prisoner's record, and was subsequently modified if the prisoner's behavior warranted it. All these were internal decisions; the prisoner learned of them only at the time of his release. This procedure enabled the Prison Authority to conduct the following controlled experiment: a randomly selected one-half of the convicts included in the experiment were released ninety days before their assessed time and were, for that time period, subject to intensive parole supervision. The result of the experiment was sobering; the sentence differential had no effect on the rate and speed with which the ex-convicts reentered the law enforcement cycle with another crime. The experiment is important, even though it did not test the issue head-on; the prisoners were unaware of the differential treatment, and the difference was obtained not by increasing the sentences as against a control group but by reducing them.[54]

Taken together, the inability of these studies to detect a change in crime rate where sentences were substantially raised or lowered should give us pause. Our own data offer only a limited, indirect perspective on the issue of deterrence by allowing us to see the low frequency with which the commission of a crime results in a jail or prison sentence. Figure 17 gives these data for three major felonies: robbery (by strangers); auto theft; and theft-burglary, that is, burglary with intent to steal.

These data emerge from linking the likelihood of arrest after committing the crime with the likelihood of conviction

54. State of California, Adult Authority, Division of Adult Paroles, Walter T. Stone, chief, Special Intensive Parole Unit, Phase I, Sacramento (November 1956, mimeographed). The experiment, it seems, was repeated in 1970, albeit with a six-month sentence differential, and reported by John E. Berecochea and Dorothy R. Jaman, *Time Served in Prison and Parole Outcome* (Sacramento: California Dept. of Corrections, June 1981). This is their closing sentence: "This conclusion lends strength to the argument that severity of punishment (among those sent to prison) is not related to recidivism."

Fig. 17
Likelihood of Being Sent to Jail or Prison after Committing One of These Crimes

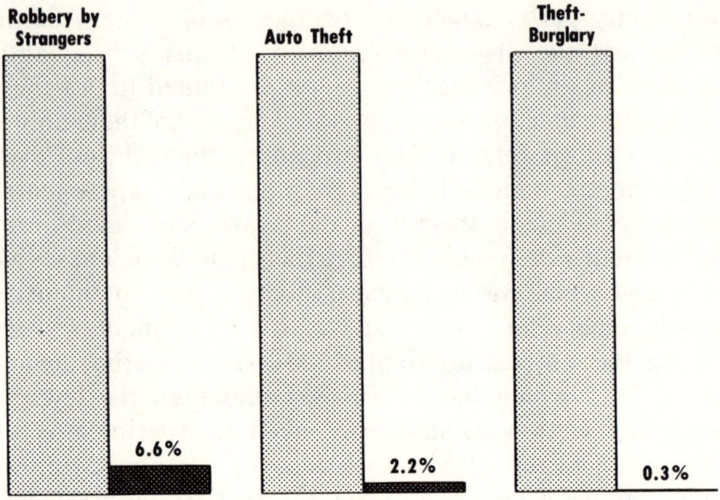

Source: See accompanying text

if arrested, and the likelihood of a custody sentence if convicted.[55] The overall likelihood of ending up in jail or prison is small; relatively larger for the crime of robbery, insignificant for the crime of burglary. The bulk of these sentences are jail sentences of less than one year; the balance are prison sentences over one year. As long as the likelihood of being sent to jail or prison is so small, why should an increase of these sentences significantly affect their deterrent threat?

There is an additional consideration that makes the threat even smaller than the numbers indicate. Students of deterrence, from Beccaria to the econometricians of our day, have taught us that, of the three elements that constitute the deterrent threat, the likelihood of being arrested has the greatest weight. If that is true, then the small likelihood of arrest, which as we saw is difficult to move upward, would make the perceived risk even smaller than it actually is.

I have bypassed here a large and crucial problem area: consideration of life in our prisons and of the efforts to devise effective penological measures outside the prison. The rehabilitative efforts of law enforcement have been moving in cycles. Right now, they are scraping bottom. But to give up, as we now almost do, the search for better prisons and for a more effective treatment of convicts in general is both immoral and unwise. The high recidivism figures are to some extent self-fulfilling prophecies: we refuse to make our prisons humane institutions, and we accept their failure as proof that to make them humane would be wasted effort.[56] In general, then, on the basis of what we

55. Arrest rates were computed from figs. 22 and 23, Chap. 2; conviction and sentencing rates from fig. 39, Chap. 4.

56. See Francis A. Allen, *The Decline of the Rehabilitative Ideal: Penal Policy and Social Purpose* (New Haven: Yale University, 1981). The report of a panel of the National Academy of Sciences, Lee Sechrest et al., eds., *The Rehabilitation of Criminal Offenders: Problems and Prospects* (Washington, D.C.: National Academy Press, 1979), generally confirmed the failure of such rehabilitation efforts as had been made. A subsequent volume points to the future: Susan E. Martin, Lee Sechrest, Robin Redner, eds., *New Directions in the Rehabilitation of Criminal*

know—as opposed to what we like to think—it is doubtful that increasing the sentences will significantly increase their deterrent effect.

The strategy, moreover, of increasing sentences in order to increase their deterrent effect raises a peculiar moral problem.

By sentencing an offender more severely, not because of what he has done but because of what others do, we use this offender as a means to an end.[57] The difficulty is aggravated by the fact that so many of the offenders whose sentences would be increased are very young. To send more of them to prison, not because of what they did but because we want to deter others, is not an easy burden to bear in view of the uncertainty that the policy will succeed. The approach is doubly grim since there is respectable expert opinion that sending a young man to prison, at least to our prisons, will make him a worse man than he was when he entered it, a consideration much on the minds of the judges who do the sentencing.

The Causes of Crime

The criminal law is based on the principle that we are responsible for our willfully committed acts. Only children who have no will yet, and insane persons who have lost theirs, are exempt. The criminal law is thus in consonance with our own immediate sense that

---

Offenders (Washington, D.C.: National Academy Press, 1981). A key sentence illuminates the present state of the problem: "The interventions studied to date have been insipid and poorly implemented." See H. C. Quay, *The Three Factors of Evaluation: What Can Be Expected to Work? (Evaluation Studies Review Annual* [1977], p. 212). See also Norval Morris, *The Future of Imprisonment* (Chicago: University of Chicago Press,1974). On the positive side, see also Robert Coates, Alden Miller, and Lloyd E. Ohlin, *Diversity in a Youth Correctional System* (Cambridge, Mass.: Ballinger, 1978).

57. The moral problem of such sacrifice forms the core of Herman Melville's tale, *Billy Budd.* See also the cautionary note in H. L. A. Hart, *Punishment and Responsibility* (Oxford: Clarendon Press, 1968), p. 172

most of what we do is the result of our own freely willed decisions. Thus, a defendant who murdered will be asked, "Why did you kill that woman?" and if he answers, "I wanted her money," the law is satisfied and we think we understand. In a deeper sense, of course, we do not understand at all why a man should "will" to murder a woman for her money. But the criminal law is basically uninterested in the question as to what caused the crime.

The irony of the demarcation is laid before us with great clarity in Samuel Butler's novel *Erewhon*. There, the judge before pronouncing sentence on a convicted defendant summarizes the law's position.

> You may say that it is not your fault. The answer is ready enough at hand, and it amounts to this—that if you had been born of healthy and well-to-do parents, and been well taken care of when you were a child, you would never have offended against the laws of your country, nor found yourself in your present disgraceful position. If you tell me that you had no hand in your parentage and education, and it is therefore unjust to lay these things to your charge, I answer that whether it is your fault or not, it is a fault in you, and it is my duty to see that against such faults as this the commonwealth shall be protected. You may say that it is your misfortune to be a criminal; I answer that it is your crime to be unfortunate. . . . I do not hesitate therefore to sentence you to imprisonment, with hard labour, for the rest of your miserable existence.[58]

Yet while the law remains disinterested, we have become increasingly aware that crime, like everything else, has causes. That awareness is a relatively recent insight, barely older than 250 years. Adolphe Quetelet, the great Belgian statistician, was among the first to see the problem. He was struck by the uncanny numerical regularity with which specific crimes reoccur year after year: the number of murders, for instance, committed in France during the six years from 1826 through 1831: 241, 234, 227, 231, 205, and 266;

58. Samuel Butler, *Erewhon* (New York: Dutton, 1917; originally published 1871), pp. 113, 116.

even more impressive, the regular frequency of special types of murders, for instance, those by strangulation: 2, 5, 2, 2, 2, and 4 for these six years. Quetelet concluded: "We can therefore from the results of the past predict what will happen in the future. This possibility of assigning beforehand the number of accused and condemned persons . . . must give rise to serious reflections on the fate of several thousand men who are driven, as it were, in an irresistible manner towards the tribunals and the convictions that await them."[59]

Quetelet went on to point to the forces that create that drive: "Society carries in itself . . . the seeds of all crimes committed later, together with the conditions that bring these seeds to maturity. . . . In some measure it is the organization of society itself that prepares these crimes, and the criminal is merely the instrument that carries them out. Every state of society thus presupposes certain numbers and certain types of crime, these being merely the necessary consequences of that organization." And finally: "As long as the same causes prevail we must expect the return of the same effects."[60]

Criminologists, ever since, have made great efforts to find the causes of crime. Judge David L. Bazelon has summarized most of what we have learned: "Those causes [of street crime] are no mystery to us. It is not news that almost all perpetrators of street crime come from the bottom of the

59. Adolphe Quetelet, *Sur l'homme et le developement de ses facultés un essay de physique sociale* (Bruxelles: Louis Hauman, 1836), pp. 11 ff. We may add to Quetelet's evidence the homicide curve in the present United States reproduced in figs. 15 and 16 of this book. The consistency of the unique shape of those curves in the various groupings of the states strongly suggests that it is determined by overwhelming societal forces. About the important role of Quetelet in the history of social science research, see Afterword to *Marienthal* (n. 9 in Introduction).

60. For today's perspective, see Daniel Glaser, "A Review of Crime Causation-Theory and Its Applications," in N. Morris and M. Tonry, eds., *Crime and Justice,* vol. 1 (Chicago: University of Chicago, 1980). James Q. Wilson does not share our view. He believes that "the problem lies in confusing causal analysis with policy analysis" ("Crime and the Criminologists," *Commentary* [July 1974], pp. 47–49).

socioeconomic ladder—from among the ignorant, the ill-educated, the unemployed and unemployable. The crime that gives us nightmares is a human problem indisputably connected with savage social and economic deprivation.''[61]

The moral problem raised by our awareness of the causes of crime is highlighted by an interesting episode in the search for these causes. Scientists are exploring the possibility that a certain congenital effect, an extra chromosome, causes some people to become criminals.[62] For our purposes, it is unimportant whether this particular theory will survive. What matters is that the theory is being seriously discussed and that one cannot exclude the possibility that someday some biological, if not genetic, condition will be found to be a cause of crime.

An intriguing question thus arises: What would such a discovery do to our notion that evil must be punished? Could we go on punishing people for having been born with an extra chromosome? To ask this question with respect to a genetic cause seems reasonable enough. But is the question less reasonable with respect to other causes? Consider growing up in a criminal neighborhood, or physical mistreatment by cruel parents, both not unlikely causes of a youngster becoming a criminal. Why do we judge such causes to be different in kind from an extra chromosome or brain damage?

One reason is that not all of us are convinced that such hereditary or social conditions do cause crime, as a virus causes illness. Our intuitive resistance to accepting such conditions as causes of crime rests on observations such as this: Why have so many youngsters, coming out of the very same settings in which one child became a criminal, grown into upright good citizens in spite of the same parental

61. Letter to *The New York Times,* October 19, 1980.

62. *Science* recently published details of a carefully executed many-authored American-Danish study that seems to support the proposition: H.A. Witkin, S. A. Mednick, F. Schulsinger, E. Bakkestrom, K. O. Christiansen, D. R. Goodenough, K. Hirschorn, C. Lundsteen, D. R. Owen, J. Philip, D. B. Rubin, and M. Stocking, ''Criminality in XYY and XXY Men,'' *Science* (1976), pp. 547–55.

mistreatment and bad company? But is that question different in kind from asking why a virus attacks some persons more effectively than others? The answer to both questions is that there was greater resilience—physical resilience against the virus, moral resilience against the temptation of crime. What caused the greater resilience? Probably better genes and better nourishment in the case of disease; in the case of crime, possibly also better genes, certainly better company, and a good job or at least the prospect of one.

Why then do we accept gunshots and viruses as causes but not bad companionship or cruel parents? There are at least three reasons why we make the distinction. First, the causes of crime have proved difficult to identify and are relatively broad in scope, such as growing up in slums and poverty without normal family support. These causes are different in kind from what we usually perceive as cause. Unlike a gunshot that causes a person to die, the causes of crime are statistical in nature. Not all children who grow up with hoodlums or have cruel parents become criminals; they are only more likely to become criminals than children who grow up in good company and with loving parents. Such proof is not necessarily less valid, but most people find it less convincing.

The third reason for our hesitancy to confront the causes of crime is our difficulty of perceiving that our own willful actions have causes. We learn only their last impact, in the form of criminal motivations, which we do not see as causes but as temptations; the ultimate decision, we feel, is ours.

If, however, we look at other persons' actions, we often have very firm ideas about what causes crime. If we learn that an unemployed youngster from the ghetto is charged with burglary, we are not surprised. But if a young man from a well-to-do suburban home stands in his place, we ask: How come, a kid from a nice family . . . ?

The growing awareness that crime has causes was one of the reasons for the humanization of the criminal law. For the last two hundred years the sentences imposed by our criminal courts were becoming less severe and less painful;

prison sentences were imposed less frequently, their duration was growing shorter; chains, hard labor, solitary confinement were becoming rarer, and the most severe sentence, the death penalty, seemed about to disappear.[63]

As long as that trend continued, our obvious need for a criminal law permitted us to overlook its moral ambiguity. But that trend is now being reversed. The country's frustration with a high crime rate that stubbornly refuses to decline has created a climate that favors a return to harsher sentences. That reversal forces us to confront the moral problem that we punish crime that is caused by conditions for which we are at least in part responsible. Even if we have not created them, we have failed to removed them.[64]

How are we to resolve the dilemma? Justice Holmes had a radical answer: "If I were having a philosophic talk," he wrote, "with a man I was going to have hanged or electrocuted, I should say I don't doubt that your act was inevitable for you but to make it more avoidable by others we propose to sacrifice you to the common good. You may regard yourself a soldier dying for your country if you like. But the law must keep its promises."[65]

The other radical solution is open only to the people of *Erewhon*. The crime for which the convict received the sentence of hard labor for life was, we are informed, having contracted pulmonary consumption. We learn from the narrator:

63. "The gradual humanization of the penal system—juvenile courts, probation, parole, open prisons, and so on—is due to our growing insight into the social roots of crime, into the influence of heredity and environment on the offender, into the causal determinants of human behaviour" (Arthur Koestler, *Reflections on Hanging* [New York: Macmillan, 1957], p. 101.

64. The relationship between the moral stance of the criminal law and the fact that crime has causes is ably analyzed in an important German study: Dr. med. Manfred Danner, "Gibt es einen freien Willen?" [Is there a free will?] (Kriminalistik Verlag, Heidelberg: Hamburg, 1977). See on this topic also Norval Morris's brilliant if despairing essay in the Orwellian manner: "The Brothel Boy" (chap. 1 of *Madness and the Criminal Law* [Chicago: University of Chicago Press, 1983]).

65. Holmes-Laski Letters, M. D. H. Howe, ed. (New York: Atheneum, 1963), p. 806.

> In that country if a man falls into ill health, . . . or fails bodily in any way before he is seventy years old, he is tried before a jury of his countrymen, and if convicted is held up to public scorn and sentenced more or less severely as the case may be. There are subdivisions of illness into crimes and misdemeanors . . . a man being punished very heavily for serious illness, while failure of eyes or hearing in anyone sixty-five who had good health hitherto, is dealt with by fine only.

If a man in *Erewhon* commits what *we* call a crime, he is "treated"—*Erewhon* was published in 1871—by his private "straightener" or in a hospital at the public expense.[66]

This road is not open to us, if for no other reason than that we know so little about how to straighten a criminal. For the time being, we rely on the criminal law to do the straightening, even if the borderline between healing and deterrence remains blurred. Moreover, the criminal law, if not by its actual correction process at least by its institutional presence, is part of the moral structure on which we base society. By threatening punishment it prevents many crimes, and it serves to remind us all that to commit a crime is a bad thing. The criminal law itself is thus a link in the causal chain that determines whether or not a person will commit a crime.

There is, however, a middle ground for reform between cynical abdication and utopian reversal, to which we are led by the realization that crime has causes and that some of them are our responsibility.

The first consequence should be that *retribution must lose its prestige as a rationale* for punishment. We should nurture some of the feeling that inspired a justice of the Norwegian Supreme Court to remark: "Our grandparents punished and they did it with a clear conscience. We punish too, but we do it with a bad conscience."[67]

66. S. Butler, *Erewhon* (see n. 58 above), p. 93.

67. As reported by Andenaes (see n. 49 above). The great German jurist Gustav Radbruch had an even more general insight. He was known to say, "To be a good jurist one must be a jurist with a bad conscience."

Second, instead of abandoning the search for alternative ways of reducing crime we should redouble our efforts to find some. This is particularly true with respect to the correction process, the one phase of a criminal's existence for which we are totally responsible. The controlled experiment that has brought us so many new insights in our fight against disease should find a greater place in our criminal law, especially during its sentencing phase.

Finally, our awareness that crime has causes should increase our efforts to locate the causes of crime and, more important, our willingness to pay for their removal.

In general, we should accept the similarity between physical and moral diseases, the other great insight of Quetelet, who considered the physical and moral pathology of society as an indivisible unit. Our disgust and horror of crime need not diminish in the process, but it will change direction. It should not be exclusively moralistic in nature but should become more objective, as our horror of the plague must have been. Thus, we might be able, without diminishing our outrage at crime, to see the tragedy that lies behind it.

The Core of the Problem

It may be difficult to bare the intricate network of the causes of crime, but at least here in the United States it is not difficult to find out where crime grows.

We obtain a first directive from the United States Census statistics on the frequency of violent crime by size of the community. Figure 18 shows that the rate of crime grows rapidly with the size of the community.

Crime grows best in the big cities, and New York City is the biggest. And within the City of New York, as the numbers in figure 19 show, it is the slums and ghettos that form the major breeding grounds for crime. To the extent to which arrest figures on the whole mirror the incidence of crime, figure 19 gives a clear picture of

Fig. 18
Violent Crime by Size of Community: Annual Rates per 100,000 Population

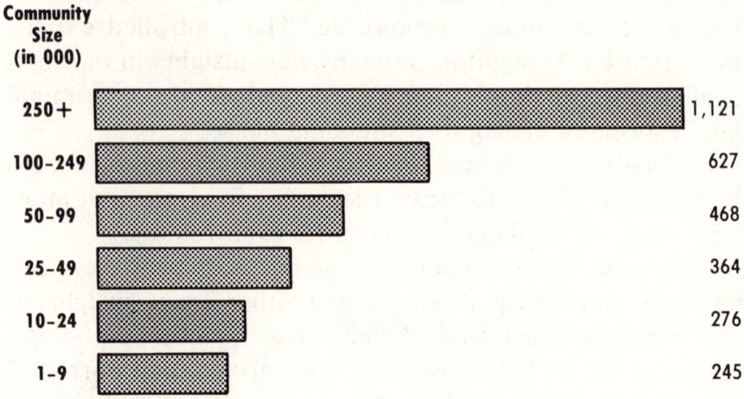

Source: 1970 US Census, Abstract Table No. 294

where crime breeds and of the age at which it becomes virulent.[68]

Figure 19 spreads over two pages; the left-hand page covers the male population of New York City, the right-hand page the female one. Each sex group is divided into three ethnic groups: blacks, hispanics, and whites; and each ethnic group is divided into seven age groups, from "up to 9," to "50 and over." The graph thus represents two (sex) times three (ethnic) times seven (age) groups, altogether forty-two subgroups of the New York population.

The *width* of each bar, or the cumulative width of several of them, represents their respective percent share of New York City's population. These population shares are listed in the second row of numbers below the bars. The *height* of each bar represents the arrest rate, the number of arrests during the year 1977 for every 100 persons in that particular subgroup of the population. The *surface* of each bar represents the amount of arrests and thereby their percent share of all felony arrests made in New York City; these arrest shares are listed in the bottom row of numbers below the bars.

Figure 19 conveys several messages:

1. Crime is still a predominantly male occupation. In every group of the population, female arrests are a negligible fraction of all arrests—on the average, 10 percent. Males provide 90 percent of all arrests.

2. Crime is an activity of the young and peaks at the end of the teenage years. From then on, the arrest rates

68. The arrest figures on which fig. 19 is based come from the New York City Police Department. The basic estimates of the population figure for that between-census year 1977 was provided by Dr. Edward Garb of Market Statistics Inc. Expert friends have directed me to him as the most reliable source for that estimate. After consultation with Dr. Garb and friends in the Bureau of the Census, I have augmented his figures as follows in order to correct for the undercount of minorities and evasion by illegal immigrants: proportionally, I have added, to make up for the undercount, 291,000 persons to the black and Hispanic population; and I have added 300,000 Hispanics to adjust for the evasion by illegal immigrants. Both numbers constitute generous adjustments, since I was anxious to avoid spuriously high arrest rates.

Fig. 19
Number of Annual Arrests per 100 Persons in 1977 in New York City by Sex, Age, and Ethnic Background

Males-Black

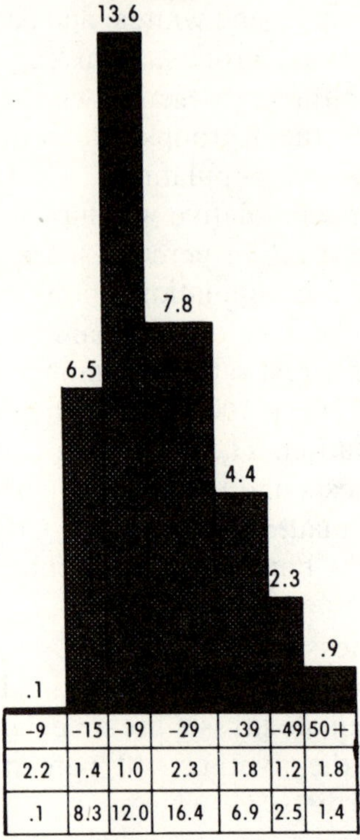

Age	-9	-15	-19	-29	-39	-49	50+	
% NY Pop.	2.2	1.4	1.0	2.3	1.8	1.2	1.8	**11.7**
% Arrests	.1	8.3	12.0	16.4	6.9	2.5	1.4	**47.6**

Males-Hispanic

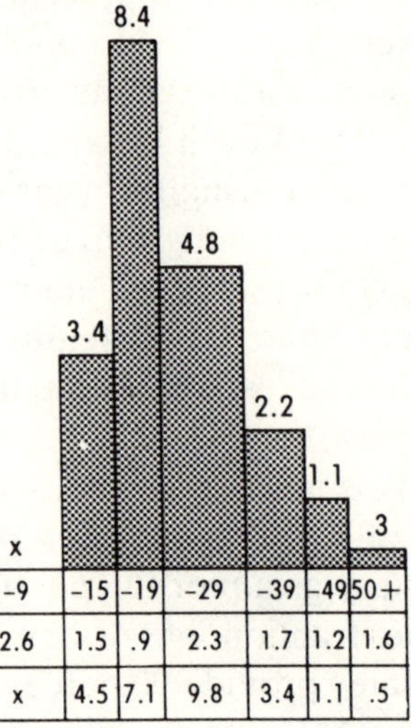

Age	-9	-15	-19	-29	-39	-49	50+	
% NY Pop.	2.6	1.5	.9	2.3	1.7	1.2	1.6	**11.8**
% Arrests	x	4.5	7.1	9.8	3.4	1.1	.5	**26.4**

Males-White

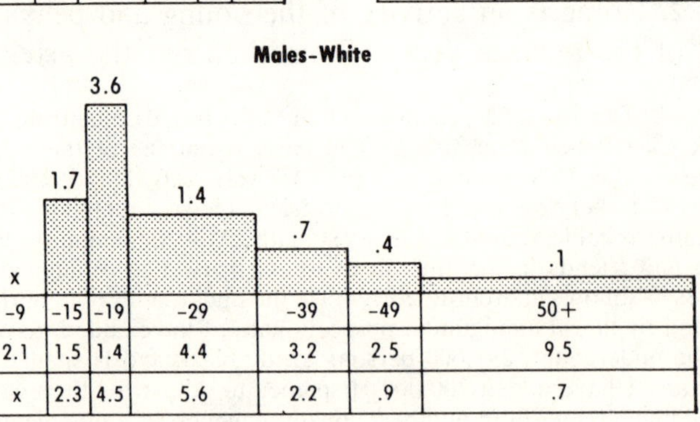

Age	-9	-15	-19	-29	-39	-49	50+	
% NY Pop.	2.1	1.5	1.4	4.4	3.2	2.5	9.5	**24.6**
% Arrests	x	2.3	4.5	5.6	2.2	.9	.7	**16.2**

Females-Black

	x	.7	1.3	1.2	.6	.3	.1	
ge	-9	-15	-19	-29	-39	-49	50+	
Y Pop.	2.1	1.3	.9	2.7	2.0	1.4	2.3	**12.7**
rrests	x	.8	1.1	3.0	1.0	.4	.2	**6.5**

Females-Hispanic

x	.2	.5	.3	.2	.1	x	
-9	-15	-19	-29	-39	-49	50+	
2.3	1.3	.8	2.7	1.8	1.2	1.6	**11.7**
x	.3	.4	.7	.3	.1	x	**1.8**

Females-White

	x	.1	.1	.2	.1	x	x	
ge	-9	-15	-19	-29	-39	-49	50+	
IY Pop.	2.0	1.5	1.4	4.3	2.9	2.7	12.7	**27.5**
Arrests	x	.2	.2	.6	.2	.1	.2	**1.5**

decline steeply with age; at age forty, crime has reached a negligible level.

3. The arrest rates of blacks are about twice as high as those of Hispanics, and about four times as high as the arrest rates of whites. Roughly 48 percent of all arrests are of black males, who represent 12 percent of the population; 26 percent of all arrests are of Hispanic males, who represent another 12 percent of the population; 16 percent of all arrests are of white males, who form 25 percent of the population.

4. Roughly 42 percent of all felony arrests are provided by teenagers. The peculiar relationship between crime and age, and the preponderance of male teenage crime is by no means an American phenomenon. The basic structure of that relationship is the same the world over; only the level of crime varies.

Several caveats for reading these arrest statistics are in order. First, the arrest rates per 100,000 are just that: the number of arrests made during one year per 100,000 population. They do not denote the number of *persons* arrested because some of them will have been arrested more than once during that year. The number of arrested persons therefore is smaller than the number of arrests. Data collected for Washington, D.C., suggest that, because of that duplication, the number of *persons* arrested for a felony charge may be around 20 percent smaller than the number of such arrests.[69] Second, the more crimes a person has committed, the greater the likelihood that he will be arrested. Finally, the likelihood of being arrested may not be the same for all lawbreakers. The police might arrest differentially more persons of certain subgroups of the population. It seems, for instance, that teenagers have a greater chance of being arrested after a crime, partly because they are more likely to act in groups.[70] There is also a suggestion

69. Unpublished data from the Institute for Law and Social Research (INSLAW) in Washington, D. C. See also Brian Forst, Judith Lucianovic, and Sarah J. Cox, *What Happens after Arrest? A Court Perspective of Police Operations in the District of Columbia* (Washington, D.C.: Institute for Law and Social Research, 1977), pp. 9–10.

that robberies by blacks are more often reported than robberies by whites, while the opposite is true for assaults.[71] In turn, professional criminals may know better than amateurs how to avoid arrest. The data concerning such differences, however, are insufficient to make numerical adjustments.

To relate figures on the frequency of crime to the ethnic background of the arrested persons raises the suspicion of a racist perspective. Nothing of the sort is involved. The statistics that show high crime rates for ethnic minorities have no racist implications because they do not show what causes these rates to be high.

The ethnic classification is a stand-in for other characteristics, socioeconomic status, parents' education, and general social conditions—data that unfortunately are not available in a form that allows them to be related directly to the people who commit crimes and the people who do not. The following three pieces of statistical information will help to document the true meaning of the ethnic classification.

First, figure 20, which presents the official statistics on the relative state of deprivation of the ethnic minority school children in New York City.

Next are two items that show that it is not the particular ethnic minorities of our day that create the high crime rates, but every ethnic minority that formed at one time or other the bottom of the socioeconomic scale. The first item comes from a 1931 report of the Wickersham Commission: "One of the most significant findings of this part of the study is the fact that, while the relative rates of delinquents in these high-rate areas remained more or less constant over a period of 20 years, the nationality composition of the population changed almost completely during this interval. As the older national groups moved out of these areas of

70. Cf. Franklin E. Zimring, "Kids, Groups and Crime: Some Implications of a Well-Known Secret," *Journal of Criminal Law & Criminology* 72 (1981): 867.

71. Michael J. Hindelang, "Race and Involvement in Common Law Personal Crimes," *American Sociological Review* 43 (1978): 93.

Fig. 20
Percent of New York City Children below Poverty Line by Ethnic Background (1976)

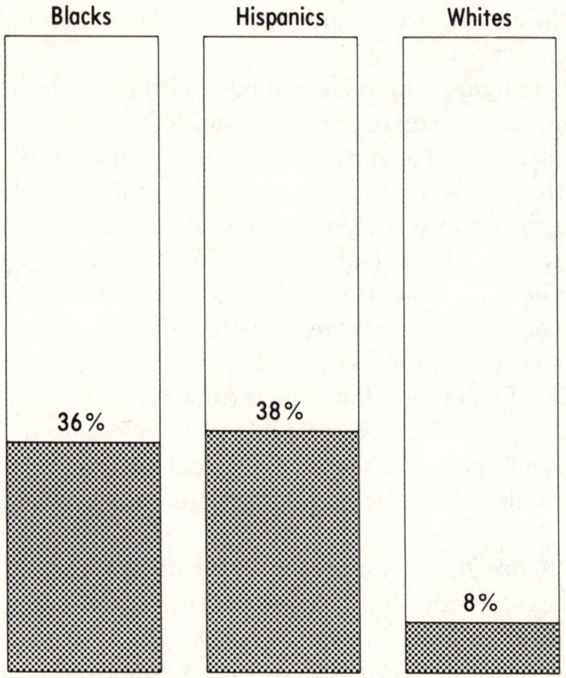

Source:
1976 Survey of Income and Education; Report of Foundation for Child Development, New York, p. 118.

first immigrant settlement, the percentage of juvenile delinquents in these groups showed a consistent decrease."[72]

The second item comes from the June 1864 (sic!) issue of *Harper's Weekly,* reporting on the activity of the New York City police during the preceding year: "Of these (54,751 arrests in New York City) over one-half were arrests of persons born in Ireland" (p. 510).

Thus, far from implying any racist origins of the high crime rate among our ethnic minorities, the statistics should leave no doubt that its true causes lie elsewhere. The crime statistics by ethnic background, however, serves one important purpose: it unmistakably shows *where* the causes of crime thrive—in the slums and ghettos of the city. And the crime statistics by age shows us that crime begins early in a young man's life. These two insights could guide us, if we cared, to the only open road to effective crime control.

Beyond Law Enforcement: Toward Preventive Crime Control

The notion that dealing with crime is the job of the criminal justice system—of police, prosecutors, courts, and prisons—is deeply imbedded in our thinking. But the reality is otherwise.

Some time ago, Karl Menninger, the distinguished doctor, testified before a committee of the United States Senate: "If crime disappears in your neighborhood it will not be due to such primitive notions as arrests and jailings but because we have found ways of preventing it from occurring. By placing them in jails we make more criminals out of youths than we cure. If the medical profession had a record like that people would rise up in wrath."[73]

Judge Bazelon reached the same conclusion: "By now it should come as no surprise that street crime cannot be

72. National Commission on Law Observance and Enforcement, U.S. Wickersham Commission Report on *Causes of Crime* (Washington, D.C.: Government Printing Office, 1931), 2:108.

73. From a personal communication.

'solved' by police, courts, or prisons. . . . They cannot begin to address the causes of crime."[74]

And here is what a thoughtful police chief has to say: "The police alone cannot solve the crime problem. Neither can the combined police and criminal justice 'system,' even if it were improved to merit the 'system' label."[75]

As long as a country's crime level is low, law enforcement can maintain the appearance of effectiveness. How limited the power of law enforcement is we see more clearly when the crime level is as high as ours. There is as little justification for crediting law enforcement systems abroad with keeping their crime rates low as there is justification for blaming ours for allowing such a high level of crime.

The power of law enforcement is limited not only because its reach is small but also because it comes too late. It is late in two respects: it acts only after the event, and it confronts the lawbreaker at a point in his life when it is usually too late to change course. That is why law enforcement alone can never solve the crime problem.

Crime control, to become effective, must look beyond enforcement. Our experience with a similar problem, controlling "murder on the highways," showed us the direction. There too our first impulse was to recommend better law enforcement, more highway patrols, more arrests, and stiffer sentences for negligent drivers. The communities that have effectively reduced highway fatalities, however, have gone a different and better route. First, they have straightened and widened the highways and have replaced crossings with overpasses, thereby removing some of the major causes of accidents. Second, they have improved the highway ambulance service. Finally, reducing the highway speed limit has proved to be the most powerful remedy. The deterrent power of stricter law enforcement has remained a subsidiary minor strategy.

Medicine provides another analogy. To heal illness when it occurs is only half of medicine's job; to prevent it is

74. See n. 61 above.
75. Patrick Murphy (see n. 7 above), p. 260.

the other half. Preventive medicine follows two strategies. One aims at *specific* prevention through such means as vaccines or the elimination of toxic substances from our food and places of work. The other aims at making us *generally* more disease resistant.

Crime control, patently impotent in its present form, coming after the event and after the cancer has obtained a foothold in the young minds, has yet to develop its preventive arm.

There are some encouraging success stories of specific crime prevention. Burglary was effectively reduced by the installation of better locks, robbery through better street lights, auto theft through indelible motor numbers and electrical antitheft devices. Theft of welfare checks was reduced by depositing them directly into the recipient's bank account. All these measures are the counterpart of redesigning our highways with the aim of reducing car accidents. The counterpart of improving highway ambulance service would be the removal of the more than fifty million handguns now in civilian hands; the measure would not necessarily reduce the number of armed assaults, but it would reduce their fatality rate; knife attack results in death only about one-fifth as often.

Of general crime prevention—the task of controlling crime by cutting off its roots—we know little, partly because we have not yet begun to think about it. Probably we are loath to think about it since the job would require great efforts and a great deal of money. And why, we hear, spend money on potential criminals when we do not have enough for the youngsters who do not threaten to break the law? Moreover, one may wonder how the task of crime prevention differs from reshaping society itself, a job so large and unfocused that its effect on crime must remain incidental.

Fortunately, what little knowledge we have of the causes of crime, or at least of its geographic concentration, allows us to narrow the job of crime prevention. For New York, as for many other cities, the crime and arrest statistics tell us where to begin: with the boys from the ghettos.

We will not solve our crime problem before we have solved the problems of our ghettos, a big task, on which so far we have worked with little diligence. But we must make a beginning, and our statistics show us where we must start. Crime, as we saw, begins early in life, and we must make a radical effort to reach these youngsters early in life before their life-style is formed.

The school statistics for Harlem allow us to come close to the target by identifying the endangered youngsters among all the boys in the slums. The absenteeism rate in some of the high schools that serve Harlem reached 45 percent for every day of the 1973 school year.[76] The actual rate was even higher because that rate excludes from its base the substantial proportion of youngsters who had dropped out of school or had been dropped.[77] The 45 percent rate, moreover, is the average absenteeism rate for boys *and* girls; the absenteeism rate for boys, who commit the bulk of the crimes, is significantly above that for girls. Hence, in Harlem the absenteeism rate for boys is likely to exceed 50 percent. If one allows for some intermittent school attendance by these boys, say for one-third of the schooltime, the official Harlem absenteeism rate implies that about 75 percent of the boys are out of school for two out of every three school days. It is a reasonable guess that among these absent, mostly truant, youngsters the proportion of present and future lawbreakers is high.[78] If this inference is correct, then we know the targets of crime prevention almost by name and address.

76. Board of Education computer printout. In addition, some students, made aware of the fact that the size of the federal school subsidies is based on attendance figures, to please the school often make sure they are recorded as attending and then leave.

77. Forty-five percent of the ninth graders who entered New York high schools in 1974 had left before graduation (report of the Board of Education, 1979, cited in *New York Times,* March 3, 1979, p. 17). There are signs that the situation in Harlem is improving. But careful auditing will be required to determine the reach of such improvements.

78. A number of studies tell us that juvenile offenders differ from their less delinquent counterparts in their greater resistance to schooling. See, for instance, Gwyn Nettler, *Explaining Crime* (New York,

In spite of its present failure, the school remains the avenue through which we must address the problem and try to reach these youngsters; it remains the only institutional point of access society has to them.

Our search for better crime control has brought us to an unexpected destination, past the many way stations of law enforcement that fail to provide relief, to the point in life where crime begins. To be sure, we might come too late. By the time boys enter high school, criminal patterns may be firmly entrenched.

The goal is simply stated: When Johnny, age eleven, tells Jimmy, age ten, "I have watched that Chevy over there for two weeks; nobody ever drove it, let's go and get it." Jimmy must say, "Sorry, John, I don't do such things."[79] If there is one point on which psychiatrists and educators agree, it is that character is established early in life and that with every passing year it becomes more difficult to change it. Crime prevention, therefore, must start early. The place to begin is the nursery school.

The obstacles will be formidable. We shall be told that we have tried everything and wasted millions in efforts to improve the school system. And we must answer that we have not tried hard enough and not the right way, that we must get out of the ruts that have led to the present dead end, that we must build schools that can become cherished centers of the children's lives.

We shall be told that the schools cannot be the whole of the children's lives, that the home remains, and the street with its present generation of youngsters, and the larger

---

McGraw-Hill, 1974), p. 164. While such correlation does not reveal which of the two factors, if any, is the cause of the other, we must act on the presumption that a better school would aid better behavior.

79. "Legal social control can only have worked well when supported by internal restraint" (from Donald T. Campbell, "Legal and Primary-Group Social Control," to be published in M. Grutes and P. Bohannan, eds., *Law, Biology and Culture*). The statistics in our text and the accompanying commentary is well illuminated by a carefully written portrait of one wayward youngster by Joseph B. Treaster, "Crime at an Early Age" (*New York Times*, November 9, 1981, sec. 1, p. 17).

society that hesitates to grant full equality to the young men from the ghetto. And we must answer that the new schools will be only the pivotal point of a beginning, the first step in an effort to remove the conditions that have brought us to the present impasse.

We shall be told that the real dangers arise after the nursery age, that statistics foretell with grim precision the onset and course of crime during growth into young manhood. And we must answer that we will appoint as teachers only the princes and princesses of the profession, who will establish bonds with their children that will hold when the dangerous years begin and will endure until they are over.[80]

We will be told that there is no money available for such a radical venture. And we must answer that, once we understand that this is the only hope for controlling the crime that wastes our cities, we will find the money.

To cite once more the great Quetelet who made us aware of the deep roots of crime: "The ability to modify the forces that determine his fate is one of man's noblest characteristics. By using all the powers of his intellect, he can master these forces to some extent and thereby bring about a better society."[81]

That we must begin with young children should make the difficult task easier; children everywhere are our friends.

80. The reform plans will have to be radical; perhaps Hank Aaron and Willie Mays should be asked to become school principals.

81. *Sur l'homme* . . . , p. 13 (see n. 59, this chapter).

Two / Crimes and Arrests

Amount of Crime

Measuring the amount of crime is more difficult than it might appear at first glance. The most widely used measure is the number of crimes reported to the police and in turn by the police to the public. Not all crimes, however, are reported to the police. Some crimes, such as violent crimes in the home, shoplifting, or embezzlement, are often privately settled and not reported. Many crimes remain unreported because the victim expects only unpleasantness from such reporting. The so-called victimless crimes, such as violations of the narcotics and gambling laws, are practically never reported; they come to light only by police surveillance or undercover work followed by an arrest. Also certain types of victim crimes often remain unreported because they remain undetected, primarily white-collar crimes (such as tax evasion or other frauds) and, for technical reasons, many acts of arson. Finally, there is the occasional awkwardness that a police department, in order to look good, will not report all the crimes that have been reported to them. There is little one can do about determining the true number of victimless crimes. But ways have been found to estimate the number of unreported victim crimes. The "dark" crime figures are determined through so-called victimization surveys, public opinion polls that inquire whether and how often the respondents have been victims of a crime.

In spite of its shortcomings, the number of crimes reported to the police has, for good reasons, remained the basic measure of crime. Such a statistic, the number of felonies reported in the City of New York during one year, broken down into the various broad crime categories, is presented in figure 21. The year is 1971, the year in which we drew the sample of felony arrests in New York City on which this study is based. During that year, 510,048 felonies—the major crimes in contrast to misdemeanors and lesser violations—were reported to and by the police, approximately 1 for every 16 of the roughly 8 million residents of New York City. The crimes are presented in three broad groups. The first two—violent crimes against the person and nonviolent property crimes—form the index crimes, so named because they are the crimes counted in the Justice Department's Uniform Crime Reports, the standard measure of crime in the United States. The third group is formed primarily by the victimless crimes, so-called because they have victims only in a figurative sense—narcotics and gambling—or in a potential sense—illegal possession of a weapon. The category "other" crimes contains also a few victim crimes, such as arson.[1]

The shares of the various crime categories come perhaps as a surprise. The two most feared and most publicized crimes, homicide and rape, together account for less than 1 percent of all reported felonies, and assault accounts for 4 percent. As in most cities, burglary is the most frequently committed crime in New York; it accounts for over one-third of all reported felonies; auto theft and other larcenies account together for another third; and robbery accounts for about one-sixth of the reported felonies.

Criminologists the world over have known for a long time that the number of crimes reported to the police are only a fraction of the number of crimes actually committed. The United States was the first country to explore systematically the "dark" crime figures. An exploratory study undertaken at the behest of President Johnson's Commission on Crime and Violence suggested that the proportion

1. See n. 2, Chap. 1.

Fig. 21
Felonies Reported to the Police:
New York City 1971

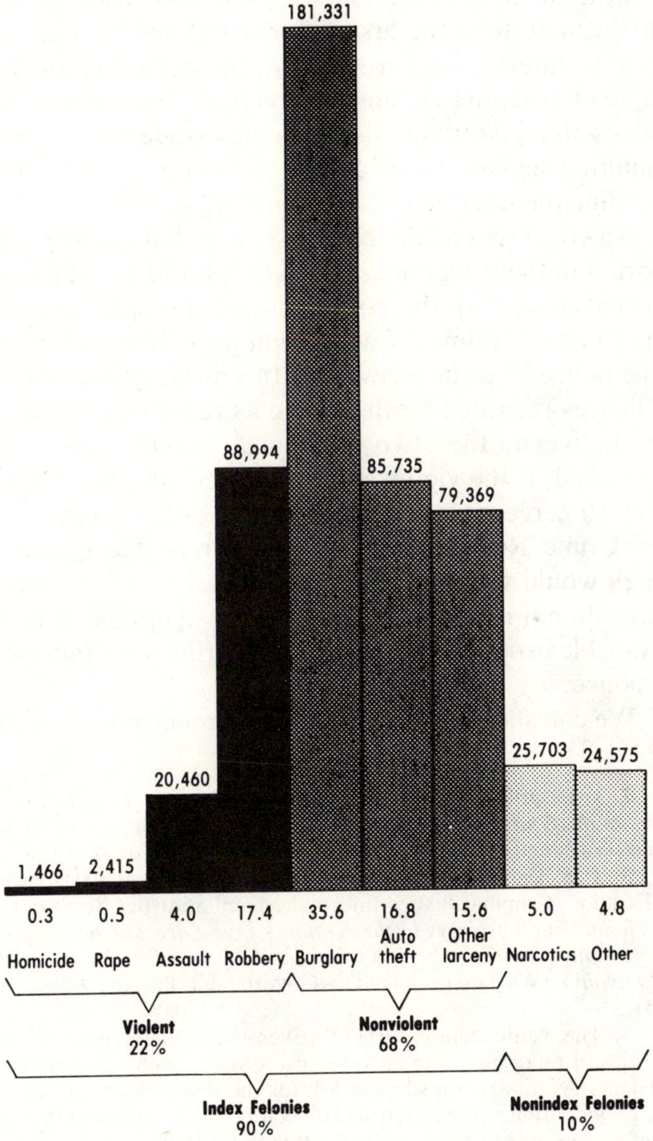

Source: FBI Uniform Crime Reports, 1971.

of unreported crime might be substantial.[2] Following up on this suggestion, the Law Enforcement Assistance Administration, in cooperation with the U.S. Bureau of the Census, undertook the first major search for the real crime figures by interviewing in each of several cities a probability sample of potential victims—individuals, households, businesses, and institutions—about the incidence of crimes committed against them during the twelve month period preceding the interview.[3]

An effort was made, of course, to link the crime figures reported in these victimization surveys to the crime figures reported to and by the police through the question, "Did you report this crime (of which you have informed us now) to the police?" If the answers to this question had matched the figures recorded by the police as reported to them, the link between the two measures would have been established. If the victim survey showed 100,000 crimes, of which 60 percent were reported to the police, and the Uniform Crime Reports showed 60,000 reported crimes, all figures would fall into place. For a variety of reasons the figures do not match.[4] It is nevertheless possible to make a reasonable estimate of the number of crimes not reported to the police.

We can show how this estimating procedure applies for

2. U.S. Office of Law Enforcement Assistance, *Criminal Victimization in the United States: A Report of a National Survey,* by Philip H. Ennis (Washington, D.C.: Government Printing Office, May 1967).

3. U.S. Department of Justice, Law Enforcement Assistance Administration, Criminal Justice Information and Statistics Service, *Criminal Victimization Surveys in the Nation's Five Largest Cities: National Crime Panel Surveys–Chicago, Detroit, Los Angeles, New York, and Philadelphia* (Washington, D. C.: Government Printing Office, April 1975).

4. The victimization surveys cover the resident population; the statistics of reported crime includes also crimes against commuters and transients. Victimization surveys ask for the respondent's recall over a time period; crimes committed shortly before the beginning of that period are often reported as having fallen within the period. And crime victims, especially in the lower socioeconomic strata, are generally difficult to locate for survey purposes. Even the U.S. Bureau of the Census has encountered these difficulties.

New York City since a special victimization survey was conducted there in the spring of 1973.[5] For our analysis we have accepted two sets of figures—the crimes reported to the police, and the rate at which persons said they had reported or failed to report to the police the crimes of which they had been the victims. From these two sets we have estimated the number of committed crimes, as shown in figure 22. Except for the number of homicides,[6] which we assume is not significantly understated, all major crime categories are underreported to some extent. Auto theft, burglary, and robbery are the crimes most frequently reported to the police, partly because these losses are often insured and require proof of report. Assault and larcenies other than auto theft are the crimes least often reported. On the average, 54 percent of these major crimes are reported to the police; 46 percent are unreported. As against the reported number of some 460,000 index felonies in 1971 in New York City, the true figure is likely to be around 850,000.

Rates of Arrests

We have estimated that somewhat more than half of all committed crimes are reported to the police. We now turn to these reported crimes and the arrests they have engendered. The rate of arrests, the ratio of arrests to the number of reported crimes, is a figure of some importance. It is a rough measure of the risk a criminal runs and, within limits, also a measure of police effectiveness. However, unless read with care, arrest rates may convey misleading information.

5. "The surveys . . . were carried out during the first quarter of 1973 and covered criminal acts that took place during the 12-month period prior to the month of the interview, a time frame roughly comparable to the calendar year 1972" (see report cited in n. 4 above). As to the future, see Albert J. Reiss, Jr., "Towards a Revitalization of Theory and Research on Victimization by Crime," *Journal of Criminal Law & Criminology* 72 (1981): 704.

6. For obvious reasons, homicide is not one of the crimes covered by a survey that interviews victims.

Fig. 22
Felonies Reported and Felonies Committed in New York City

	Number Reported to Police (a)	Percent Said to Be Reported to Police (b)	Est. Number of Committed Crimes (a÷b)
Homicide	1,466	100 (est.)	1,466
Rape	2,415	61	3,959
Assault	20,460	41	49,902
Robbery	88,994	60	148,323
Burglary	181,331	67	270,643
Auto theft	85,735	73	117,445
Other larceny	79,369	31	256,029
Total	459,770	54	847,767

Sources: for (a), FBI Uniform Crime Reports, 1971
for (b), LEAA Victimization Surveys

Of the 510,048 felonies reported in 1971 to the police, 102,148 resulted in an arrest, an average arrest rate of 20 percent, one arrest for every five reported felonies. The arrest rates for the various crime categories, as figure 23 shows, differ widely around this average, from 6 percent for larceny other than auto theft to over 90 percent for the victimless (nonindex) crimes. The arrest rate for homicide, 78 percent, is high for two reasons. The police allocate comparatively more resources to the investigation of this most serious crime, and suspects are more easily found because in the majority of homicide cases the offender in one way or another was related to the victim. Similar reasons account for the relatively high arrest rates for assault and rape. The arrest rate for robbery is lower (20 percent) because the crime is normally committed by strangers and often with but one witness, the victim, making it difficult to trace the perpetrator. The average arrest rate for violent crimes against the person is 26 percent; for nonviolent property crimes, it is 8 percent. The arrest rate for all index crimes, combining both these categories, is 12 percent.

This average contrasts sharply with the arrest rates for narcotics and "other" crimes, in which the arrest rate is close to 100 percent (89 and 96). This contrast does not reflect higher police efficiency or higher risks on the part of the criminal. For the victim crimes, the arrest normally follows the report to the police that a crime has been committed. For the victimless crimes it is as a rule the police arrest that causes the crime to be entered as "reported to the police." The same is true for violations of the weapons laws or for such clear victim crimes as arson: as a rule it is only after somebody is arrested for arson or for illegal possession of a weapon that the police will enter those crimes into the list of "felonies reported to the police." We have no way of knowing the true number of committed narcotics crimes or of illegal possessions of a weapon. Thus, the arrest rates for these crimes are meaningless as measures of police effectiveness and must be excluded from all average arrest rates.

Fig. 23

Arrest Rates (as Percent of Reported Crimes) for Major Crime Categories

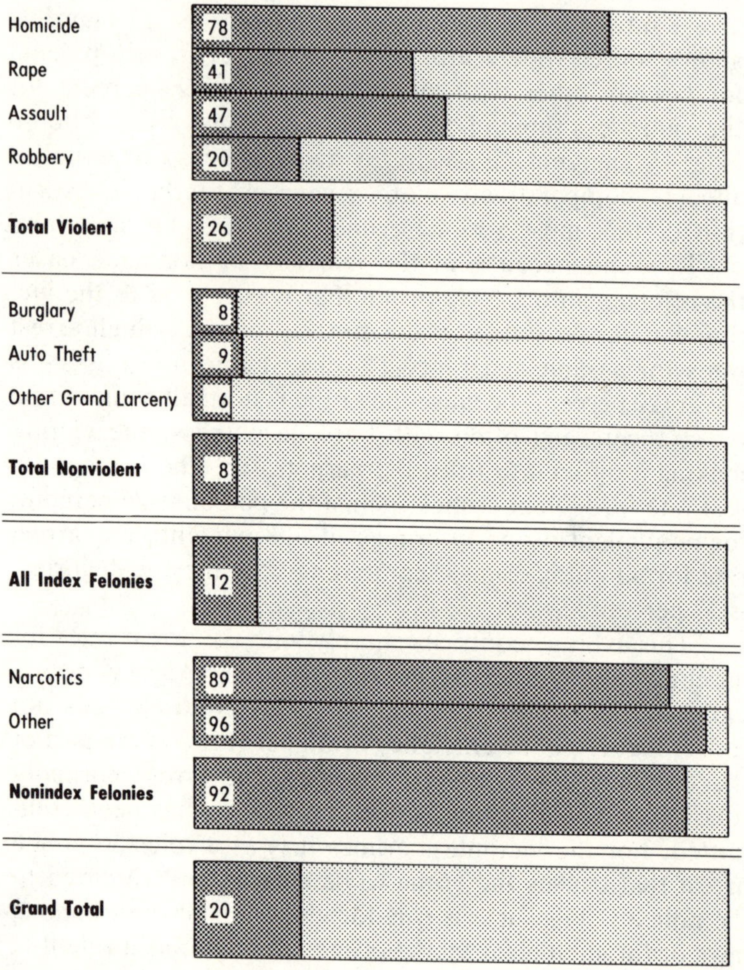

Sources: N.Y. City Police Department and 2000 Sample

Figure 24 shows another aspect of the relationship between arrests for index crimes and for victimless and "other" crimes. The index crimes constitute 90 percent of all crimes reported to the police, but only 55 percent of all police arrests. The 10 percent narcotics and "other" crimes account for 45 percent, almost one-half, of all police arrests.

Felony arrests, however, as figure 25 shows, are only part of the enforcement activity of the New York Police Department; they account for less than half of all the arrests made by the police. The remainder are arrests for misdemeanors and for what the law calls violations and infractions. Moving traffic violations, which far outnumber crimes proper, are not included. In addition, the courts obtain cases through police summonses, which may be issued in lieu of arrests to persons charged with no more than a misdemeanor. The majority of the prosecutions for lesser offenses are initiated by such a summons. In this wider context, felony arrests account for 19 percent of all processed cases.

Who is Arrested?

The statistics about the persons arrested and charged with a crime provide most of our knowledge about who commits the crimes. We record the age, sex, ethnic background, and other demographic characteristics of the persons we arrest and take that collection of facts to represent by and large the population of persons who commit these crimes. Such projection rests on a number of tenuous assumptions which were discussed in the text accompanying figure 19 above.

Figure 26 gives the demographic profile, by sex, age, ethnicity, and criminal record of the persons arrested on a felony charge. The vast majority of these persons were male. Thirty-one percent were under 20 years old; 12 percent were under the age of 16, and therefore by New York law did not come under the authority of the criminal courts;

Fig. 24
Contrast between Arrests and Reported Felonies: Index Felonies and Other Felonies

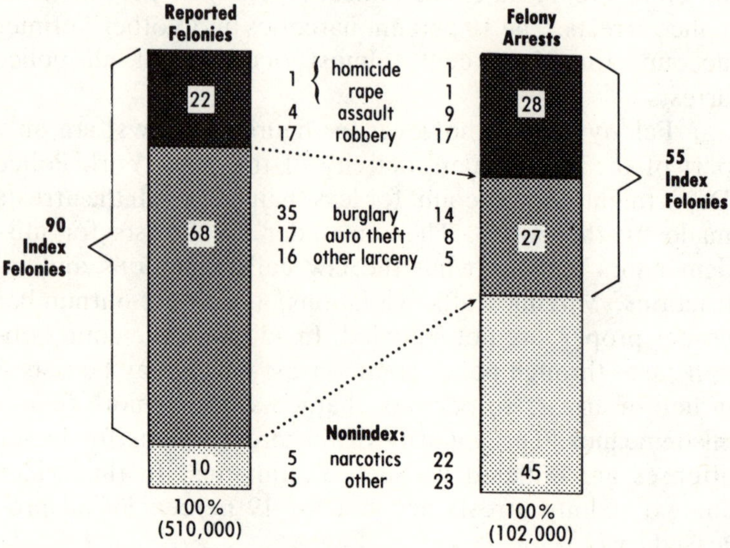

Sources: N.Y. City Police Department and 2000 Sample

Fig. 25
Police Apprehensions for All Penal Code Violations

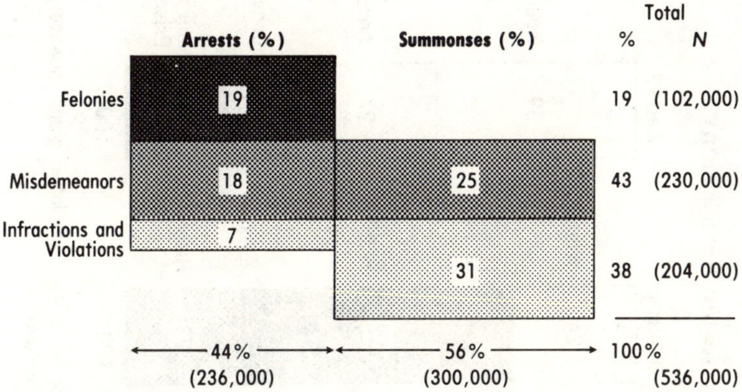

Source: N.Y. City Police Department

Fig. 26
Demographic Profile of Persons Arrested for a Felony

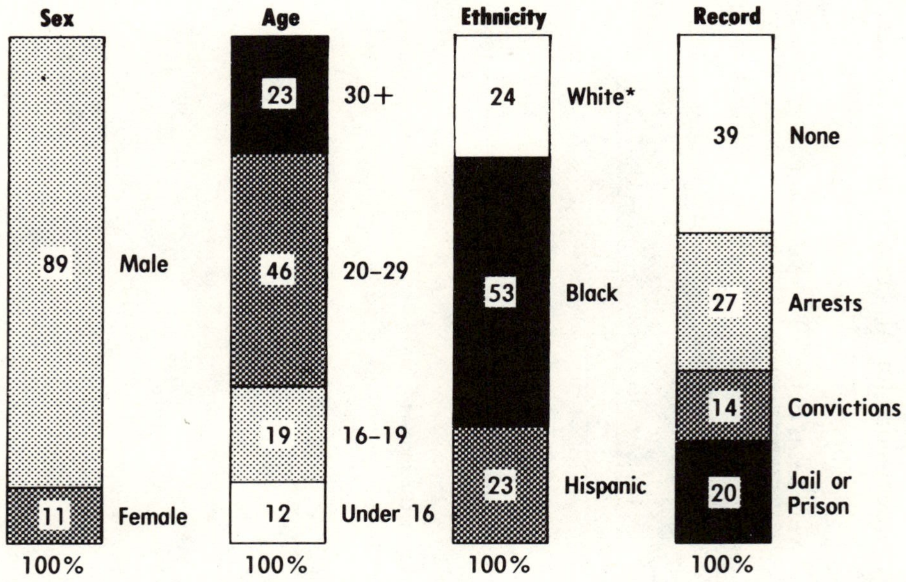

*More precisely, "white and other than Blacks or Hispanics." The latter group, however, constitutes less than one percent of the arrested defendants.

Source: 2000 Sample

19 percent were between 16 and 19 years. Almost one-half of all arrested persons were in their twenties; fewer than 10 percent were over 40. The distribution by ethnic background was approximately one-quarter Hispanic, one-quarter white, and one-half black. Thirty-nine percent of the defendants had never been arrested before; 27 percent had been arrested but not convicted; 14 percent had been convicted but had not served time in jail or prison; 20 percent had served time. Thus, approximately 60 percent of the persons arrested for a felony had at least an arrest record.[7]

Crime, it appears, is a preoccupation of men, of young men at that, and often of young nonwhites. This demographic statement fails to consider two important stratifications, information for which is unavailable, those by income and by education of the parents. Ethnicity is largely a stand-in for the distribution by income and education of the parents. If we had these arrest rates, we very probably would have concluded that crime is a preoccupation of the young men from poor and hence uneducated families.

We now consider in figure 27 the demographic profile as to sex, ethnic background, criminal record, and age for each of the eight major crime categories. These crime categories are listed across the top. Under each heading four bars represent the distribution of the arrested persons by sex, ethnicity, criminal record, and age. To simplify the picture, we have made each of the four distributions dichotomous, female/male, white/nonwhite, prior conviction/no prior conviction, under twenty years/twenty years and older. Only one of the alternatives is shown (in the shaded section); the other occupies the space difference to the 100 percent level. Thus, if the first bar shows that 4 percent of the persons charged at arrest with homicide were female, this means that (100−4=) 96 percent were male. The dotted line across each of the four sets of eight bars represents the average sex, ethnic, etc., distribution for all arrests, taken from figure 26. These lines facilitate the

7. See also the section Problems of the Criminal Record in Chap. 1.

Fig. 27
Demographic Profiles of Felony Arrests by Type of Crime

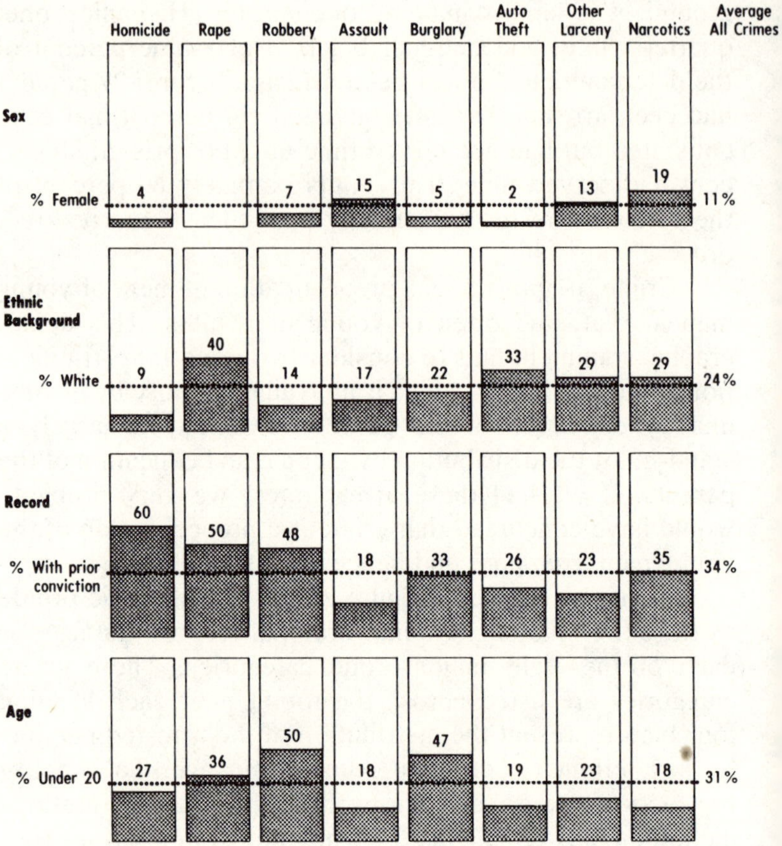

Source: 2000 Sample

visual analysis by allowing us to see how far each crime category deviates from the average for all crimes. Thus, the bars can be read vertically or horizontally. Vertically, they show the four profiles for each crime.

Reading the top row of eight bars across, we learn that the share of female arrests is far below average for homicide and auto theft, and still below average for robbery and burglary. The female share is above average for assault, for larceny other than auto theft, and for violation of the drug laws. Eleven percent of all persons arrested for a felony are female.

Reading ethnicity across: the share of white arrests is above average for rape and below average for the other three violent crimes; it is close to the average for burglary and above the average for auto theft, other larceny, and narcotics violations. Reading the third row across, we see that persons arrested for homicide, rape, and robbery have a record far more often than the average of 34 percent, in contrast to assault, where only 18 percent of the arrestees had a record. The age distribution of homicide and rape is not far from the average; the share of teenagers in robbery arrests reaches a record high of 50 percent; the teenager share in assault is relatively small, 18 percent.

Figure 27 can also be read vertically. For instance, of the persons arrested for homicide, only 4 percent are female (the average for all crimes is 11 percent); only 9 percent are white (the average for all crimes is 24 percent); but the frequency of a criminal record is 60 percent, almost twice the average of 34 percent; the proportion of teenagers is 27 percent, slightly below the average of 31 percent. Persons arrested for rape are white in higher proportion than the average for all crimes, have a criminal record more often than the average, and are teenagers slightly more than average. Burglary shows a relatively low share of females, an average share for whites and for persons with prior convictions, but a near-record 47 percent share of teen-agers.

Three / **The Dispositions**

Reasons for Dismissal

We know from Chapter 1 that only 55 percent of all felony arrests that reach the criminal court system end in conviction. We also know that this is not a pecularity of New York City, that the loss of close to one-half of all suspects is not only the rule in other American jurisdictions but most likely in all legal systems that distinguish between the amount of proof sufficient for arrest and the amount of proof required for conviction. Since only 1 percent of all felony arrests end in acquittal after trial, the bulk of the loss comes about through dismissal of the cases. The problem, as figure 28 shows, pervades all crime categories. Dismissal rates range around the average of 43 percent from 18 percent for homicide charges to 75 percent for rape charges. These variations become understandable as we explore just what the main evidentiary problems were that prompted the dismissals.

We have asked prosecutor and defense counsel of each dismissed case why the case was dismissed. Their reasons refer in the main to evidentiary difficulties, some already apparent at the time of arrest, others developing later. Table 2 shows that the major reason for dismissal is the withdrawal of the complaining witness, a problem we will consider more closely in the next section. Also nonevidentiary circumstances occasionally affect the decisions to dismiss, albeit always in conjunction with evidentiary consideration.

Table 2 lists the grouped reasons for the sixty-six dismissals for which we were able to determine reasons. They

Fig. 28
Percent Dismissals by Type of Crime

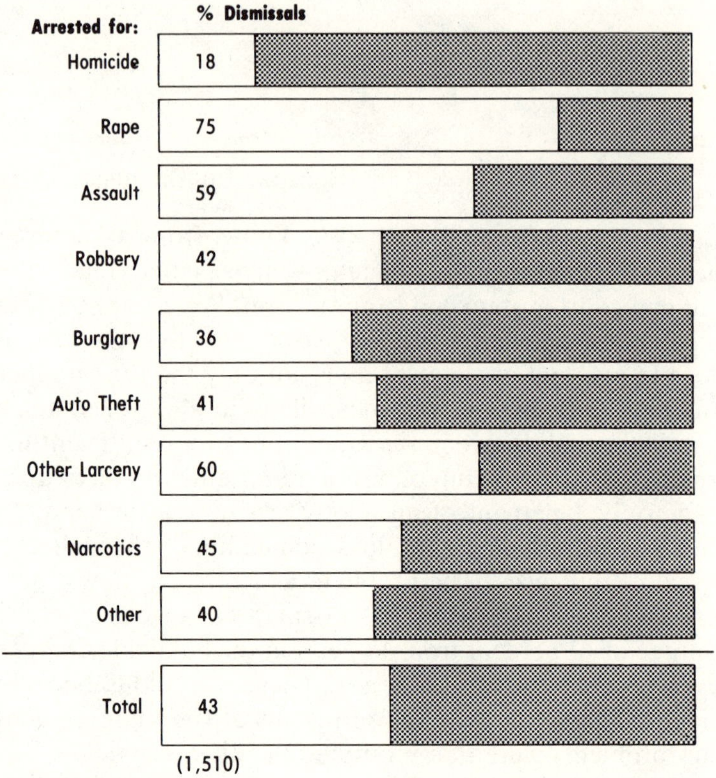

Source: 2000 Sample

Table 2
Reasons for Dismissal

	No. of Cases	
1. Evidentiary reasons		
General		
Complaining witness withdraws	33	
Complaining witness lacks credibility	8	
Gave conflicting testimony (3)		
Weak identification (1)		
Was prostitute (4)		
Codefendant assumed responsibility	1	
Codefendant, tried separately, was acquitted	1	
Cross-complaints	1	
Specific		
Delayed return of rented car (criminal intent doubtful)	6	
Mentally incompetent	2	
Consent to rape	1	
Possession or ownership difficult to prove	6	
Did not fire gun	1	
Self-defense	2	
Had bill of sale	1	
Only a rider	2	
Only a joke	1	
Total		66
2. Managerial reasons		
Defendant was tried on a more serious charge elsewhere	1	
Defendant was arrested as courtesy to out-of-town police	1	
Total		2
3. Personal considerations (in conjunction with evidential reasons)		
First offense	6	
Made restitution	4	
Employed	1	
Family responsibilities	5	
Old age	1	
Student	1	

(cont.)

Table 2 continued

	No. of Cases	
Very young	1	
Minor crime	3	
No injury	1	
Family relationship; domestic dispute	8	
Performed well in drug rehabilitation program	1	
Served some time in pretrial detention	1	
Victim partially culpable	1	
Total		34

are but a fraction of the 159 dismissed cases in the 400 sample. They nevertheless illuminate the problem. The evidentiary reasons are conveniently classified into general and crime-specific, idiosyncratic reasons. In half of all cases (thirty-three out of sixty-six) the dismissal was prompted by the withdrawal of the complaining witness. Doubts about the complaining witness's credibility are frequent. In two cases the codefendant prompted dismissal, in one by assuming sole responsibility for the crime and in another by obtaining an acquittal in a separate trial, thus demonstrating the weakness of the case. At times, formal considerations inform a dismissal that does not free the defendant from prosecution but delivers him to another case or another jurisdiction. The decision to dismiss a case is at times helped along by the fact that either the defendant or the alleged crime, or both, were not particularly dangerous.[1]

Figure 29 brings into sharper focus the fact that occasionally also the presence of other than evidential reasons affects the decision to dismiss. If the defendant was

1. Peter W. Greenwood and Marvin Lavin reported a similar finding from California: "The likelihood of conviction is not significantly affected by the arrestee's prior record, although those with less serious records are more likely to be released without formal court proceedings" ("The Disposition of Felony Arrests: Prosecuting and Sentencing Policies in California and Their Effects on Crime," RAND publication no. 10061-1-DOJ [mimeographed], 1977, p. 59).

Fig. 29
Dismissal Rates by Defendant's Record
(Excludes Cases in Which Complaining
Witness Withdrew)

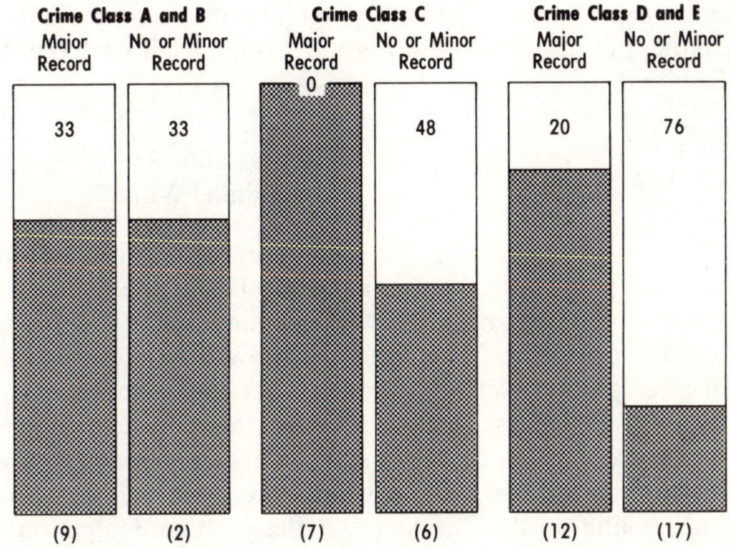

Note: The percentages are not always natural fractions of the number of cases because they come from a stratified, and correspondingly weighted, sample.

Source: 400 Sample

arrested for a class A or B crime, the dismissal rate remained unaffected by the defendant's criminal record. But if he was arrested for a lesser felony, having no record or only a minor record facilitated dismissal. Defense lawyers know this. As one of them, defending on a minor felony charge, put it: "If my client is a first offender, I try to get a dismissal."

Withdrawal of the Complaining Witness

Withdrawal of the victim from the prosecution is the major reason for the dismissal of cases. It occurs primarily when victim and offender had been living together, or at least had known one another, had an altercation which led to the arrest, and subsequently decided to make up. The prospect that this may occur is one of the considerations that may guide the police officer's decision on the scene about whether to make an arrest. At times, withdrawal is due simply to the great burden put on a complaining witness by the need for repeated court appearances, a burden aggravated by waiting time.

In theory, a witness can be forced to testify, but a reluctant witness sharply reduces the prospects of successful prosecution. The great majority of the arrests for victim crimes are initiated by the complaint of the victim, who then, as a rule, becomes the key witness in the case. Yet before the case reaches disposition, as we saw in the preceding section, many complaining witnesses stop cooperating, either by simply failing to appear in court or by formally withdrawing the complaint. Such withdrawal weakens the prosecutor's case and often brings about its dismissal.

Table 3 shows the distribution of reasons that led to the withdrawal of the complaining witness. In some cases these reasons were given to defense counsel who reported them to us; in some cases we inferred them. The most frequent reason for the victim's withdrawal is the existence of a prior

Table 3
Reasons for Withdrawal of Complaining Witness (No. = 98)

	Percent
Victim and defendant related in some way (family, ex-lovers, etc.)	25
Victim and defendant companions (drinkers, junkies, etc.)	9
Rape not by a total stranger	6
Cross-complaint (washout), fear of self-incrimination	15
Victim was "reached"	12
Restitution was made	9
Victim was a "John"	6
Victim took pity	3
Victim resides out of town	3
No reason discovered	12
	100

bond between victim and offender: they may have been friends, or lovers, or even members of the same family. Some victims lose interest in the prosecution of a property crime because restitution has been made, or of a violent crime because the first wave of anger has subsided. In some cases, it appears that withdrawal occurs because the victim has been "reached" and discouraged from further prosecution by friendly or not so friendly intervention. On occasion the motive for withdrawal is the threat of a countercomplaint, very much as civil suits and countersuits are occasionally abandoned by consent. In a number of cases the complaining witness imply refused to testify, citing fear of self-incrimination; it is difficult to determine in these cases whether this fear is real or merely a legal excuse for abandoning prosecution for other reasons.

In a considerable number of cases we could find no specific reason for abandoning prosecution.[2] We know,

2. It must be remembered that in this study we did not talk to the complaining witnesses.

however, from other studies[3] that many complaining witnesses give up simply because their interest wears thin and at some point is no longer sufficient to sustain the considerable burden of being a witness. The following cases provide some of the illuminating details of the circumstances that led to withdrawal. Here, first, are some cases that illustrate the withdrawal in a family setting.

> The defendant and his common-law wife had lived together for ten years. They had their share of quarrels and sometimes these got rough. One night the defendant had been drinking and he and his wife fought over money. When she refused to give him her pay check, he hit and injured her. She called the police; the defendant became frightened. Convinced he would go to jail, he offered the police $20. They charged him with robbery 1, assault 2, and bribery. The complainant was taken to the hospital, where she received stitches for a cut on her head. In court, she requested that the charges be dismissed. The prosecutor insisted on a plea to bribery, a misdemeanor, and the defendant was sentenced to a conditional discharge. The judge explained, "They were standing arm in arm. She told me he was a good man and a good provider. They had been together 10 years and they had every appearance of staying together another 10."
>
> The probation department had recommended discharging the defendant on condition that he stay away from the complainant. "They don't understand what's going on," the legal aid lawyer said, "to recommend that they stay away when it would be impossible to separate them." [Case 53]

A "family" crime may be a "property" crime as in the following two cases.

> A grandfather returning home found his son and grandson ransacking his apartment; outraged, he called the police. Although the son had twenty-five arrests, the case

3. Frank J. Cannavale, Jr., and William D. Falcon, eds., *Witness Cooperation: With a Handbook of Witness Management* (Lexington, Mass: D.C. Heath & Co., Lexington Books, 1976).

was dismissed at the preliminary hearing when the complainant withdrew [Case 101]

Two young men were caught by a policeman appropriating several hundred pairs of stockings from a moving van; they were charged with grand larceny. But the owner of the merchandise, who was the father of one of the defendants, refused to sign the complaint and never came to court. [Case 311]

Neighbors and acquaintances have a propensity to withdraw after the heat of battle has cooled.

The defendant and her husband, homeowners, had fought with their neighbor for years. One summer evening the feud erupted into battle. The defendants charged into the neighbor's yard spraying mace, and the complainant retaliated with a baseball bat. The police who were called in attempted to calm things down, but the irate complainant, in an "exhilarated state," stole one of the officer's guns intending to use it against the defendant. Everyone was arrested. In the end there was a private settlement assuring dismissal of both parties. [Case 86]

A cross-complaint seems to be a potent motive for withdrawal.

Two women were fighting, apparently over a man. Both had to be hospitalized. The legal aid attorney reported, "The police officer made sure both women filed complaints, knowing that these complaints would then be dismissed." [Case 97]

Prosecutions for property crimes are likely to stall because the victim has lost any financial interest in the prosecution.

In the course of a routine checkup, a defendant's fingerprints were found to match those found at the scene of a burglary commited two years earlier in a clothing store. In spite of the fingerprints, the case was dropped because the store owner, probably reimbursed by his insurance company, had no interest in prosecuting. [Case 66]

Car thefts are primary examples of such withdrawal after restitution; several such cases involved auto rental companies. Once the car is returned and the rental fee paid, the complainant urges dismissal of the charges. Remarked the prosecutor, "The company is using the court as a collection agency."

The 12 percent of the withdrawals in which the complaining witness was reached may not involve more than a plea by the defendant or his family.[4] But it may involve more.

> A man had kept his former girl friend secluded for twelve hours against her will and beat her, fractured her nose and some of her teeth. When his apartment was searched, a gun and gambling slips were found. A motion to suppress was denied. He was charged with kidnapping, assault, possession of a dangerous weapon, and possession of gambling records. The woman was so reluctant a witness that she was kept in civil jail as a material witness before appearing. She refused to testify saying she was threatened. The man was allowed to plead guilty to an E felony (the lowest grade) with a promise of probation. The probation report, according to the judge, was very favorable and described the defendant as "a very likable person." When it was found that he was on probation on a federal court sentence, the sentence was changed to a conditional discharge. [Case 25]

> According to the complainant, four defendants had beaten him and taken his welfare check; two days later they were arrested. The complainant did not show up for subsequent appearances and notified the welfare department "not to tell the police when he registers." The police thought the complainant witness had been "reached."[5] [Case 12]

4. I know of a case (not connected with this study) in which a New York woman who had been robbed of her purse by some juveniles was urged by their families and social workers to drop the complaint.

5. The *New York Post* (September 15, 1974) reported that in the Queens criminal court robbery charges against two youths were dismissed when the restaurant's night manager and waitress failed to appear. Shortly after the two suspects were arrested, an unidentified teenager had entered the restaurant and told the manager, "I hear that you are supposed to go to court. I don't think it would be a good idea for you to show up."

Finally, there is the case of a woman for whom it was clearly not worth returning to the city (probably more than once) in order to help the prosecution.

> According to the complaint, the defendant, unemployed and drunk, allegedly jostled a woman from out of town as she emerged from Macy's, and tried to snatch her purse. The woman suffered minor injuries and called a detective, who charged attempted robbery 3, assault 2, and public intoxication. The complainant agreed to sign a complaint at the station house but never showed up in court. She probably left town shortly after the incident. The case was reduced to public intoxication, for which the detective's testimony sufficed. [Case 247]

Occasionally, the prosecution's case survives withdrawal of the complaining witness. Often a gradual realization that the complaining witness may not reappear in court provides time for a negotiated settlement.

Disposing of Felony Arrests in the Misdemeanor Court

Few felony arrests ever reach the Supreme Court, which alone can convict a defendant of a felony. This section examines where, on their way through the court system, felony arrests are disposed of and convictions are obtained.

Felony arrests, as a rule, are made by the city's police department, a centralized agency that covers the entire city. Its chief, the commissioner of police, is appointed by and responsible to the mayor. Occasionally an arrest is made by one of the other police agencies in the city, the Housing Authority Police, the Transit Authority Police, and the Port Authority Police.

In contrast, the city's criminal court system is decentralized and consists of two tiers. There is one central citywide Criminal Court with divisions in each borough (each borough being also a county), and five separate Supreme Courts, one in each of the boroughs: Manhattan

(New York County), the Bronx (Bronx County), Brooklyn (Kings County), Queens (Queens County), and Staten Island (Richmond County). Each county has its own elected district attorney, an autonomous official answerable to the electorate.

The itinerary of a felony arrest through the courts may be long if the case goes all the way to trial; it may end, however, at the police station, as early as a few hours after the arrest or at arraignment, or anywhere along the way to trial. The Criminal Court, the lower court, arraigns the arrested defendant and decides on bail, conducts as a rule a preliminary hearing to determine whether a felony charge should be bound over to the grand jury. The Criminal Court judge has jurisdiction to try and dispose of misdemeanors; the maximum sentence he may impose is, therefore, one year in jail. The Supreme Court has sole jurisdiction over felony indictments, although it too, of course, can convict for the lesser crime usually included in felony charges.

The process begins with the police officer's report of the arrest to the precinct station house or to a central booking unit, where formal arrest charges are leveled. Under the law, the police may drop the arrest charge at booking, but this rarely happens.[6]

From the station house, the arresting police officer brings the case to the complaint room, a branch of the district attorney's office, where an assistant district attorney draws up the legal charges. The complaint room offers the office of the district attorney its first opportunity to review the charges, discuss the case with the arresting officer, and talk with the complainant and other witnesses. The assistant district attorney who at this point writes up the charges is empowered to raise, reduce, or dismiss the charges drawn by the police, except in Queens, where this reviewing decision is left to the clerk of the court. In 85 percent of the cases in our study, the police charges were accepted

6. We did not sample the frequency of this event, but others have done so (see Floyd F. Feeney and James R. Woods, "A Comparative Description of New York and California Criminal Justice Systems: Arrest through Arraignment," *Vanderbilt Law Review* 26 [1973]: 973).

without change; in 12 percent of the cases they were reduced; in less than one-half of 1 percent of the cases the charges were dismissed outright; in only 3 percent of the cases were they increased.

If the suspect is under the age of sixteen, the case is transferred automatically to the family court; cases of child neglect or child abuse may start in Criminal Court and be transferred later to family court, and so may felony charges originating in disputes among adult family members. Assault or attempted assault, disorderly conduct, harassment, or reckless endangerment between spouses, between parent and child, or between members of a family or a household may be transferred to the family court unless the complaint (1) is withdrawn within three days, (2) has originated in family court and been transferred to criminal court, or (3) is dismissed for legal insufficiency. On weekends, when the family court is closed, family felony cases are arraigned in Criminal Court and later routed to the family court. Fourteen percent of the 1971 felony arrests found their way into the family court.[7]

From the complaint room the case is sent to Criminal Court arraignment, where the charges are read and bail is set. In addition to the charges, the judge usually has before him at that time the defendant's criminal record, transmitted from Albany via teletypewriter, and the release on recognizance (ROR) report prepared by the court's pretrial service.

Here in the Criminal Court, as at any later stage, the case may be disposed of by dismissal or by a guilty plea to a misdemeanor or lesser violation. Unless the case is thus disposed of, the judge decides on bail. The defendant may be released on recognizance, that is, without bail, or the judge may set bail, at an amount he deems appropriate. In some instances the law allows the judge to hold the defendant without bail.[8]

7. See fig. 1 in Introduction.

8. See fig. 52 and the accompanying text in the section on Setting and Making Bail in Chap. 5.

The next stop on the itinerary through the court is the preliminary hearing before a judge of the Criminal Court, to determine whether there is "probable cause" to bind the defendant over for indictment to the grand jury. That hearing must be held within seventy-two hours of the arrest if the defendant is in custody. If the defendant is not in custody, the hearing is likely to be held within a few weeks of arrest, depending on the calendar and availability of witnesses. The preliminary hearing is part of the many-tiered process designed to weed out cases that would not justify felony conviction or possibly any conviction. It provides prosecutor, judge, and defense counsel another opportunity to review and evaluate the case, to dismiss it, or, if the prosecutor consents, to dispose of it by guilty plea to a misdemeanor. No preliminary hearing is held if the prosecution moves directly for indictment by the grand jury, or if the defendant waives his right to the hearing because he is certain that the case will move to indictment and he wants to speed up the process.

The grand jury, an arm of the Supreme Court, as a rule will indict the defendant, but it has the option of reducing a felony charge to a misdemeanor charge, thereby returning the case to Criminal Court, or of dismissing the charge outright. If the grand jury indicts, the case is arraigned in the Supreme Court. A pretrial conference is then held, and from there the case moves to trial.

At any one of these stages the case may be disposed of without trial either by dismissal or by the defendant's pleading guilty. Figure 30 gives a quantitative overview of the stages at which the criminal court system disposes of its felony arrests.

In the complaint room only a small fraction of the cases, 0.4 percent, were disposed of by dismissal. At arraignment (5.1+8.9=) 14 percent of the cases were disposed of, two-thirds of them by guilty plea which had to be be to a misdemeanor or less. More than half of all dispositions (31.5+21.4=), 53 percent, took place at preliminary hearing; the ratio of dismissals to guilty pleas there

Fig. 30
Stages at Which Felony Arrests Are Disposed of
(Percent of All Dispositions)

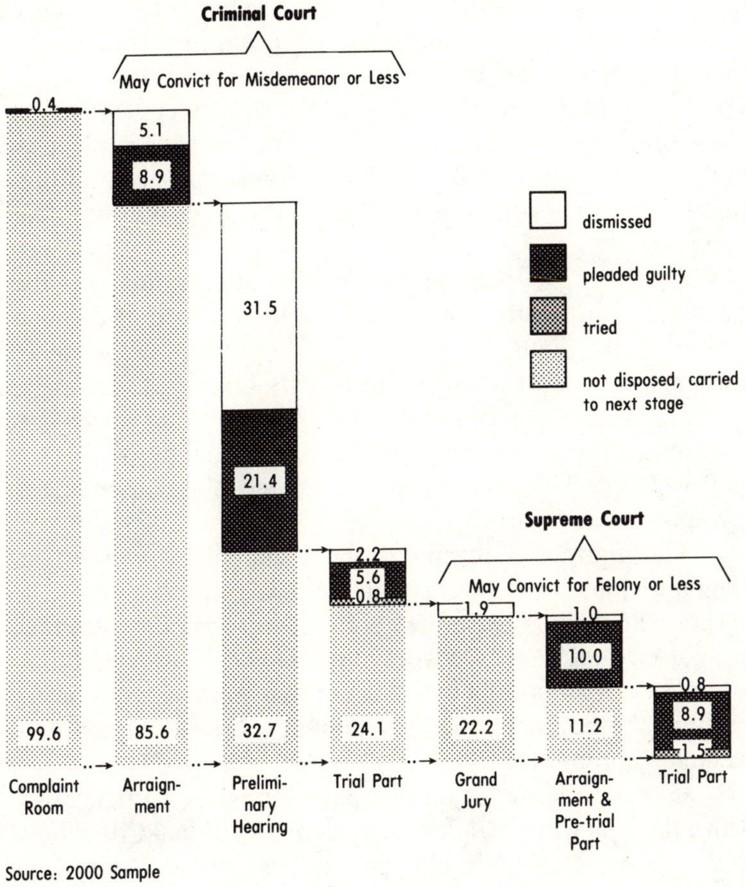

was about three to two. Almost 9 percent of the cases, cases in which the charge had been reduced to a misdemeanor or less, were disposed of in the trial part of the Criminal Court, although only 0.8 percent were actually tried. Once a case is indicted by the grand jury (which dismissed 2 percent of the cases), the chance of dismissal is greatly reduced. Only 2 percent of the cases were dismissed thereafter; most of the remaining 20 percent were pleaded guilty in the felony court but by no means all to a felony; only 1.5 percent of the arrests reached trial in the Supreme Court.

Figure 31, with decimals rounded off, summarizes the data found in figure 30 with respect to the type of disposition and the court in which the disposition was made. Seventy-six percent of all felony arrests are disposed of in the Criminal Court; (39 out of 43=) 91 percent of all dismissals take place there, but only (36 out of 55=) 66 percent of all guilty pleas. The few trials are divided about evenly between the two courts.

The many convictions in the Criminal Court raise intriguing questions: Are so many cases convicted in the Criminal Court because they were meant to end in less than a felony conviction? Or were some of these cases disposed of as misdemeanors because there was a managerial desire to limit the number of cases "going up" to the highly congested Supreme Court?

Our data allow at least a partial answer to that question. If cases were pleaded down to the Criminal Court level only to prevent their clogging the Supreme Court, one would expect the guilty pleas to be for the highest crime class for which the criminal court can convict—an A misdemeanor. Figure 32 shows that a considerable portion of criminal court convictions are below that level; 40 percent of all convictions in the criminal court were for less than A misdemeanors. If one considers in addition that about one-third of all guilty pleas in the Supreme Court were for less than a felony, the conclusion is inescapable that the pattern of reduction of the original charge is largely in-

Fig. 31
Amount (Percent) and Type of Dispositions in the Two Courts

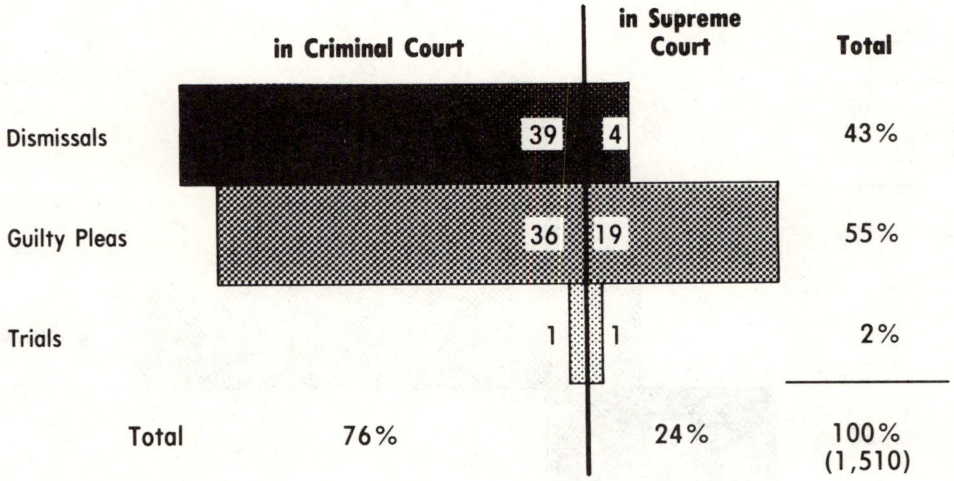

Source: 2000 Sample

Fig. 32
Crime Class of Conviction (Percent) in the Two Courts

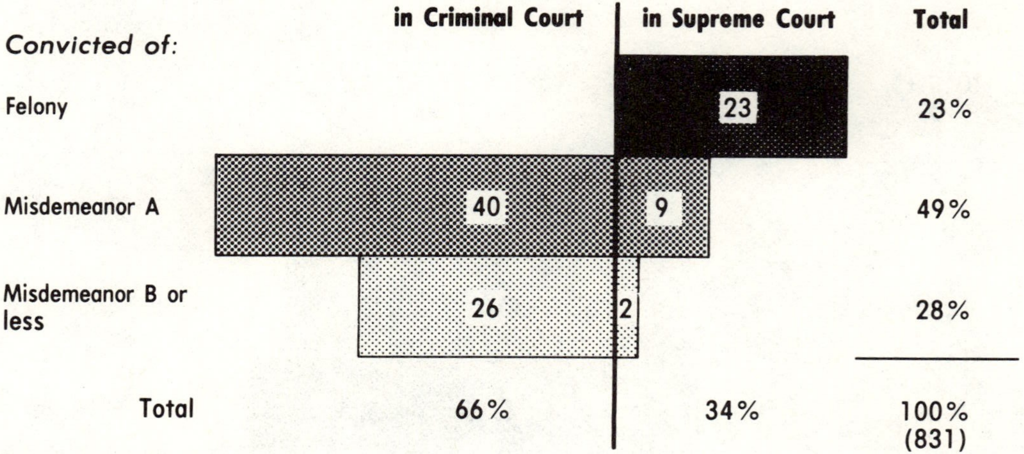

Source: 2000 Sample

dependent of the court in which it happens to take place. The reductions are primarily determined by the prosecutor's judgment as to the appropriate disposition of the case.

Plea Bargaining: Charge Reduction

Plea bargaining is a paradoxical institution. It is an important, integral part of our court procedures, but the average citizen has a hard time appreciating its merits; he cannot understand how bargaining and justice can mix. All he is told is that trying every case would be too expensive, would in fact bring the law enforcement system to a standstill. And some scholars tell us that such bargained justice negotiated between prosecutor and defendant or his counsel even has merit because it replaces the rigid letter of the law by more flexible and often more "just" arrangements. Be that as it may, the United States Supreme Court has declared plea bargaining necessary, beneficial, and legal. The fact remains that it is a peculiarly American institution, without parallel anywhere in the world. The following analysis does not discuss the merits of the system; it merely sheds some light on the substance and the form plea bargaining takes in the courts of New York City.

Plea bargaining potentially involves two types of concessions: a reduction of the crime charges and a reduction of the expected sentence. This section begins the description of the bargaining process with the first of these two concessions.

The New York Penal Law at the time of our study distinguished nine classes of crimes of differing severity and established for each the legal sentencing frame—the minimum and maximum sentence—within which the imposed sentence must fall. Table 4 summarizes the classification. Conviction for an A felony brought a minimum sentence of fifteen years and could bring a sentence of life. For all convictions below class C felony the

Table 4
Sentencing Frames for Crime Classes of New York Penal Law

	Maximum Sentence	Minimum Sentence	Available Alternatives
Felonies:			
A	Life[a]	15 years	
B	25 years	1 year	Probation (no discharge or fine only)
C	15 years	1 year	Probation and discharge[b] (no fine only), drug treatment[c]
D	7 years	1 day	Probation, discharge[b] fine, drug treatment[c]
E	4 years		
Misdemeanors:			
A	1 year	None	All alternatives permitted[c]
B	90 days		
Violations[d]	15 days	None	Conditional discharge, [b] fine (no probation)
Infractions	(As specified in the code)		Conditional discharge, fine (no probation)

[a]Indeterminate sentences are not allowed for A felonies; all other felonies permit indeterminate sentences, in which the courts can set minimums as well as maximums. If the court fails to set a minimum, the Parole Board may consider release after one-third the maximum is served.

[b]Except for narcotics crimes.

[c]Drug treatment in closed institution (NACC) optional for certified addicts on felony conviction, mandatory for misdemeanor conviction. (Sentence no longer available.)

[d]Parking violations and the bulk of traffic violations are technically not criminal and are handled by the Parking Violation Bureau, and administrative agency, not a court.

law prescribed practically no minimum sentence. The judge was free to grant probation, except after conviction for an A felony. He could even discharge the defendant without sentence unless the crime was a narcotics crime. While minimum sentences thus hardly differed, the maximum sentences were steeply graded: life for an A felony; twenty-five years for a B felony; fifteen years for a C felony; down to four years for the lowest felony, E. The maximum sentence for a conviction below the felony level is one year. One of the options open to the sentencing judge, but not any longer, was to send an offender convicted of a felony, if he was a certified narcotics addict, to the Narcotics Addiction Control Commission (NACC) for period of three or five years.[9]

Figure 33 shows the distribution of the charges for the 98 percent of all convicted offenders who pleaded guilty. On the left-hand side are the charges at the time of arrest, on the right-hand side the charges to which these defendants pleaded guilty. At the time of arrest (2+13+21=)

9. Table 4 reflects the New York law prior to September 1973. The main changes enacted since are as follows: class A felony was split into classes A-I and A-II, with murder 1 being a special class of A-I. The death sentence to follow conviction for murder in the first degree was made mandatory, but that provision was held unconstitutional in People v. Davis, 43 N.Y.2d 17, 400 N.Y.S.2d 735, 371 N.E.2d 456 (1977). For class A-II, the minimum sentence must be not less than three years and not more than eight and one-third years; the maximum is life. Classes B through E were divided into violent and nonviolent felonies. The maximum sentences for all class B crimes remains twenty-five years, with the minimum period to at least six years for violent and three years for nonviolent crimes; the minimum for B violent must be one-third the maximum but may go as high as one-half the maximum. For all of class C the maximum sentence has remained fifteen years. For violent crimes in class C and for some enumerated nonviolent ones, sentence must be at least four and one-half years, and for all other C crimes at least three years. For all crimes the minimum sentence is one-third the maximum. Imprisonment is mandatory for conviction in classes A-I (except murder 1) through C violent and for some enumerated crimes in lower classes, with the exception that lifetime probation is permitted in return for the defendant's material assistance in connection with a drug felony in specified categories (New York Penal Law §§55.00-85.15, 125.27 [McKinney 1975 & Cum. . Supp. 1980–81]).

Fig. 33
Crime Classes at Arrest and at Conviction
(Percent of Cases in Which Defendant Pleaded Guilty)

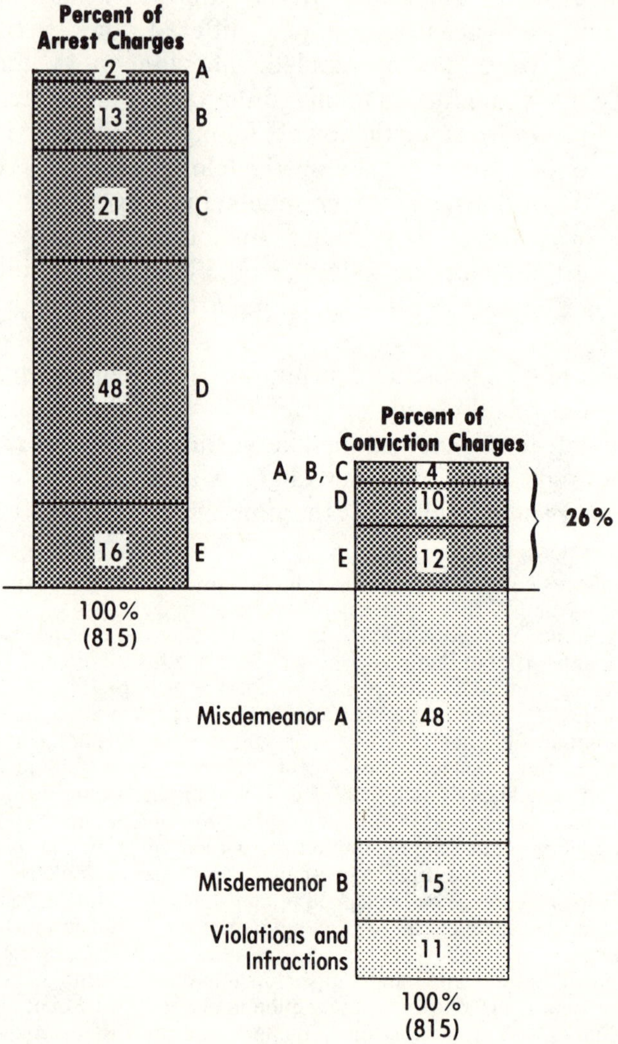

Source: 2000 Sample

36 percent of these offenders had been charged with either an A, a B, or a C felony. At the time of disposition, only 4 percent of the defendants were convicted of one of these major felonies. Only 26 percent were convicted of any felony. Three-fourths of all convicted defendants originally arrested on a felony charge were convicted of only a misdemeanor or less.

Figure 34 shows the downgrading of the charges between arrest and conviction separately for each of the five felony classes charged at arrest, for persons convicted after pleading guilty. Of the defendants charged at arrest with a class A felony who eventually pleaded guilty, only 11 percent were allowed to plead guilty to a misdemeanor or a lesser offense. As the crime class descends, the proportion of guilty pleas below the felony level (marked by the horizontal line on the graph) increases rapidly. Those originally charged with a D or E crime show 85 and 87 percent guilty pleas below the felony level.

The average for all defendants pleading guilty (the summary bar at the right-hand side) shows the same distribution as the right-hand bar in figure 34, with one difference. Figure 33 shows what share of the felony guilty pleas was for the crime class originally charged. Of all defendants pleading guilty, only 7 percent pleaded guilty to the crime class with which they had been originally charged; notice, however, that for class A crimes, a tiny fraction of all crimes, that proportion was 31 percent.

The bottom row of numbers in figure 35 indicates the average class reduction between arrest and guilty plea. On the average, the arrest charges for the convicted defendants are reduced by 2.3 classes. The amount of reduction is again related to the severity of the arrest charges. Arrest charges of class A crimes are reduced, on the average, by 2.1 classes; class B charges by 3.0 grades, declining from there to a reduction of 1.5 classes of E felony arrests. The decline is likely to be due to the fact that the lower the arrest charge, the smaller the number of remaining classes to which the charge can be reduced. The relatively higher per-

Fig. 34
Charge Reduction for Defendants Who Pleaded Guilty by Class of Crime at Arrest

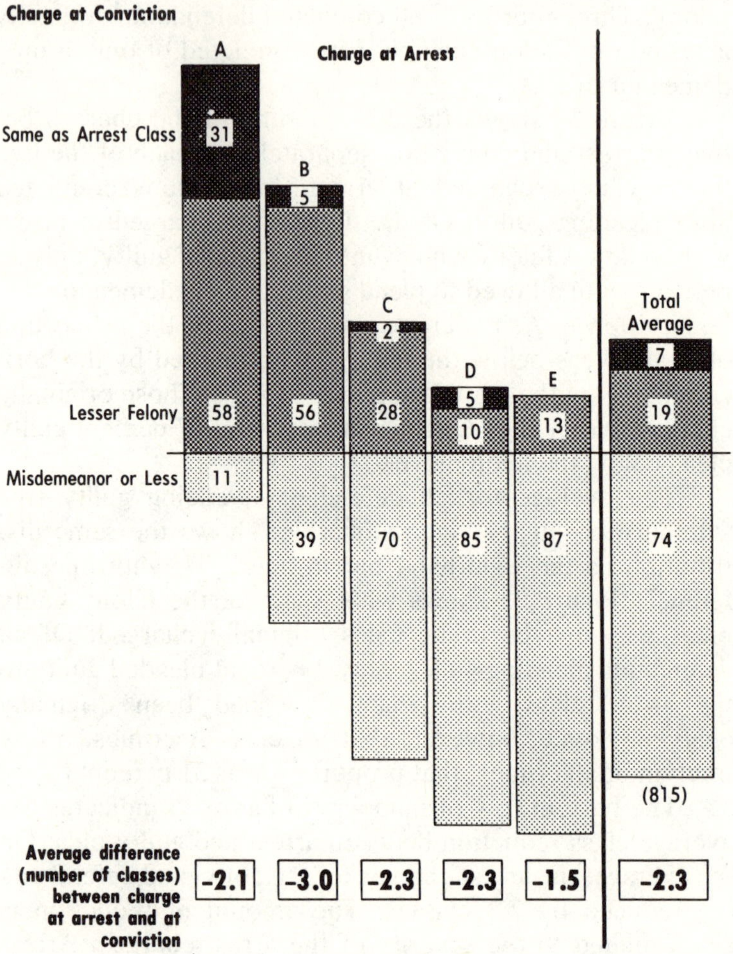

Source: 2000 Sample

Fig. 35
Frequency and Type of Sentence Assurance as Part of Guilty Plea

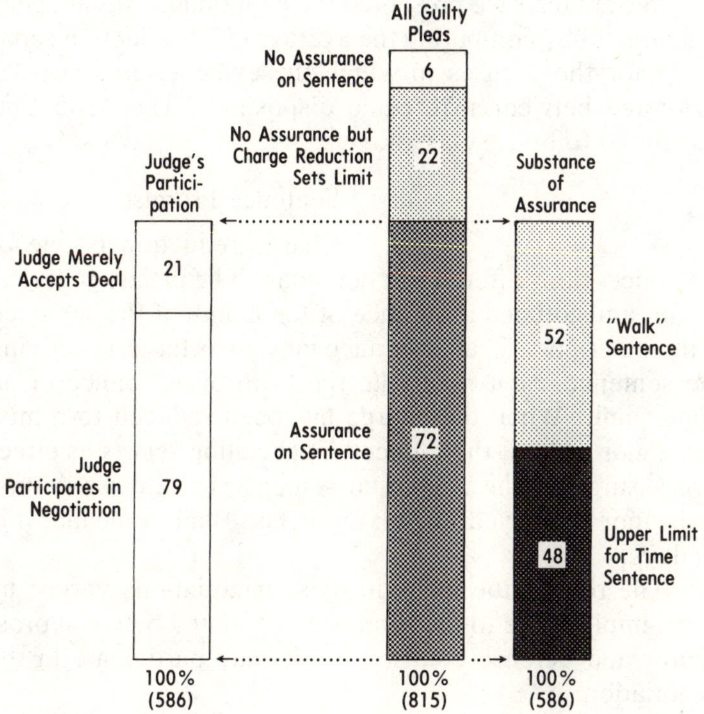

Source: 2000 Sample

centage of "no charge reduction" after an E felony arrest is due to the fact that, if the prosecutor is unwilling to allow a plea for less than a felony, he has no felony class left to which he can reduce the charge.

In Chapter 1 we presented the endpoint of this analysis in figure 10, by computing the average class reduction separately for those cases in which the evidence had not deteriorated between arrest and disposition. That reduction was found to be 1.6 classes.

Sentence Promise

Charge reduction is one of the concessions offered to a defendant if he pleads guilty; as a rule, a negotiated assurance of the length of the sentence is the other part. That assurance may go as far as specifying the sentence, or it may take the form of assurance of an upper limit. When the charge has been reduced to a misdemeanor or less, the reduced legal ceiling serves as effective assurance; the maximum sentence for a class A misdemeanor is one year in jail; for a class B misdemeanor it is 90 days.

The role of the judge in these negotiations varies: he may simply agree to the sentence negotiated between prosecutor and defense counsel, or he may participate in the negotiation.

Figure 35 shows the extent to which the sentence is part of the plea bargain. In 21 percent of the negotiated sentence assurances, the judge merely accepted the deal worked out between prosecutor and defense counsel; in 79 percent of these cases the judge took part in the negotiating process.

In 72 percent of the guilty pleas, the defendant had some assurance as to what his sentence would be. In the remaining 28 percent of the cases, the defendant did not have precise assurance of his sentence. But in the 22 percent in which he was allowed to plead guilty to a misdemeanor or a lesser offense, he thereby knew the much reduced upper limit of the sentence—one year in jail if the

Fig. 36
Severity of Sentence by Seriousness of Arrest Charge and Defendant's Criminal Record

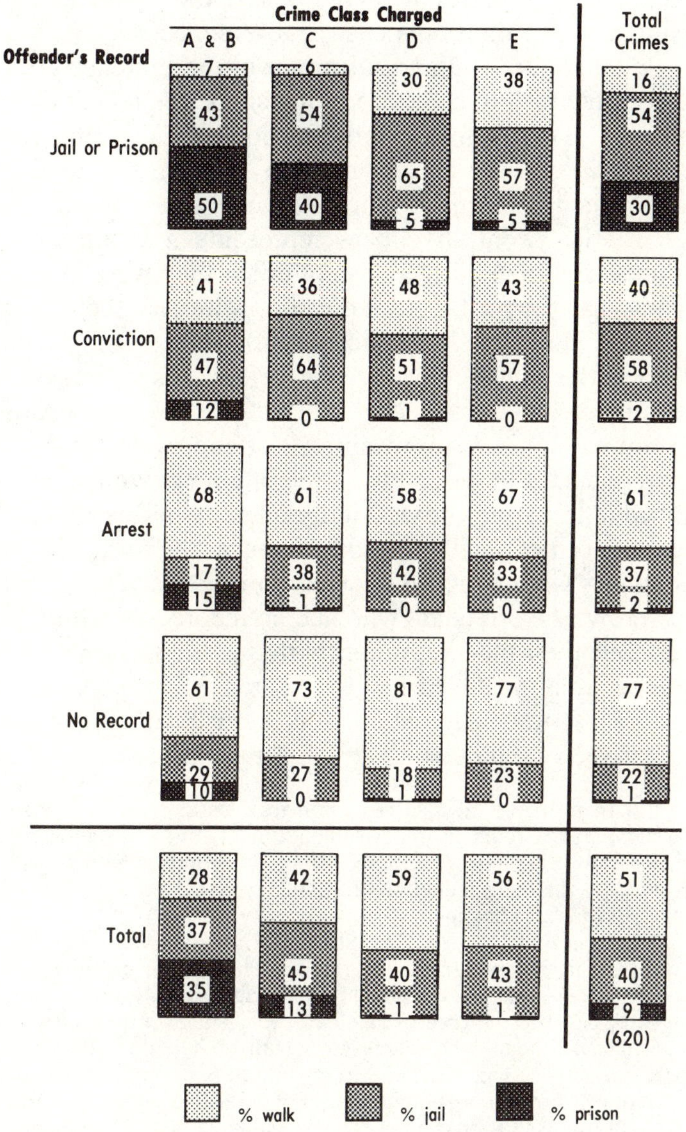

Source: 2000 Sample

plea was to an A misdemeanor, three months if it was to a B misdemeanor.[10] In 52 percent of the cases the promise involved the assurance that there would be no custodial sentence, and in 48 percent of the cases, the agreement involved an upper limit on a custodial sentence.[11]

So much for form and substance of the sentence promise. We now turn to the factors that shape the length of the sentences. Two factors emerge as powerful determinants: the severity of the crime and the convicted offender's criminal record, if any. Figure 36 shows the relationships. Each of the twenty-five bars represents a group of defendants identified by the class of crime they were charged with (across the top) and by the seriousness of their criminal record (down the left-hand margin). Thus, the upper-left bar gives the sentence pattern for defendants with a jail or prison record and arrested on a class A or B felony charge. The top row of bars represents all offenders with a jail or prison record; the second row, the offenders whose record showed at least one conviction for a felony or misdemeanor but no record of a jail or prison sentence; the third row, the defendants whose record showed no more than arrest; the fourth row, the offenders who had no record, for whom this arrest was their first encounter with the criminal law.

The relationship between sentence and conviction crime class, not unexpectedly, is more pronounced than that between sentence and arrest crime class, shown in the

10. In principle, also, a reduction to a lesser felony gives some information on a reduced upper-sentence limit; but since felony sentences hardly ever reach the upper limit, little information is in fact conveyed by the mere reduction of the felony class, unless a "sentence tariff" prevails and is known to counsel.

11. Joan E. Jacobi, in "The Standard Case Set: Measuring Prosecutor Decision-making" (in B. R. Price and Ph. J. Baunach, eds., *Criminal Justice Research,* [Beverly Hills, Calif.: Sage, 1980]), offers a hint—not more, because the control sample is very small—to the effect that rewarding a defendant who pleads guilty with a reduction of the criminal charge may be encountered more frequently in New York than in other jurisdictions. The author submitted a set of cases to a sample of assistant district attorneys in Brooklyn, N.Y., and Wilmington, Md., with, among others, this question: "At what level will this case be disposed of?" In Wilmington 38 percent of the cases were predicted to be disposed of below the felony level; in Brooklyn 75 percent.

bottom row of figure 36. Sentences of one year or more in prison decline with each successively less severe crime class, as do the jail sentences up to one year. This sharper profile is partly the result of having nine crime classes in figure 37, as against only five classes in figure 36. Since all arrest charges in our study were by definition felonies, only the five felony classes appear in figure 36; since many convictions were for offenses less than felony, figure 37 includes also the four lesser categories.[12]

The Offer That Cannot Be Refused

The workload of a criminal court is primarily determined by the number of cases it must try. Time spent on cases that are pleaded guilty is measured in hours, often in fractions of an hour; trials are measured in days or weeks, even in months. For the prosecutor who must also count the time needed for preparation of the trial, the contrast is even greater. Aside from avoiding trial, the guilty plea gives the prosecutor another advantage—it assures him of a conviction since a trial always involves some risk of acquittal.

Altogether, only 2.3 percent of the felony arrests were disposed of by trial, an exceptionally low proportion by any comparison. Figure 38 shows how this average varies with the type of crime charged. Homicide cases were most likely to go to trial, followed by charges of assault. In all the remaining crime categories (84 percent of the felony arrests), the frequency of disposition by trial remained below the average of 2 percent. What caused trial to be such a rare event?

As a rule, as we have seen, in order to obtain a guilty plea the prosecutor offers to reduce the charges and makes a sentence offer. The defendant and his counsel must then decide whether to accept the offer or to reject it and to go to trial. The calculus involved in this decision—provided it is rational, which it is not always—compares what is offered

12. See table 4, this chapter.

Fig. 37
Severity of Sentence According to Crime Class for Which Defendant Was Convicted

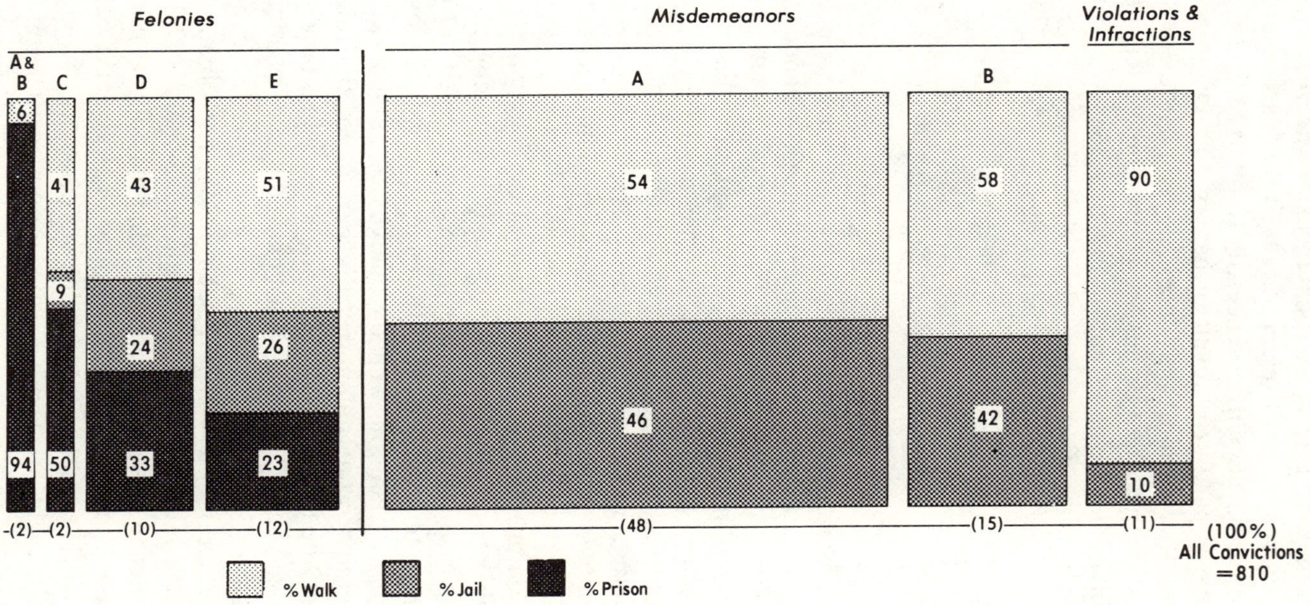

Source: 2000 Sample

Fig. 38
Percent of Arrests Reaching Trial by Type of Charged Crime

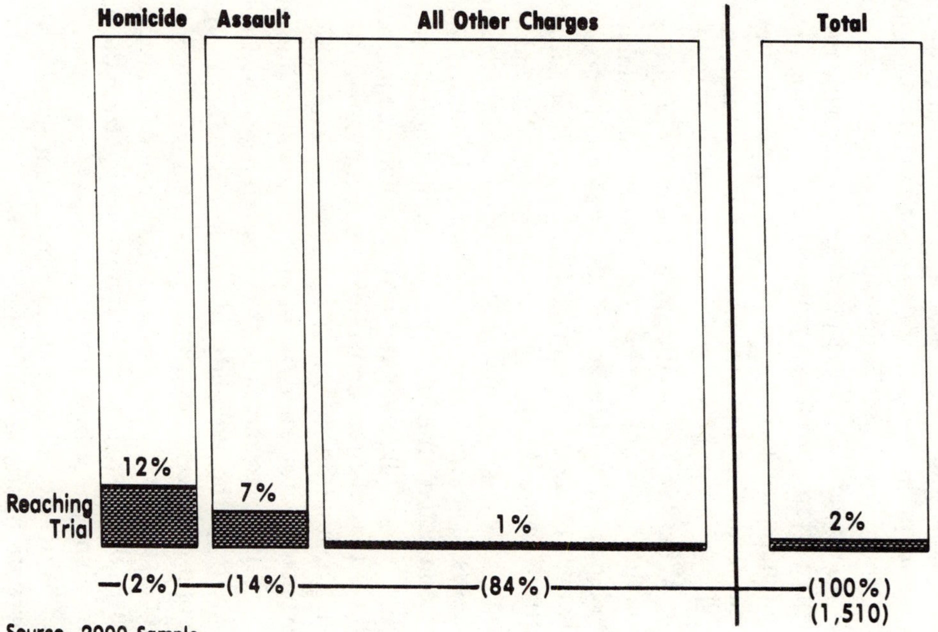

Source: 2000 Sample

for a guilty plea with what is expected after trial.[13] The comparison involves three elements: (1) the likelihood that the trial will end in the defendant's conviction as charged; (2) a comparison of the pending charge with the reduced charge offered for a guilty plea; and (3) a comparison of the sentence promised, or likely to be imposed after a guilty plea, with the sentence likely to follow conviction after trial.

What kind of verdict to expect after trial is a calculation the defendant and his counsel will base primarily on the evidence they foresee. If the defendant considers his chances of acquittal very good, points (2) and (3) will have little weight. He will refuse to plead guilty and will go to trial, unless of course, the prosecutor subsequently dismisses the case. But if there is some likelihood that he will be convicted after trial, he will be inclined to consider an offer for a guilty plea that involves a charge and a sentence lower than the one he would face if convicted after trial. In such a situation the magnitude of the difference between the expected verdict and the offered plea will be important.

Efforts to measure these differences have been hampered by the difficulty of comparing, for a comparable group of cases, the sentences after a guilty plea with the sentences after conviction at trial. The difficulty is that the cases that go to trial are different in kind from the cases that are disposed of by guilty plea.

Our data allowed us to circumvent these difficulties in part. In figure 12 of Chapter 1, for cases in which a plea offer was made and rejected and the defendant subsequently convicted at trial, we have measured the difference between the two sentences. On the average, they more than doubled in severity. To be sure these cases form a biased sample because they do not include the cases in which the plea offer was accepted. A complete sample

13. Plus a consideration of the cost of going to trial. In the case of the indigent defendant, these will become priority considerations of the legal aid lawyers.

would require knowing for these cases what the sentence would have been after conviction at trial.

A tentative effort in that direction failed. The defense lawyers tended to overstate the size of the differential in order to magnify their achievement; prosecutor and judge had the opposite tendency because too large a differential seemed difficult to justify. A better way of obtaining a realistic estimate of the sentence after trial would be to ask the question with respect to a particular case, but not of the immediate participants in the case and not by comparing it with the sentence after guilty plea. Prosecutors, defense lawyers, and judges should be asked: "If in this case the jury would find the defendant guilty, what sentence is he likely to get?"

For the time being, the data reported in Chapter 1, figure 12 provide the best estimate of the difference as it is practiced in the criminal court system of New York City.

Trial: Failure of Plea Bargaining

Every defendant has the choice between pleading guilty and going to trial. The rational calculation for making the choice would weigh the conditions of the offered guilty plea against the expected sentence after trial, modified by the likelihood that the trial would end in acquittal or conviction for a lesser charge.

Also, the costs of going to trial may enter the calculation. This section explores the details of this decision process for the defendants who took the rare step of deciding for trial in New York in 1973, who refused the offered guilty plea or did not even explore the possibility of such an offer. The analysis, based on the trial cases in the 400 sample, for which we have detailed information, offers the opportunity of comparing the motivations that actually determine the decision process with the rational model. The results, interesting by themselves, also throw some light on the general relevance of rational decision models.

Table 5 summarizes the information for the twenty cases in the 400 sample in which the defendants went to trial.[14] The table arranges the cases in three groups according to the main motive for going to trial. In group I are the seven defendants who, for a variety of reasons, thought they had a reasonable chance of being acquitted or of being at least partially acquitted; in group II are eight defendants who thought the offered guilty plea was insufficient, either because the specific goal of the defendant (e.g., avoiding a felony conviction) was not met or because the sentence after conviction at trial could not be much worse; in group III are two defendants who went to trial for extraneous reasons (9a out of loyalty for her codefendant, 18 because his mother insisted), and four defendants whose decisions to go to trial we were unable to discover.

In the first of these cases, the defendant was fairly certain that he would be acquitted because he knew that the complaining witness, the only witness in the case, would not testify. He had made sure of it by filing a cross-complaint, which he then withdrew.

(1)

W was found in his car with a knife wound in his chest. The police arrested the defendant, who W claimed had been the assailant. The defendant filed a cross-complaint, claiming he had stabbed in self-defense when W had pulled a gun on him; a gun was found in W's car. As the judge reports it: "It was a very short trial; both sides withdrew their complaint. Nobody testified. There was nothing to do but acquit the defendant. There never was an offer to plead guilty."

In the second case, the defense was so much better prepared than the prosecution that the defendant must have considered his chances for acquittal to be high:

(2)

The defendant worked in a building in which an office equipment company had been burglarized. When, a few

14. The proportion of defendants reaching trial in the 400 sample was 6 percent.

Table 5
Synopsis of Reasons for Going to Trial: 20 Cases

Case	Likelihood of Acquittal	Verdict	Perceived Difference Between Offered and Expected Sentence	Sentence Offered before Trial	Actual Sentence after Trial	Remarks
Group I: reasonable chance of at least partial acquittal						
1	Good	Acquittal	?	?		Had made certain that complaining witness would not testify; cross-complaint
2	Good	Acquittal	?	?		Well prepared; had superior defense and knew prosecution was ill prepared
3	Some	Acquittal	Small	Probation		Defendant war veteran without criminal record

(cont.)

Table 5 continued

Case	Likelihood of Acquittal	Verdict	Perceived Difference Between Offered and Expected Sentence	Sentence Offered before Trial	Actual Sentence after Trial	Remarks
4	Some	As charged	Considerable	Probation	3 years	Had been acquitted elsewhere of similar charge
5	Good for lesser offense	Guilty of misde-meanor	Small	E-felony	Probation	Not clear why case was tried in supreme court
6	Good for lesser offense	Lesser offense conviction		?	15 days	Complaining witness did not appear at trial; defendant possibly knew she would not
7	Poor	Lesser offense conviction	Some	4 years	4 years	Realistic hope for partial acquittal

Group II: guilty plea offer insufficient						
8	Some	Acquittal	Small	E-felony probation		Felony plea would have meant loss of job. No criminal record plus good defense preparation
9	*a*) Some	As charged	Small	?	25 years	Hoped to benefit from the refusal of codefendant to plead guilty
	b) Some	As charged	Considerable	Probation	2 years	Refused to plead guilty out of loyalty to (lover) codefendant
10	Good for lesser offense	Lesser felony conviction	Considerable	?	Probation	Only goal was avoiding felony conviction (which meant job (loss). Plea offer insisted on felony
11	Poor (charge reduced to misdemeanor	As charged	Small	Approx. 1 year	10 months	No sentence assurance after plea because of long record

(cont.)

Table 5 continued

Case	Likelihood of Acquittal	Verdict	Perceived Difference Between Offered and Expected Sentence	Sentence Offered before Trial	Actual Sentence after Trial	Remarks
12	Poor	As charged	Small	Plea to misde-meanor or without assurance of no jail sentence	Probation	Avoiding jail was the goal; defendant, who had no record, felt he could not be worse off at trial
13	Poor	As charged	Relatively small	10 years	15 years	
14	Very poor	As charged	Small	25 years	30 years	
15	Very poor	As charged	Small	B-felony—no sentence assurance	15 years	Defendant hoped for judge's sympathy since he had granted motion to suppress (later reversed)

Group III: other, or no discernible reason						
16	Poor	As charged	Relatively small	15 years	25 years	Irrational; even an erroneous earlier offer of 4 years had been rejected
17	Poor	Acquittal	Small	10 years		During trial unexpected defense offered itself
18	Poor	As charged	Considerable	C-felony	B-felony 2–7 years	"Powerhouse" mother of defendant insisted on trial
19	Very poor	As charged	Considerable	Max. 4 years	7 years	No discernible reason
20	Very poor	As charged	Considerable	E-felony		No discernible reason

days after the burglary, he returned the keys to a rented truck that contained some of the missing merchandise, he was arrested. The defendant claimed he had returned the truck for another man, X. The rental contract was in the name of X, but the truck owner testified it was the defendant who had signed the name. X was never produced, but two witnesses said they knew him and that he resembled the defendant. Two out-of-town witnesses provided an alibi for the defendant.

An early effort to obtain a plea failed; the defendant insisted on trial. On the day before the trial, the D.A. sensing the weakness of his case, asked the judge for a postponement so that a handwriting expert could examine the signature on the rental contract. The judge declined: "I refused to let him do it; he should have done it earlier. In any event, if I had allowed him to call an expert, the defense would have called one too."

During the trial only the rental car owner testified for the prosecution. The jury acquitted, and the judge commented caustically, "On the evidence they did the right thing."

The interesting point about this case was that the original arrest was the result of information obtained from the defendant's wife and a man who claimed that they had seen the defendant put the stolen merchandise into the truck. The informants refused to testify in the trial, saying they were afraid of the man, and the prosecution did not force them to testisfy.

In the third case, the felony charge had been reduced to a series of misdemeanors and the defendant had been offered probation if he pleaded guilty. Since he had no criminal record, he probably did not risk a more severe penalty if convicted after trial. He refused to plead, and after a six-day trial in the criminal court he was acquitted:

(3)

Alerted by a radio call, the police stopped an allegedly stolen car. The man driving it, subsequently the defendant, had a stab wound and was "rambling incoherently." The complaint was that the man had jumped into the open car while the owner was outside and had driven it away, trying to run over the owner. The charge, theft and assault, was reduced to a misdemeanor by the grand jury. ("Theft of a five-year-old car does not deserve supreme court treatment.") The defendant nevertheless refused to plead guilty, insisting that the complainant had attacked him and, to save his life, he had jumped into the car and driven away.

At the trial both complainant and defendant testified. The judge had dismissed the assault charge; the jury acquitted the defendant, a twenty-two-year-old Vietnam veteran with seven medals and no criminal record.

Then there is the man accused of fraud who had some grounds for expecting an acquittal. A short time earlier, in a neighboring county, he had been acquitted of a very similar charge. It turned out that he misjudged his prospects; he was convicted and sent to prison:

(4)

The defendant was an elderly insurance broker, charged with filing fictitious claims for hospital and medical bills totaling over $30,000. The offer was for a plea to an E felony, which the D.A. thought would not have resulted in a custody sentence. The defendant refused the offer, his confidence bolstered by his recent acquittal on a similar charge in a neighboring county. Here, however, he was convicted and sentenced to three years in prison by a judge who explained, "I thought of deterrence, which is particularly important in white-collar crimes."

There are three cases where the defense must have considered the chances for partial acquittal to be reasonably good. The first of these is the rare case of an indictment for attempted burglary:

(5)

The complainant was startled from his sleep by two youths rummaging on his porch. He testified that he saw them trying to get into his house "using a bar of some sort to pry open the window." The defendant was arrested by the

> police a block away. He admitted trying to steal a chair from the porch but denied burglary. He had no prior record and no bar was found.
>
> The case was indicted for attempted burglary and only a felony plea was offered. The defendant, on advice of his counsel, refused. The complainant's testimony did not suffice to sustain the burglary charge, and the jury convicted only of the B misdemeanor of attempted petty larceny; the sentence was probation.

In view of the prevailing practice, one does not quite understand how this case, in which nothing was in fact stolen, against a man without a record, got all the way to an overloaded supreme court.

The second of these cases developed from a fracas with two security guards, a situation which typically results, as it did here, in an overcharge by the police:

> (6)
>
> The case developed from a visit of two friends to a prostitute's apartment in a housing development that had its own security guards. For some reason the woman wanted the men to leave; they refused. The guards came and removed them with handcuffs and nightsticks. In the process the defendant, one of the men, spit at the guard and threw a brick, but not at the guard. The original charge was for aggravated assault, harassment, and trespass.
>
> At the preliminary hearing the aggravated assault charge was reduced to the misdemeanor charge of simple assault. The defendant refused to plead guilty. At the jury trial in the criminal court, the defendant, insisting on his innocence, was acquitted of the assault charge, and the trespass charge was dropped because the complainant failed to appear. He was convicted of harassment; the sentence was fifteen days, of which eight had been served in pretrial custody.

This case was tried in the lower, Criminal Court because the felony charge had been replaced by a misdemeanor charge.

In the third of these cases, the defendant had some

ground for believing that he could win at trial and actually did win a partial acquittal. The sentence, however, was close to what he could have expected after a guilty plea:

(7)

The police testified that the defendant was observed carrying a gun. He fled in a car. When he was arrested, drugs and a gun were found in the car. The defendant claimed the police had put the drugs and gun on him a second time because in an earlier arrest he had convinced a judge that the police had tried to frame him. The assistant D.A. offered a D felony plea with a four-year maximum sentence. The defendant refused and was tried in narcotics court. He was acquitted on the gun charge and convicted on the D felony drug charge. The sentence was four years.

The eighth case went to trial because the prosecutor insisted on plea to a felony, which the defendant refused because a felony conviction would mean automatic loss of his job:

(8)

Defendant and a codefendant, who subsequently jumped bail, were charged with robbing an elderly woman in the hallway of her apartment building. The defendant, a Vietnam veteran with a family, had no criminal record. The prosecutor offered the defendant a plea to an E felony with probation. The defendant was prepared to plead to a misdemeanor but not to a felony, which would have cost him his job.

At the trial, the defendant came up with the surprising defense that he was trying to dissuade his codefendant from committing the robbery and apparently convinced the jury. The judge commented, "The assistant D.A. did not expect this defense and was no match for it."

In the next case, the two defendants charged with a number of heinous crimes who went to trial out of a variety of motives. The female codefendant, who played a minor role, refused to plead guilty out of loyalty to her lover, the main defendant. He refused to plead guilty, one may infer, because with his codefendant refusing to testify against him he had some hope. More important, although we do not know whether a sentence offer had been made, it could not have been an attractive one:

(9)

Two women had come to the city to sightsee over the weekend. In the park they met a man and his girl friend, who became the defendants in this case. They persuaded the women to come to their apartment, where they offered them drugs. Then the women were forced to perform deviant sex acts with each other, after which the man raped both of them with the help of his girl friend. Eventually the women escaped and went to the police.

The man (9a) claimed the women had been "high" when he met them in the park and that all their activities had been voluntary.

The woman codefendant (9b), whose case also fell into the sample, was offered a plea for a minor offense and probation if she would turn state's witness against her codefendant. She refused, and since he too refused to plead guilty, they both were tried and convicted on all counts; rape, assault, sodomy, and coercion. The man was sentenced to twenty-five years in prison; the woman to two years.

In the next case, the decision to go to trial turned on the expected sentence. Conviction of a felony would have meant for this defendant, a subway train operator, the loss of his civil service job. When the prosecutor refused to accept a plea below the felony level, the defendant, who had no criminal record, went to trial:

(10)

The charge in this case developed from a bedroom scene in the man's apartment. With a knife he had ripped the woman's clothes off and slashed her buttock. Also a gunshot was fired but not aimed at her. The woman ran naked into the wintry street and was eventually sheltered and clothed. There were two versions of what happened. His was that he told her their affair was at an end. Hers was that he demanded that he pimp for her. He was charged with attempted murder, assault, robbery, and larceny.

> In the trial all charges but the aggravated assault were thrown out. The jury convicted of the felony charge; the judge gave probation. The D. A. explained, "This assault was more serious than those we sometimes reduce to a misdemeanor when there was a prior relationship and no criminal record."

For the remaining ten defendants, the prospects of a favorable verdict ranged from poor to very poor. The motive for going to trial, therefore, had to lie elsewhere. In seven cases, the difference between the sentence offered during the guilty plea negotiations and the reasonably expected sentence after conviction was small. In this context it is important to remember that the pronounced sentence is not the sentence the convicted defendant will have to serve. As a rule, it is the parole board that makes the final sentencing decision; for the board, differences between long prison sentences are less important than the difference in years appears to indicate, because its decisions are more dependent on how its members judge the convict's rehabilitation prospects.

In the first of the remaining cases the charge had been reduced to a misdemeanor, but no particular sentence was offered for a guilty plea. The defendant, who had a long record, could be reasonably certain that the sentence would be close to the maximum misdemeanor sentence of one year:

> (11)
>
> The defendant was found in a three-year-old car, stolen twenty-four hours prior to the arrest. He claimed a friend, who could not be located, had asked him to park it. The car owner lived in Westchester County, which apparently created difficulties. In exchange for the defendant's stipulation that he drove the car without the owner's permission, the charge was reduced to the A misdemeanor of unauthorized driving.
>
> Since the defendant had a long list of auto theft incidents—eleven arrests and one conviction—the prosecutor refused to give any assurance about the size of the

sentence. The defendant apparently feared that because of his record the sentence after a plea would be close to, if not at, the maximum of one year. So he decided to go to trial, was found guilty and sentenced to ten months.

In the other relatively minor case, the plea offer was refused because it did not include the assurance that the defendant would not go to jail. Since the plea offer was for a misdemeanor and the defendant had no record—a combination that hardly ever brings jail—it is puzzling why he was not offered a "walk" sentence:

(12)

A fairly new Buick, on which the serial number had been altered, was found registered in the name of the defendant. The car had been stolen; the defendant claimed he had bought it for cash from a third party. The charge was forgery and unauthorized possession of a stolen vehicle, a D felony. The prosecutor offered an A misdemeanor but would not agree to probation. Thereupon the defendant insisted on a trial, was convicted, and sentenced to probation.

The typical case that goes to trial appears to be the one which involves a major crime and a major sentence. If in these cases the prosecutor does not offer attractive conditions for a guilty plea, the defendant may decide to go to trial even if he sees only a slim chance of a favorable verdict. There are five such cases (13 through 17), all ending in conviction and sentences of more than ten years. In the first one, it seemed the defendant and his counsel had some real hopes, which disintegrated as the trial developed:

(13)

The defendant and two other men were charged with attempted robbery of a store at gunpoint. A radio alarm had brought the police in time. Some shots were fired, and one of the men was killed by the police. The defendant was found tied up, but the prosecution claimed he himself had done this to mislead the police. The original charge was attempted murder of a police officer and robbery.

A plea offer of ten years was refused. The defendant, protesting innocence, would have accepted a plea for an E felony. In this he seemed to have been backed by his attorney, who thought he had a chance of winning an acquittal. ("He disappointed me. He was one of the most articulate clients I ever had. . . . Unfortunately, when he got the stand, he froze. I could not understand it, he had practiced so much, he had told the story so many times. We had rehearsed the whole thing—how he was to say that. . . etc.") Apparently, he had a number of outstanding similar robbery cases. There was some talk about a Robin Hood crusade against store owners who fronted for the narcotics trade. The defendant belonged to a religious militant sect; his minister and wife attended the trial. The sentence was fifteen years.

In the following case the likelihood of a favorable verdict must have looked small, but apparently so did the difference between the plea offer of twenty-five years and what the defendant could expect after trial:

(14)

The defendant, who had a long criminal record, was charged with forty-five counts of rape, sodomy, robbery, and sexual misconduct against six women in four separate incidents. The D.A.'s offer was a plea to the major charge, a B felony, and twenty-five years. The defendant refused; the maximum sentence he faced after conviction at trial (if concurrent sentences were imposed) was thirty years. An alibi defense failed; the movie he claimed to have watched was not on at the time. He was convicted and sentenced to thirty years.

In the next case the plea offer did not specify the sentence. But since it was a trial in narcotics court and the defendant had a felony drug record, he must have known what to expect:

(15)

The police were informed that the defendant was a dealer in drugs and had a large amount of heroin in his possession. When the police arrived, they found nineteen envelopes of heroin. The defendant, to protect his wife, said, "Don't take her; this is all my stuff." His sole defense was that the search warrant was not signed by the police. The motion to suppress was granted, but the decision was reversed. Meantime, the defendant, who had been out on bail, was arrested on another drug possession charge.

The offer was a plea to a B felony to cover both indictments, without any sentence promise. The defendant refused and went to trial. He waived a jury, because he had received a break from a judge (on the motion to suppress) and was also afraid that the large amount of heroin found would prejudice the jury. He was found guilty and sentenced to fifteen years. It appears that on a B guilty plea, since he had a felony drug record, he would not have received less.

The following case offered hardly any hope at trial. For reasons unknown, the defendant rejected a very favorable plea offer, made before the prosecutor learned of the defendant's long criminal record:

(16)

The defendant, a man in his fifties, had lured a nine-year-old girl into his apartment (he was the superintendent of the building) and raped her. The medical report corroborated the charge, and neighbors said they had seen the girl leaving the man's apartment disheveled and crying.

The first offer for a plea was an E felony with four years. This offer was made and rejected before the defendant's record was discovered, which included child rape and rape. After that, a C felony, with ten years, was offered. The defendant refused and kept repeating, "Only D with four." During the trial a last offer was made: C, with fifteen years. At this point the defendant accepted, but the judge refused. The record did not come out in the trial since the defendant did not take the witness stand, but the judge had it before him at sentencing. The jury, after hours, found the defendant guilty of all charges: rape, sexual abuse, sexual misconduct, and endangering the welfare of a child. The sentence was twenty-five years.

In the next case it is just possible that the defendant went to trial because counsel had an inkling that the codefendant might provide an opening for his client's escape:

(17)

The testimony was that the defendant and two other men entered a store, pulled guns, and took $150. A plainclothesman nearby heard the commotion and arrested two men on the run. They had no money and no guns. The third man got away. The two men were booked for attempted murder, armed robbery, and possession of a gun. The attempted murder charge was dismissed at the preliminary hearing. When the legal aid attorney discovered there were two other armed robbery indictments against this defendant, he asked the court to assign counsel. Defendant had a record of seven prior arrests, including robbery, burglary, and a pending weapons charge.

The D.A. offered ten years for this one case. The defendant declined. He was then offered fifteen years for all robbery cases pending against him. Again he declined, although counsel advised him that the chances for acquittal at trial were minimal. On the other three charges counsel saw some chance for acquittal because of identification problems. During the trial, as defense counsel described it, an unexpected defense developed: "For some reason, the codefendant told something I believed was a lie. He said he did not know my client. It was a man named Joe with two other men who proposed to rob the store. He did not know where Joe was. But with the help of his testimony and some contradictions in the other evidence, I suggested to the jury that my client was merely a junkie who happened to be in the store at the time of the robbery. It created enough reasonable doubt for the jury to acquit. So my advice to him had been wrong after all."

The last three cases also involved major crimes. They all ended in conviction and prison sentences ranging from two to seven years. In the first of these cases the likelihood of acquittal was slim and the expected sentence differential large. In this case it was the defendant's mother, "a powerhouse of a woman,'' who insisted on the trial of her ''innocent'' son:

(18)

The defendant, with two other men, had gained admittance to the residence of a man whom he had known from earlier business dealings. The two men, on instructions from the defendant, pulled knives, and eventually the three left with cash and jewelry without hurting anybody. The defendant was an addict and in spite of his youth (he was only nineteen) had a long record of arrests, including a pending case for an earlier robbery.

Efforts to obtain a plea—a C felony had been offered—were thwarted by the defendant's mother, a ''powerhouse of a woman.'' The defendant was convicted of the original B felony and sentenced to two to seven years in prison.

In two cases we have no hint as to why the defendant refused to plead guilty. Both prosecutors and defense attorneys tell us that such cases are not rare; defendants at times insist on trial for irrational reasons that they cannot articulate and their counsel cannot perceive.

(19)

To all but the defendant it seemed an open-and-shut case of purse snatching. The defendant was arrested after the police had heard ''stop the thief'' cries and observed a tug-of-war between him and the victim.

The defendant was offered a reduction from robbery D to robbery E (maximum four years). Claiming he found the bag after some children had thrown it away, the defendant refused to plead guilty, against the advice of his legal aid counsel. He was convicted and sentenced to the maximum of seven years.

(20)

The defendant was arrested with two others in a car that was slowly cruising in a high-crime area. The policemen claimed they found a gun between the feet of the defendant. (There is legal presumption, rebuttable by the defense, that a gun found in a car is in the possession of riders.) A motion to suppress because the search was illegal was denied. An offer to plead guilty to an E felony without promise of time was refused. After a trial in which the defendant, who had a long criminal record, did not take the stand, the jury convicted of the possession charge, a C felony. The sentence was three years.

Four / Close-Ups

Sentences by Crime Charged at Arrest

This chapter presents a closer look at three major and one minor crime category, that is, the disposition process after arrest for robbery, burglary, auto theft, and the illegal possession of a weapon. As an introduction, figure 39 presents the sentences following conviction after arrest for the ten major felonies, and thereby gives a general idea of their relative seriousness as reflected in these respective sentences: convictions after an arrest for homicide and rape result as a rule in a prison sentence; the "walk" sentences for these crimes result from convictions for reduced charges. The only other arrest charge that shows a relatively high share of prison sentences is robbery. In all other categories the likelihood of a prison sentence is 9 percent or less.

The highest percentage of walk sentences after conviction occurs after arrest for assault and for the illegal possession of a weapon.

Robbery

Robbery by a stranger is the act that more than any other represents our notion of the feared street crime. The sentences that follow conviction after arrest are severe, especially if the defendant had a criminal record. A surprisingly large proportion of robberies, however, is not of that sort. They are committed not by strangers but by a person whom the victim knew. These

Fig. 39
Sentences by Type of Crime for Which Arrested

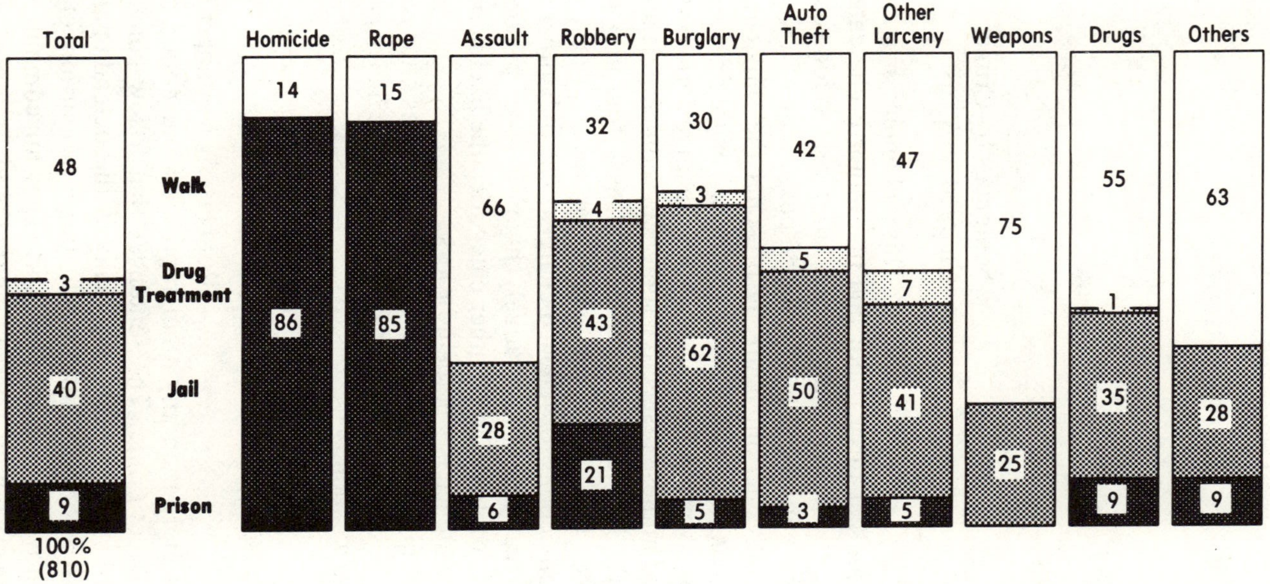

Source: 2000 Sample

defendants commit a very different kind of robbery and end up with a very different kind of disposition.

Robbery is stealing by force or by the threat of force. The crime is feared not so much for its objective, the theft, but for its unpredictable amount of violence. The law reflects this emphasis: the three degrees of robbery are not distinguished by the value of the stolen goods but by the amount of force used. The crime is *robbery first degree,* a B felony, if serious injury was caused, or if the defendant was armed with a deadly weapon, if he used or threatened with a dangerous instrument, or displayed what appeared to be a firearm, unless defendant can prove that it was not loaded. It is *robbery second degree,* a C felony, if the defendant was aided by another person, if injury (not serious) was caused, or if the defendant displayed what appeared to be a firearm, even if it was unloaded. *Robbery third degree,* a D felony, consists of any other forcible stealing.

A related crime is *jostling* (a misdemeanor): placing, in a public place, one's hand near a person's pocket or handbag, or jostling a person when somebody else places a hand near a person's pocket or handbag.

Figure 40 shows the overall disposition of robbery arrests. Altogether 42 percent of the robbery arrests ended in dismissal or acquittal. Of the convicted offenders, 32 percent walked, 68 percent received a custody sentence, 21 percent a prison sentence of over one year, a relatively high proportion.

The high dismissal rate is related to the curious fact that robbery, more often than one would think, is committed by a person whom the victim knew or was even close to. In the 400 sample that allowed us to determine that proportion, 39 percent of the robbery victims knew their attacker. Those victims, as we have seen,[1] have a high propensity to cease cooperation with the prosecutor. The defendant in these cases often claims that he took only what belonged to him, as in the following:

1. See section on Reducing the Dismissal Rate in Chap. 1.

Fig. 40
Disposition of Robbery Arrests

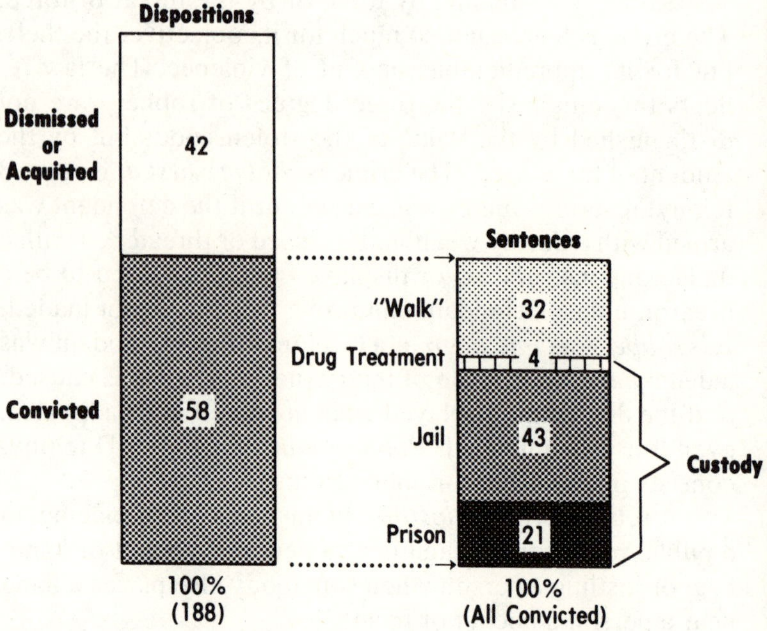

Source: 2000 Sample

> The victim complained at the station house that the defendant had robbed her of some money and given her a black eye. Defendant was arrested and charged with 3d degree robbery. It turned out that complaining witness and defendant had lived together. Defendant claimed it was a "debt collection." There was also a second witness. Defendant had a long record. He was in jail and pleaded guilty to a B misdemeanor. Both he and the complaining witness were drug involved; he was conditionally discharged. [Case 104]

Figure 41 shows the main differences between robbery by strangers and robbery by persons whom the victim knew.[2] Robbery by nonstrangers is less likely to be committed on the street, less likely to be a first-degree (armed) robbery, and more likely to be dismissed: 61 percent of the nonstranger arrests are dismissed against only 9 percent of the stranger robberies. Stranger and nonstranger robbers, however, do not differ significantly with respect to their criminal record; few have none, and many have a major one.

The sentencing pattern of persons convicted after a robbery arrest is shown in more detail in figure 42 where it is related to the degree of robbery charged at arrest and to the offender's criminal record.

Only first offenders, provided they were not arrested for first-degree robbery, have a reasonable chance of getting away with a walk sentence. Offenders arrested on a first-degree charge have a high expectation of going to prison. Depending on the defendant's record, the expectation is 14 percent if this was a first offense, but 40 percent if there was a prior felony conviction. Even if the charge was only for lesser degree robbery, the chances for a walk sentence are small if the defendant had any kind of record.

Burglary

The crime of burglary is the most frequently committed felony.[3] It is also the one seri-

2. The disposition of robbery cases in the 400 sample differs somewhat from that in the 2000 sample.

3. If auto theft and other larcenies are counted separately.

Fig. 41
Differences between Robbery
by Strangers and by Nonstrangers

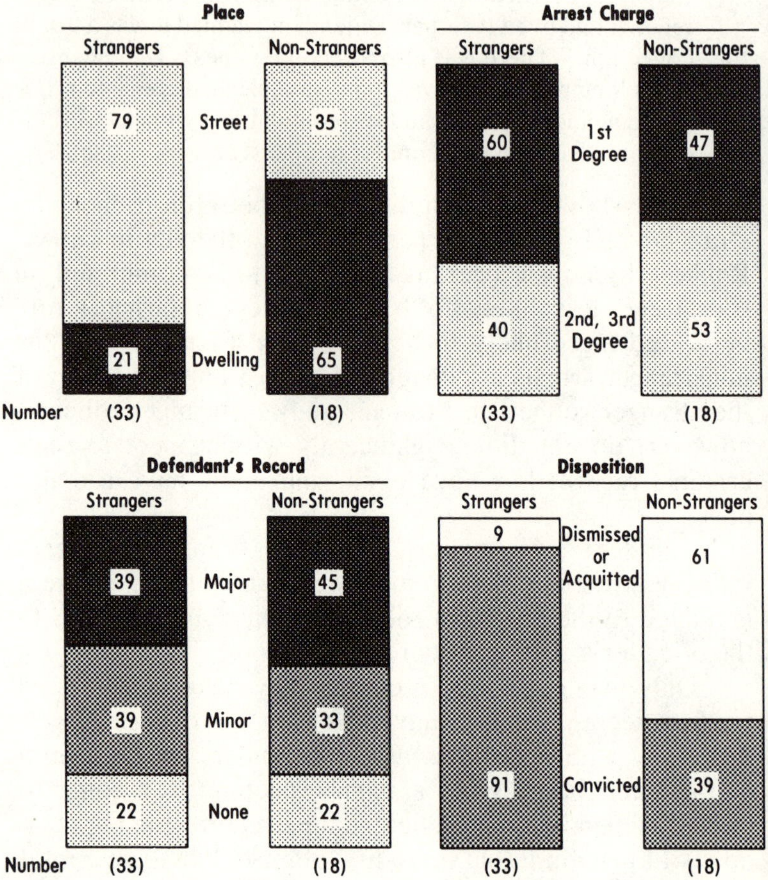

Source: 400 Sample

Fig. 42
Sentences of Persons Convicted after Robbery Arrest by Degree of Robbery and Offender's Record

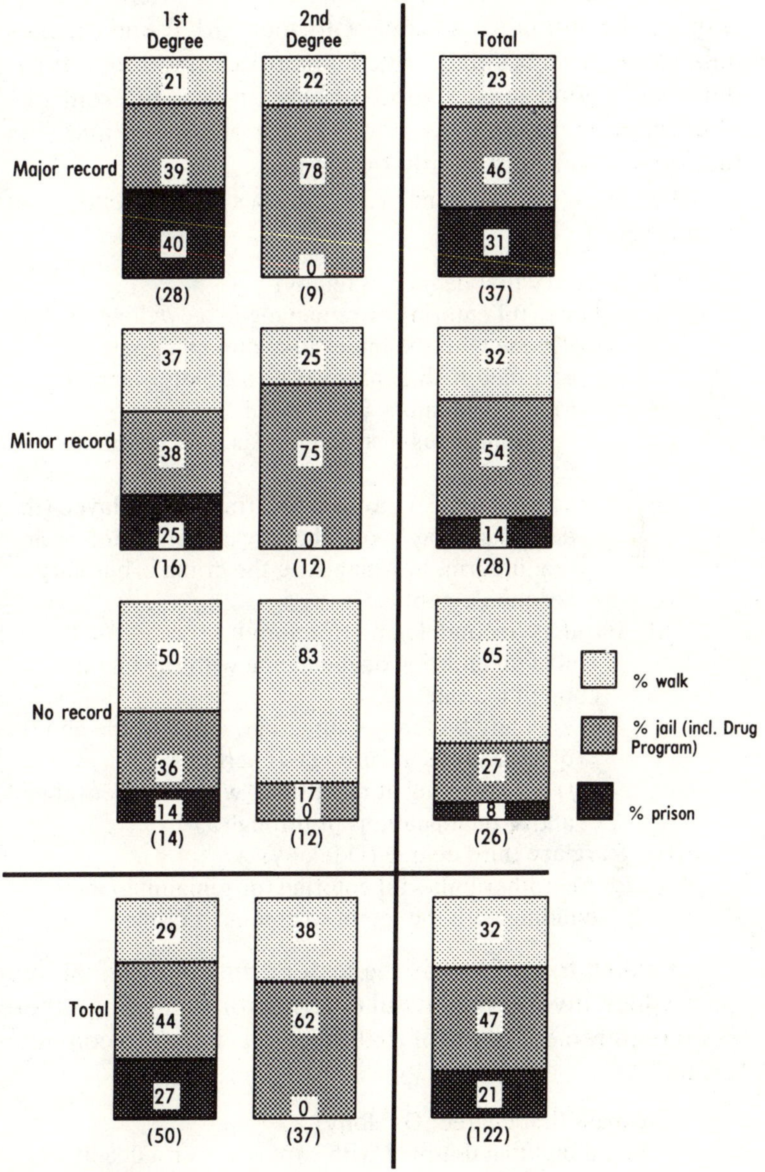

Source: 2000 Sample

ous crime whose legal definition does not match the layman's notion of what it means. For the layman, burglary is the unlawful breaking in or entering with the intent to steal. For the law, *any* criminal intent, for instance, the intent to assault a former girl friend, makes unlawful entry a burglary. The layman's distinction, it turns out, makes good sense. Nontheft burglary is a different sort of crime, committed by a different sort of person, and is in fact treated very differently by the law.

The New York Penal Law knows three degrees of burglary:

I. Burglary first degree (B felony)
  Unlawful entering or remaining in a dwelling at nighttime with the intent to commit a crime, if:
  a) armed with explosives or a deadly weapon
  b) physical injury was caused
  c) a dangerous instrument was used or threatened with
  d) what appears to be a firearm was displayed (the defendant may prove that it was not loaded or no real firearm, in which case the crime is burglary second degree)

II. Burglary second degree (C felony)
  Unlawful entering or remaining with the intent to commit a crime:
  e) in any building at any time, if one of the above qualifications (*a* through *d*) pertains
  f) in a dwelling at night time, without any of the above qualifications (*a* through *d*)

III. Burglary third degree (D felony)
  Any other unlawful entering (or remaining) in any building with the intent to commit a crime

Related to burglary is the lesser crime of criminal trespass which involves unlawful entering (or remaining); there is no requirement of proof that there was intent to commit a crime.

Trespass first degree (D felony)
  into a building if armed with explosives or a deadly weapon

Trespass second degrees (A misdemeanor)
into a dwelling (no qualifications)
Trespass third degree (B misdemeanor)
into a building or fenced-in place (no qualifications)

In addition, there is the crime of

Possessing burglary tools (A misdemeanor)

Figure 43 shows the overall disposition of burglary arrests. Roughly one-third of the burglary arrests end in dismissal. Of the convicted offenders, one-third walk, two-thirds receive a custody sentence; there is an overwhelming number of jail sentences under one year.

Figure 44 shows how the degree of the burglary charge and the defendant's criminal record affect the sentence. Prison sentences, with rare exceptions, are reserved for defendants arrested for first degree burglary. Even defendants with a major record have only a small chance of being sent to prison if the arrest was for second- or third-degree burglary. Defendants with a major record receive substantially higher sentences than other defendants; on the other hand, the sentence difference between defendants with a minor record and no record is minimal.

The rules that govern the sentencing of theft-burglary arrests cannot be seen clearly from our sample. Occasional communications from assistant district attorneys suggest that there are a variety of internal guidelines concerning the desirable disposition of burglary arrest. Thus we hear from one prosecutor: "Commercial burglaries . . . are generally reduced to a misdemeanor unless a large amount of property is involved or the defendant is a professional burglar."

Perhaps the disposition picture would emerge with greater clarity if we had a sufficiently large sample of cases for every borough, that is, for each of the four district attorneys who might have differing policies concerning the prosecution and sentencing of the crime of burglary.

We now turn to the important distinction between theft-burglars and burglars with a different intent. Here, first, are some examples of these nontheft burglaries:

Fig. 43
Disposition of Burglary Arrests

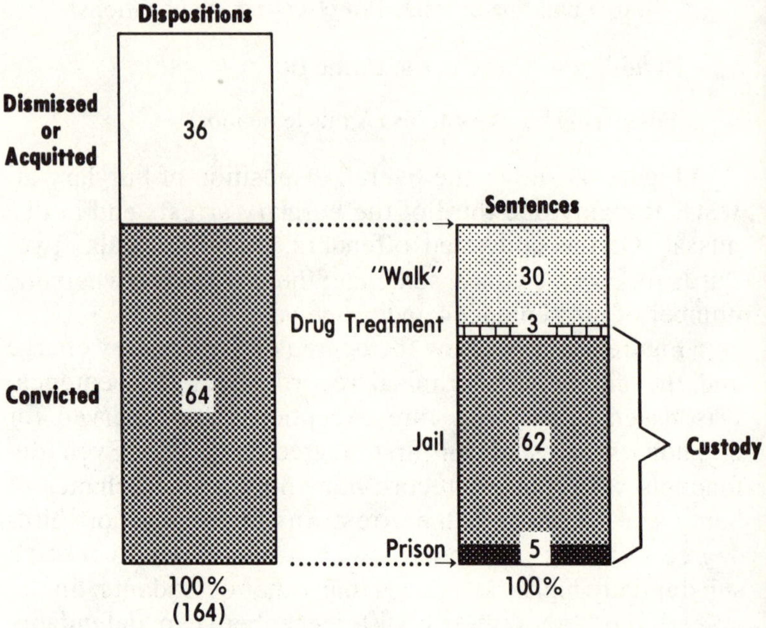

Source: 2000 Sample

Fig. 44
Sentences of Persons Convicted after Burglary Arrest by Degree of Burglary and Offender's Record

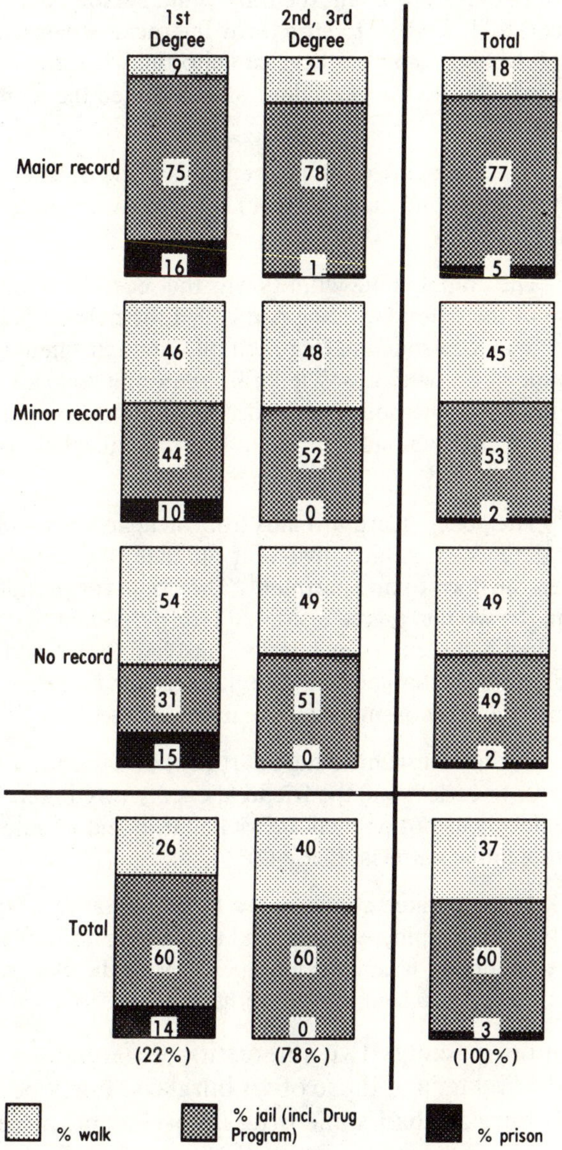

Source: 2000 Sample

The defendant was in a hotel room with a woman who had complained to the manager that the defendant had entered the room by force, held and beaten her. [Case 190]

An elderly woman, the only white person on a black street, told children to stop throwing rocks at her window. At this point some mothers came to the woman's door, allegedly broke the glass door and assaulted the woman. [Case 425]

A woman called the police because the defendant, a former boyfriend, had kicked in her door and tried to assault her. [Case 254]

The complaining witness was the recently divorced wife of the defendant. She had called the police, charging that her ex-husband had broken into her apartment and wounded her with a Bowie knife, requiring hospital treatment. When the police arrived, the defendant was sitting at the table (on which there was a Bowie knife), talking to his son. [Case 322]

The police heard screams from an apartment and found the defendant, a thirty-five-year-old man, trying to break open the door to an apartment. The door was partially broken; the woman on the inside said the defendant (with whom she had had some prior relationship) had threatened to kill her. He was charged with burglary (second degree), a C felony, and harassment (a violation). [Case 302]

Defendant went to the apartment of a friend, a security guard, to collect $50 the friend allegedly owed him. When the door was not opened, he kicked it in and threatened the complaining witness. [Case 206]

The separated common-law husband, father of the child of the complaining witness, had kicked the door of her apartment and taken a camera and TV set he claimed were his; the woman said they were hers. [Case 267]

Figure 45 shows two interesting differences between the theft burglars and these other burglars. Forty percent of the theft burglars had some drug involvement, none of the others had; 45 percent of the theft burglars had a major

Fig. 45
Differences between Theft Burglars and Other Burglars

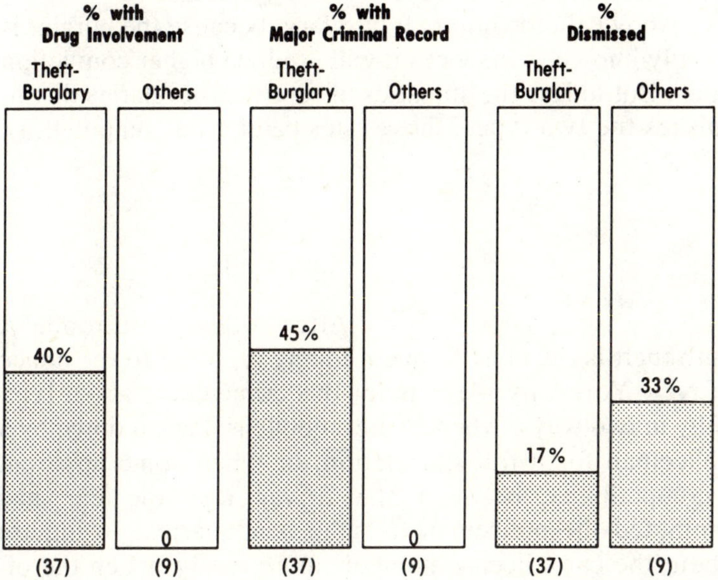

Source: 400 Sample

criminal record, and, again, none of the others had such a record. While larger samples would surely replace these zero numbers, the differences are suggestive.

Above all, the nontheft burglary, because the burglar is usually known to his victim, will produce higher conviction rates. But unless the statistics of reported burglaries distinguishes the two types, these rates cannot be computed.

Auto Theft

After burglary and robbery, auto theft is the most frequent felony reported to the police of New York City. Arrests for this crime come about typically in two ways: when an automobile is flagged down by a policeman for a traffic violation, or when some apparent incompatibility between the driver and the car had prompted the policeman to radio headquarters to inquire about the car's license number; more rarely, when the offender is observed in the act of breaking into a car or trying to dismantle it.

For a variety of reasons, arrests for auto theft are least likely to end in a felony conviction and hence in a prison sentence. First, it is a pure property crime, with no possible personal danger to the victim. Second, it is beset with a variety of evidentiary difficulties. Third, the arrest as a rule brings with it the restitution of the car and thus makes both the victim and his insurance company lose interest in the further pursuit of the case.

Normally, the defendant driving or otherwise in possession of the stolen automobile is routinely charged with three crimes in the expectation that at least one of the charges will stick:

1. Stealing the automobile,
2. Knowingly possessing a stolen automobile,
3. Use of an automobile to which he was not authorized by its owner.

Occasionally, if circumstances warrant it, a fourth charge is added:

> 4. Altering the license plate (also a felony), or possessing a burglary tool.

The first of these four crimes are felonies if the value of the car exceeds $250, which it normally does;[4] the last two crimes are misdemeanors. The crime is grand larceny in the first degree, a D felony, if the car's value exceeds $1,500; otherwise grand larceny in the second degree, an E felony. Whether it is the one or the other is the arresting policeman's decision, which in turn is informed primarily by the car's age, as shown in figure 46. As it turns out, the distinction between auto theft first and second degree makes little difference. Figure 47 shows the disposition pattern for auto theft arrests; it is close to the average disposition pattern for all crimes. The dismissal rate is in the 40 percent range; a little less than one-half of all convictions receive a walk sentence.

Prosecutors talk about the peculiar evidentiary difficulties of auto theft cases. As a rule there is no witness who saw the defendant steal the car found in his possession, and there is at best only circumstantial evidence that he knew the car was stolen. References to the difficulty of proof in these cases abound, as for instance in the following case, in which, had it come to trial, the defendant simply would not have testified, and the jury would never learn of his long arrest record for car thefts:

> Defendant was stopped driving a stolen car. He had twenty-two prior arrests all related to car thefts. Even the judge thought him a professional car thief. The defendant was allowed to plead guilty to unauthorized use, and since he had spent seventy days in pretrial detention he was discharged under condition that he join a drug rehabilitation program. [Case 235]

4. In only one case in the 400 sample (the car was a twelve-year-old Chevrolet) was there a justified doubt as to whether its value reached the felony level of over $250. Continuing inflation is shifting these figures.

Fig. 46
Age and Value of Stolen Cars

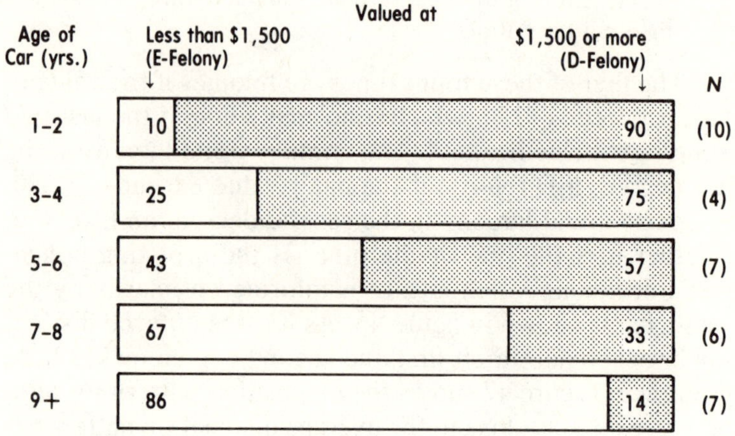

Source: 400 Sample

Fig. 47
Disposition of Arrests for Auto Theft

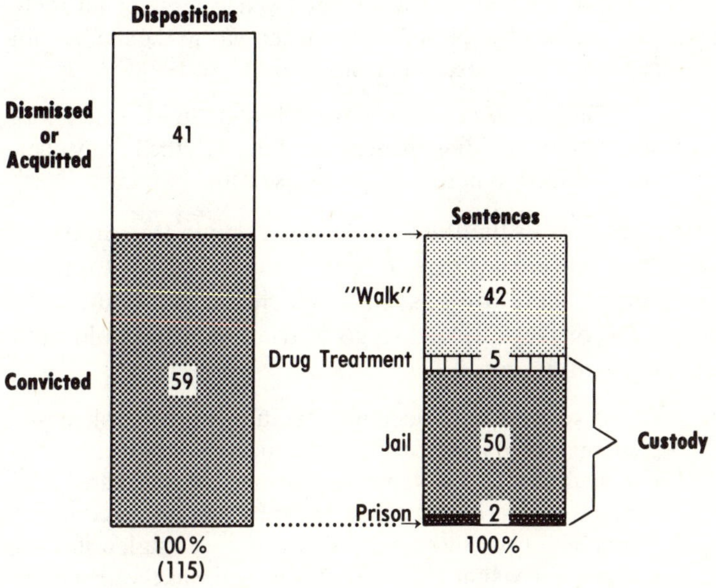

Source: 2000 Sample

Difficulties may also arise if the car was stolen from out of state or even only from outside of New York City:

> The 1963 Buick was owned in New Jersey. A form to be signed by the New Jersey owner was in the file but not executed. The case was dismissed. [Case 192]

> The car was owned in Westchester. In exchange for a stipulation regarding ownership of the car, the felony charge was reduced to petit larceny. [Case 210]

None of these difficulties, however, explain the almost universal reduction of the felony arrest charge to a misdemeanor. There are cases for which the prosecutor, if he wanted to or were forced to go to trial, clearly could obtain a felony conviction.

> A policeman noticed an alteration on the car license plate on a 1970 Buick while it was in a repair place. The car, it turned out, was stolen. The "owner" was arrested and charged with criminal possession and unauthorized use. He claimed he had not known that the car was stolen, his son had given it to him as a present. The son was thought to be a professional car thief. The defendant was indicted by the grand jury. He refused to plead guilty to a misdemeanor and went to trial. The jury found him guilty as charged. Since he had no criminal record, he was given probation. [Case 477]

There is other evidence that it is not primarily difficulty of proof that prompts the prosecution to accept misdemeanor pleas. Every so often the crime is clear, as in the following cases where there was either a witness to the theft itself, or the defendant's observed behavior provided strong circumstantial evidence, yet the accepted plea was for a misdemeanor.

> Defendant and another man were seen by the car's owner driving away his 1971 Cadillac. When he yelled at them, they stopped the car and ran away. The complaining witness and friends made a citizens' arrest after catching the two men. The charges were attempted grand larceny second degree, petit larceny (they had actually stolen some minor items from the car), third-degree criminal possession of

stole property, and criminal trespass since the car was taken from a closed-in parking lot. Within a week of arraignment, defendant pleaded guilty to criminal trespass, third degree, a misdemeanor, and received a thirty-day jail sentence. [Case 217]

The police officer observed and arrested the defendant when he tried to break into the trunk of a 1968 Ford with burglar tools. The car had been reported stolen one week prior to the arrest. Defendant was charged with grand larceny, possession of burglar tools, and criminal mischief. The charges were changed at the arraignment to petit larceny, unauthorized use, and criminal possession. Defendant was a parole violator after conviction for a drug offense and was allowed to plead guilty to unauthorized use of a vehicle and sentenced to a conditional discharge for one year. [Case 372]

Defendant and another man were observed by the police stripping a 1967 Cadillac. Since the car had been stolen just two hours earlier in New Jersey, the circumstantial evidence was strong. The defendant, who had no record, pleaded guilty to the misdemeanor of petit larceny and was given a $150 fine. [Case 277]

Even auto thefts that have a professional flavor may end in conviction for a misdemeanor:

The arresting policeman observed the defendant entering first one, then another car (a 1964 Chevrolet), and starting it up. The defendant had used a General Motors master key. He had a long record of arrests for auto theft. The D.A. thought him a professional car thief. He was nevertheless allowed to plead to unauthorized use and received a five-month jail sentence. [Case 207]

The defendant had been arrested twice in connection with two stolen cars. In the first arrest, he was charged with criminal possession of a 1970 Ford Mustang. The car was stolen only shortly before. Two days later, he was again arrested for selling a 1968 car for $850 without having title to it. That car had been stolen from New Jersey almost a year earlier. He was charged with larceny second degree. The arresting officer thought defendant was a vendor of stolen vehicles and identified the person for whom he thought defendant had worked. Defendant pleaded guilty to the misdemeanor of criminal possession of stolen property. Since he had no prior record, sentence was set at three years probation. [Case 62]

Seeing how misdemeanor convictions persist even when the theft was reliably observed, and even professionalism was suggested, one must conclude that it is the internal rule of the system to treat auto theft generally as a misdemeanor.

It appears that it is not the prosecutor alone who wants these auto theft cases disposed of in the Criminal Court. In this policy he is assisted by the grand jury. The prosecutors report that acceptance of a misdemeanor plea for car theft is so deeply rooted that the grand jury often refuses to indict and returns the case to be presented on the misdemeanor level.

Defendant was observed with another man (not caught) by the arresting policemen pushing a 1967 Buick, which was reported stolen. Defendant also had another stolen car, a 1968 Oldsmobile, in a nearby shop. The charges were two counts each of grand larceny third degree. The grand jury returned the case to criminal court on petit theft. [Case 217]

Defendant was seen by police to be driving a 1972 Plymouth, which had been reported stolen by AVIS for its JFK car facility a month earlier. He was charged with grand larceny. The grand jury reduced the charges to petit larceny. Defendant pleaded guilty to unauthorized use and received a conditional discharge. [Case 320]

A policeman observed defendant's brother driving a 1971 BMW with an altered number. The car had been reported stolen two months before. The brother protested that defendant had bought the car for $800 and displayed a bill of sale. The police charged him with larceny because he should have known that $800 was too low a price for a car worth $4,000, especially since he was a European and familiar with the value of a BMW. Defendant had bought the car from a man, never caught, who could have been part of a pro-

> fessional car ring because he had sold several other cars, according to defendant. The case was sent to the grand jury, which converted the charge to a misdemeanor. Defendant pleaded guilty in criminal court to attempted criminal possession of stolen property, a B misdemeanor, and sentenced to a $250 fine. [Case 314]

The following case shows why the prosecutor may be hesitant to bring a case before the grand jury if he risks rejection. Failure to obtain a felony indictment reduces his plea bargaining power:

> The defendant was stopped for a traffic check and unable to produce registration; the car had been stolen two days earlier in Westchester. The ignition was damaged. Defendent was charged with grand larceny, possession of stolen property, and unauthorized use. In exchange for stipulation regarding ownership of the car, the felony charge was reduced to petit larceny. Since the defendant had a lengthy record of car arrests, no further offers were made. He went to trial, was convicted of two misdemeanor counts, and sentenced to ten months concurrently with a two-year sentence he owed on a violated parole. It seems the defendant went to trial because he had little to lose once the felony charge was dropped and the plea offer was a nine-month sentence. [Case 210]

Normally, since one car theft is not much different from another, the defendant's criminal record is the major determinant of the resulting sentence. Defendants with a record, as a rule, go to jail, although there are exceptions:

> Defendant was stopped in a routine traffic check while driving a 1961 Chevrolet. A radio call revealed the car was stolen. Defendant was charged with grand larceny and pleaded guilty to petit larceny. Since the car was twelve years old, it was probably not worth $250, the misdemeanor limit. The defendant received a conditional discharge on the condition of entering a drug program, although he had a lengthy arrest record. [Case 260]

Given the workload pressure on the system and the need for assigning priorities, it should not be a surprise that auto theft ranks low on the crime scale. Arrest of an auto thief, as a rule, returns the automobile, seldom worse for the wear. The owner typically becomes irate only when the car is seriously damaged, which at times happens in the course of the attempted arrest:

> The defendant was driving a stolen 1971 Mercury when he was waved down by the police. He tried to flee, damaged another car in the ensuing chase, and was eventually apprehended. He was indicted for grand larceny, reckless driving, etc. He pleaded guilty to grand larceny third degree (E felony) for which he received a conditional discharge, and to reckless driving ("to reward the woman owner of the damaged car who had come into court") for which he got three years in the drug program. He had a minor property crime record and several narcotics arrests; he was a certified addict. [Case 427]

> Defendant was a passenger in a 1968 Chevrolet. The defendant and four other youths under twenty-one were caught in a stolen car which was wrecked after being driven off the road. Two of them worked at a service station and took the car for a joy ride after the car was left there overnight for maintenance. The police observed the accident and arrested the five when no registration was produced. The arrest charges were grand larceny. The evidence was clear—the participants admitted to the theft. The complaining witness pressured the prosecutor because the car was wrecked. In the Supreme Court, the defendant pleaded guilty to unauthorized use and received three years probation. Judge thought the case overcharged and overindicted. "This case, a joy ride with kids and not a felony, should take 5 minutes in Criminal Court."[Case 304]

Thus it is understandable why auto theft is treated gingerly. The crime is beset with proof problems, and it is perhaps the only crime where normally the arrest brings full restitution to the victim.

Illegal Weapons

New York City is one of the few places in the United States with stringent restrictions on the ownership of handguns. To obtain a handgun, a person needs a license, and to obtain a license, the applicant must show a specific need. It is the type of law most other developed countries have enacted, but few other places in the United States have it.

It was, therefore, of particular interest to see how the courts treated violators of that stringent system of gun control, especially since it was the police commissioner's statistics on that crime that spawned the present study.[5]

New York State law makes the unlicensed possession of a handgun and other concealable weapons a crime, as shown in table 6. The crime is a D felony if the defendant has a prior conviction for a misdemeanor or more, or if, without such a record, he was found in the possession of a firearm with ammunition anywhere except at his home or his place of business. The sentence frame for a D felony extends from a conditional discharge to seven years in prison.

All other forms of illegal possession of a firearm or other dangerous weapons constitute an A misdemeanor, for which the maximum sentence is one year.

The cases dealt with in this chapter are cases in which the weapon charge was the highest charge leveled against the defendant; cases where a felony was committed with a dangerous weapon, and the weapon charge was collateral to the felony, are not included.

Figure 48 presents the disposition pattern in these weapons cases: In one third of the arrests the case was dismissed; of the two-thirds convicted, 75 percent obtained a walk sentence, 25 percent a jail sentence.

We had twenty-four weapon cases in the 400 sample on which we have detailed information. In ten of these, the weapon charge could not be sustained. The weapon was either not a dangerous one within the meaning of the law or the defendant could not be shown to have legal possession. Synopses of these ten cases follow. Their disposition is summarized in table 7.

5. See n. 3 in Chap. 1.

Table 6
Illegal Posession of a Weapon in the New York Penal Law

<table>
<tr><th></th><th></th><th colspan="2">Possession of</th></tr>
<tr><th>Prior Record</th><th>Place of Gun</th><th>a loaded firearm with fitting ammunition</th><th>a firearm (without ammunition) gravity knife, switchblade knife, cane sword, billy, blackjack, bludgeon, metal knuckles, sandbag, sand club, or slingshot</th></tr>
<tr><td rowspan="2">If no prior conviction for a misdemeanor or felony</td><td>If at home, or at place of business</td><td>A-misdemeanor</td><td rowspan="2">A-misdemeanor</td></tr>
<tr><td>If anywhere else</td><td>D-felony</td></tr>
<tr><td colspan="2">If such a prior conviction</td><td>D-felony</td><td>D-felony</td></tr>
</table>

Fig. 48
Disposition of Arrests for Illegal Possession of a Weapon

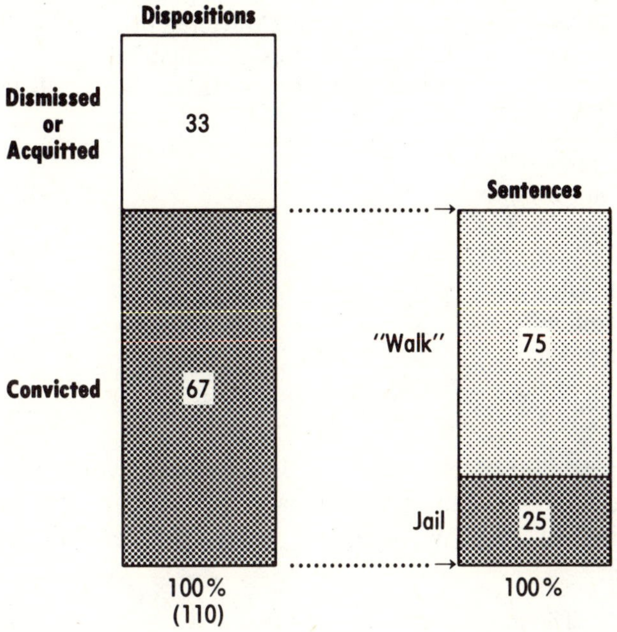

Source: 2000 Sample

Table 7
Evidential Reasons for Dismissal or Dropping of the Weapon Charge

	Dismissed	Convicted of Lesser Collateral Offense	Total
Either no weapon or no "dangerous" one	2	3	5
Possession could not be proved	3	2	5
Total	5	5	10

Here, first, are cases in which there was either no weapon or a weapon that was not "dangerous" in the meaning of the law, the two cases that ended in dismissal:

> The police radio reported that in a street fight a car driver had pulled a gun. The police located a man in a car fitting the description. He admitted the fight with a drunkard over a parking space but denied owning a gun. The search was negative. The complainant never appeared, and after two months the case was dismissed. [Case 214]

> The defendant appears to have been held under a not fully supportable weapon charge as a courtesy to the New Jersey police, who came to pick him up for having stolen an automobile; the weapon charge was dismissed. [Case 178]

In the following two cases, the defendant pleaded guilty to a lesser, connected charge:

> The defendant's knife was just an ordinary pocket knife; but he was also a petty thief, and the evidence was clear. And since he had a substantial record, he received a jail sentence upon his guilty plea to petty theft. [Case 159]

> A woman was originally arrested for urinating on the sidewalk; a knife in her pocketbook led to a felony weapon

charge. When it turned out that it clearly did not qualify as a dangerous weapon, the case ended in a guilty plea to the original "crime." [Case 471]

Then there are the cases where the gun found was real enough but where the proof of possession ran into difficulties. There were altogether seven such cases (28 percent). Three of them ended in dismissal.

> The defendant and another man stepped outside their parked car when they were apprehended by the police, who suspected them of possessing stolen property. The police said they heard a metallic sound in the dark and immediately flashed a light on the ground. There they saw a loaded pistol. The judge, in the preliminary hearing, thought "the police version a bit fabricated"; in any event, there was not sufficient proof of possession, and the case was dismissed. [Case 291]

If a weapon is found in an automobile with several occupants, the law establishes a (refutable) presumption that all occupants are in possession of the weapon. In the following case, that presumption was refuted:

> Three men, the driver and two others, were sitting in the front seat of a car; under the driver's seat a gun was found. All three men were charged with possession. Subsequently, a policeman testified that he had seen the driver throw the gun into the car, whereupon the possession charge against the other two men (one of them was in our sample) was dismissed. [Case 417]

Again, some of these cases where possession was in doubt ended in guilty pleas for lesser crimes and lesser sentences.

> The defendant, age seventeen, and his older brother were apprehended by the police in a public toilet; in one of the stalls a hypodermic needle, some envelopes with heroin, and a gun was found. The charge was illicit possession of a gun and of drugs, both felonies, and loitering, a violation. [Case 141]

To judge from the disposition of the case, the evidence was considered insufficient to prove possession. At arraignment, the two major charges were dismissed; the defendants pleaded guilty to loitering and were sentenced to conditional discharge. Some doubts, nevertheless, seem to have remained. Said the assistant district attorney: "For the boy it was the first arrest. Loitering and a conditional discharge was better than dismissal. There is at least some hold on him; I was not happy with this case." Said the defense counsel: "His brother is on probation, he had a record. Conditional discharge might keep him out of trouble and clean for a while."

In a third case, the situation was more confused:

> In connection with some gypsy cab dispute, a minor street riot broke out in which several Molotov cocktails were thrown. A plainclothes police officer charged the defendant with having thrown one at him; he pursued him, lost him, and then found him again. It was dark at the time of arrest. . . . The defendant denied the charge. He was twenty-one years old, had no record, was working, and lived with a wife and two children. He pleaded guilty to reckless endangerment, an A misdemeanor, on a promise of probation. [Case 429]

Finally, there are the cases in which there could be neither doubt over the dangerous character of the weapon (it was always a real gun) nor doubt over possession. In two of these cases the defense moved to suppress the evidence because, it alleged, there was an illegal search. In both cases, the motion was denied. It seems, nevertheless, that the lingering suspicion of an illegal search moves the plea bargaining in favor of the defendant. Two stock phrases in a report tend to raise such doubts: When the police officer noticed a weapon "protruding" from the defendant's pocket, and when "information was received" from a not further identified person. Here are a few of these cases:

> The defendant was observed by a policeman to have a weapon protruding from his pocket and was subsequently arrested. A gun was found on him and a minor quantity of heroin. He was charged with possession of a dangerous weapon (D felony) and of drugs. A motion to suppress was

> denied. The judge recalls, "The policeman was not a very convincing person, but I did not feel I could dismiss the case. I thought it was a question the jury could resolve, as to whether the police officer was telling the truth or not. After the hearing, the defense attorney and the ADA approached the bench. The prosecutor because of the problem in the case was willing to accept a plea to an E felony [attempted possession of a gun] and would go along with a sentence promise of one year if I agreed. The defendant had a long record of violent crimes and prison."[Case 528]
>
> The defendant worked at a gas station. An off-duty policeman was a customer when he noticed a gun, found to be loaded, in the defendant's back pocket. The man was arrested and indicted. In that county the policy was not to reduce a gun charge below the felony level, so there was no choice for the defendant. There was, however, no doubt that this defendant would not be sent to jail. He was fifty-five years old, had only a minor record—one arrest—had a family with children, and had been working steadily for twenty years. He pleaded guilty to an E felony and was given probation.
>
> In the "rumble" case (#483), the policeman said he saw a gun "sticking out of the defendant's pocket." That gun was subsequently identified as a teargas gun.

The second hint of a bad search is the "unidentified complainant."

> An unidentified pedestrian . . . went up to a police officer and said he believed one of the men had a gun. [Case 146]
>
> The police said, " . . . a passing motorcyclist informed us that a fellow in a car had pulled a gun on him." The motorcyclist had ridden away and was never identified. In this case the suspicion of an illegal arrest was buttressed by indications of the real motive: The police found the man fitting the description in a car displaying a police shield (badge). They arrested him and found a gun on him. There was a suspicion that it was the police shield that led to the arrest. The defendant eventually pleaded guilty to a

> misdemeanor weapon charge with the assurance of a conditional discharge. [Case 336]

Here is one of the two cases in which the quality of the search was put to a court test; in each the motion to suppress was denied.

> At 3 A.M. a policeman observed a parked gypsy cab with three men in the front seat. Since the car did not move for quite a while, the policeman approached it for a routine check of the licenses. One of the men (the defendant), the policeman reported, suffered from uncontrollable sniffles which made him suspect of using cocaine. A search brought forth a loaded gun and seventeen packages of cocaine. [Case 511]

It would appear the motion argued that, since the licenses were in order, there was no ground for suspecting a crime and that the "sniffles" were fabricated by the police, or that that symptom of itself did not establish "probable cause." In any event, the judge denied the motion. The defendant pleaded guilty to the felony charge; yet, in spite of a lengthy record the sentence was only probation. Possibly this was a compromise sentence reached in view of the possibility of a bad search.

The general sentencing rule suggested by our data is that a defendant with a prior conviction record is either sent to jail or is at least convicted of a felony. The defendants without such a conviction record are invariably spared a jail sentence and as a rule permitted to plead to a misdemeanor. The law, as will be remembered, makes a weapon charge a misdemeanor only under two conditions: if the weapon was not a firearm with ammunition, or if such a firearm was kept at the defendant's home or place of business. In the cases in the 400 sample for which we know these details, neither of these conditions was present.

Five / Problem Areas

Overcharging by the Police

In the dialogue in which the police have accused the courts of allowing guilty offenders to walk away, the courts have accused the police of bringing poor arrests to the courts. Many of these arrests, it is argued, either cannot be prosecuted at all, or only for an offense below the one the police have charged, because the arrest was not accompanied by sufficient evidence to prove guilt beyond reasonable doubt.

To some extent, this reproach is borne out by our data, but they must be evaluated against the well-established and to some extent defensible police practice of lodging the maximum charge against a defendant that is compatible with the available or expected evidence. Often the facts in the case are not clear at the time of arrest, partly because the police officer often has no more to go on than the complaining witness's allegation. Occasionally, additional evidence is available: another witness, burglary tools, a weapon, an injury, possession of the allegedly stolen goods, very seldom fingerprints, but often the officer's own observation.

In these situations of varying uncertainty, the police officer charges the reasonable maximum. This practice is ingrained in police routine for at least two reasons. The police assume that it is always easier to reduce a charge than it is to raise it; and, aware of the plea negotiation process likely to follow, the police want to enhance the prosecutor's bargaining position. The second incentive—perhaps it is the main one—for the police to charge the maximum derives from the fact that the seriousness of the arrest is part of the officer's productivity record. An arrest that clears a felony counts for more than one that clears a misdemeanor.

Also, the structure of overtime pay encourages officers to make arrests for felonies rather than for misdemeanors. A felony arrest requires the officer's presence at arraignment unless he is excused at Central Booking; this often guarantees overtime pay. A misdemeanor arrest can be processed through a summons which discharges the officer from further involvement. As a rule, such extra incentive is hardly necessary. When the police find a man in a room with a broken door and he can give no good reason for his being there, the charge will be burglary.

The following case, for instance, was not classified as overcharge but rather as an instance at the upper limit of the maximum charge rule:

> The defendant was observed stealing from a building a box of tiles worth about $50. At the station house some marijuana was found on him, and he was charged with petit larceny and criminal possession of drugs, a D felony. The police officer himself reports, "I was only a rookie cop at the time, not very experienced. We could not say how much it was, but we thought it was about felony weight." The weight turned out to be clearly below the felony level. [Case 199]

The maximum-charge rule must be distinguished from the deliberate overcharge, where the police know that the facts will not sustain the charge. In these cases, it turns out, the police inflict a kind of pretrial punishment on the defendant who made the police function more difficult than it is anyway by resisting arrest or worse. In such cases the police are liable to "throw the book" at the suspect.

According to our count, 7 percent of the arrests were overcharges in the sense we propose the term be used. They arise typically when the police officer's anger is aroused either because the arrest does not go smoothly or, more important, if the police in one form or another consider themselves attacked by the suspect.

A special kind of overcharge occurs with some frequency but is more in the nature of a standing dispute between police and prosecutor over the classification of a very specific crime, the forging of a driver's license by altering the name or expiration data. Police in these cases consistently charge the D felony of possession of a forged document (Section 170-25 of the Penal Law); prosecution and court, with equal consistency, treat this crime as driving a car without a license (Section 501.3 of the Traffic Code). In view of this established policy, court and prosecutor consider the police label an overcharge. These driver's license cases are all more or less the same as a prosecutor tells us: "Every possession of a forged instrument case I ever had was a possession of a forged license. All the cases I know of were sent back from the grand jury with the instruction to prosecute the case for a 501.3." There is even something like a standard sentence for first offenders, as a judge reports: "I fined him fifty dollars; that is what the fine would be in traffic court."

The genuine overcharges run the gamut of crimes. Following are some of the scenarios that occasionally engender this overstepping of the rule.

The extreme situation is reached with a charge of attempted murder of a police officer. The New York Penal Law generally makes the attempted crime rank one class below the completed crime. This is normally true also for the crime of murder; completed murder is an A felony, attempted murder a B felony. The law makes one exception from this general rule; attempted murder of a police officer while in performance of his duty remains an A felony. The special provision of the homicide law, designed to discourage this particularly heinous form of murder, is at times too easily invoked by the police. There were three attempted murder charges of a policeman in the 400 sample; two of them ended in outright dismissal; in the third the defendant pleaded guilty to a misdemeanor. As one prosecutor summarized these incidents: "Here we get attempted murders when they should actually be harassments. It is preposterous to look at some of the complaints that officers crank up." Undoubtedly, one of the reasons the police occasionally go to such extremes is the hope that it will discourage the all too many attempts of real and at times deadly violence against the police.

At other times, the conflict with the policeman arises from little more than the defendant's, at times justified, protestation of innocence; in the process the fine borderline between protest and resisting arrest is transcended.

> The defendant, an employee of a rental company, was stopped in a car of his company and the officer tried to arrest him. The defendant protested, and the officer charged him with both larceny and resisting arrest. The officer later called the rental company who did not consider the car stolen since the defendant had taken it out only that evening and, as he said, only for that evening. The defendant, who had no record, claimed that he never had intended to keep the car. At the preliminary hearing all car charges were dropped. The defendant pleaded guilty to the resisting arrest charge and was sentenced to a fine. [Case 212]

> A man, obviously drunk, drove his automobile in a way that "he almost caused the death of three police officers" as reported by the arresting officer. He was charged with reckless endangering, a D felony, ("evincing a depraved indifference to human life"). All it seems to have been was drunken driving, and he so pleaded guilty. [Case 295]

The same felony charge was leveled against a defendant who, as the complainant victim (an off-duty policeman) reported,

> had struck his car repeatedly from the rear. He was also charged with drunken driving and leaving the scene of an accident. The felony charge was dismissed, but the defendant refused to plead guilty to any of the charges and went to trial, in which he was found guilty of drunken driving. [Case 459]

> Juan R. was charged with felonious assault and resisting arrest. The incident occurred in a bar, where the officer saw the defendant swallow a substance he thought to be cocaine, grabbed him, and tried to force him to cough up the substance. The defendant resisted. From this point on, the ver-

> sion told by the policeman and by the defendant, as transmitted by his counsel, differ. The officer said he knew that the swallowed stuff was cocaine because the bar was a trade center for it. He knew the defendant who had been arrested previously on drug charges and was frustrated over the lost evidence. As the officer told the story, as he approached the defendant and accused him of swallowing cocaine, the defendant retaliated by shouting obscenities and assailing the officer. As the defendant told the events, the officer after their colloquy beat him up so that he was bruised and bandaged. The officer charged him with resisting arrest and felonious assault, probably an overchange since the policeman did not claim that he was injured. "I was endangered," he said. [318]

Occasionally, a minor violation may grow in this fashion into a felony.

> The defendant was seen urinating on the sidewalk by a police officer who arrested her for disorderly conduct and public lewdness (a violation). When she told the officer to fuck off he searched her, and when he found a knife in her pocketbook he charged her with possession of a dangerous weapon, a D felony. She was also charged with possession of a drug syringe. The case ended in a plea to a B misdemeanor and conditional discharge; the condition was participation in a methadone program. [Case 471]

Drug Involvement

The relationship between drugs and crime other than the direct involvement in the sale or use of drugs has been a concern of long standing. Figure 49 gives an overview of that relationship as it emerged from the 400 sample.

A little more than one-fourth of all defendants, 28 percent, had some drug involvement: 12 percent were addicts; 6 percent were in some drug program; 10 percent had some record of drug arrests. The proportion of drug involvement was highest for the defendants arrested for burglary, 45 percent, and robbery, 40 percent.

At the time this study was made, but not any longer,

Fig. 49
Drug Involvement of Persons Arrested for an Index Felony

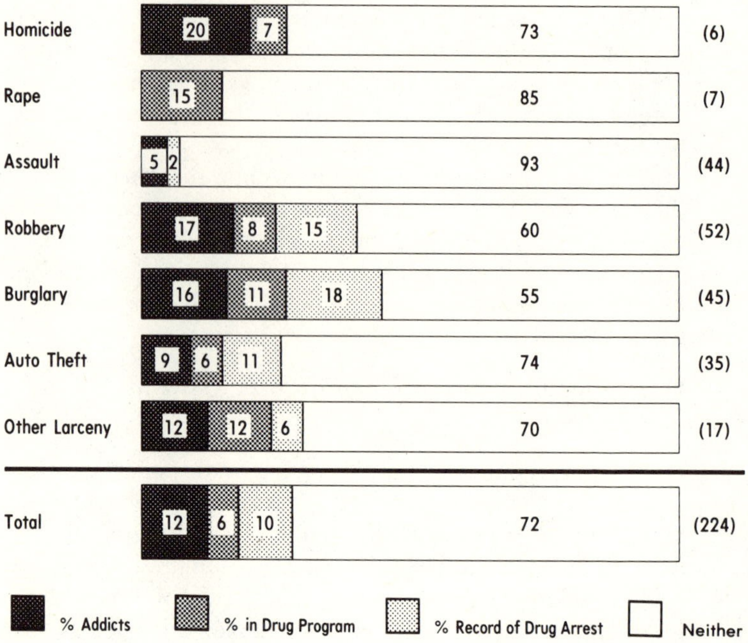

Source: 400 Sample

the law prescribed that a drug addict convicted of a misdemeanor could not be sent to prison but was to be committed to the Narcotic Addiction Control Commission (NACC), a closed institution for the treatment of narcotics. If the conviction was for a felony, the judge had the option to commit the defendant, but he rarely made use of it. By statute, NACC sentences were thirty-six months for misdemeanors and sixty months for felonies. Our interviews, however, suggested that NACC often released inmates after they had served less than a year, in some cases much less than a year, a scenario that occasionally tempted defense attorneys into all kinds of games. For those and presumably other reasons the statute was rescinded in 1975. Explained one attorney: "If my client is a first offender, I try to get a conditional dismissal, but if he has a prior record, that's out of the question. In that case, I try for a drug program." Another attorney: "God forbid that your defendant isn't an addict. I press my clients: 'Do you ever use heroin?'"

Of all convicted defendants originally arrested on a felony charge, 4 percent were sent to NACC. Among the offenders convicted after a robbery or burglary arrest, there were eight who claimed to be drug addicts but were refused that status after examination. This claim reflected the advantage the addict status could bring to a convicted offender. Figure 50, although based on a minimal sample, shows the structure of this effect.

The convicted offender with a major record had a smaller chance of being sent to jail if he was an addict than a similar defendant without drug involvement. The convicted offender with a minor record was better off if he was not an addict; instead of being sent to NACC, as the addict was, he obtained a walk sentence. This explains why offenders with a major record occasionally tried to claim addict status, but defendants with minor records made no such claim.

Setting and Making Bail

Although the law vigorously insists on the presumption of innocence, and although only

Fig. 50

Sentence of Persons Arrested for Burglary by Offender's Drug Involvement and Criminal Record

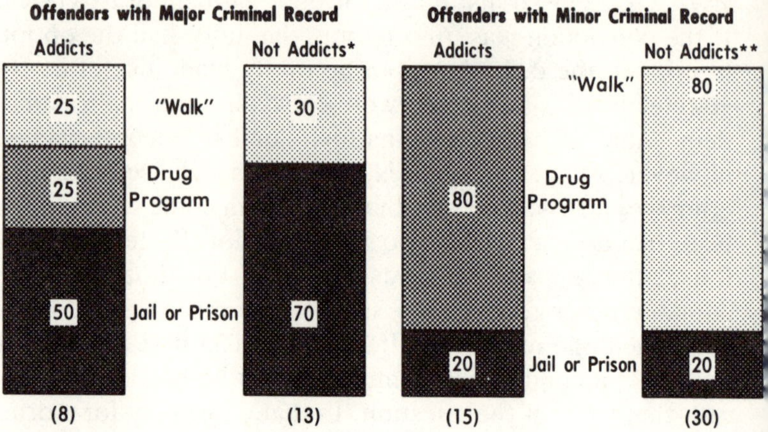

*3 Claimed to be Addicts
**None Claimed to be Addicts

Source: 400 Sample

about one-fourth of all felony arrests end in a custody sentence of any sort, the law enforcement routine begins with the suspected defendant's being taken into custody.[1] To be sure, within a relatively short time (within twenty-four hours in New York), this preliminary custody must be reviewed by the arraignment judge. But even at that point, long before any evidence is produced, the majority of the defendants arrested for a felony are kept in custody, albeit conditionally, until such time as they can post the bail set by the judge. For the defendants who cannot make bail, the judge's bail decision may be the most important step in the entire enforcement process.

Denial of bail is a rare event, although New York law allows the judge under certain conditions to hold without bail a defendant charged with a felony.[2] As a rule, the judge either sets bail or releases the defendant on his own recognizance (ROR). The law lists the circumstances the court must consider in making its bail decision: the defendant's (1) character, reputation, habits, and mental condition; (2) employment and financial resources; (3) family ties and length of residence in the community; (4) criminal record; (5) record of previous adjudication as juvenile delinquent or youthful offender; (6) record in responding to court appearances when required or with respect to flight to avoid criminal prosecution; (7) the weight of evidence against defendant and any other factor indicating the probability or improbability of conviction, or, on appeal, the merit or lack of merit of the appeal: and (8) the sentence that may be or has been imposed.[3]

Figure 51 gives the overall pattern of the bail decisions for defendants brought into the court on a felony charge. In 34 percent of the cases, the judge released the defendant on recognizance, that is, without bail; in 3 percent of the cases

1. This holds true only for felony arrests; arrests for lesser crimes may be initiated by a summons. See fig. 25, Chap. 2, above.

2. N.Y. Crim. Proc. Law §530.20 (McKinney Cum. Supp. 1978–79).

3. N.Y. Crim. Proc. Law §510.30 (2) (a) (McKinney Cum. Supp. 1978–79).

Fig. 51
Frequency (Percent) of Various Bail Decisions

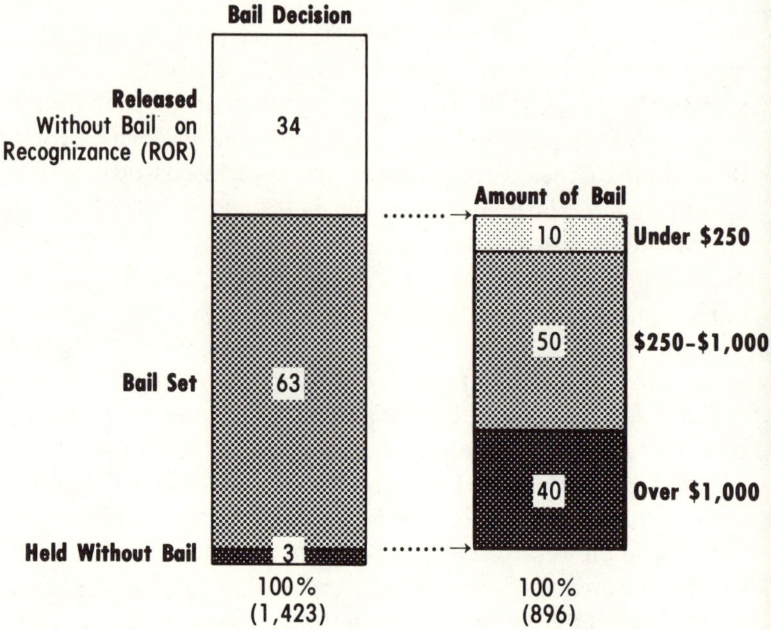

Source: 2000 Sample

the defendant was held without bail; in the remaining 63 percent the judge set bail. Of these, in 10 percent the bail was below $250; in 50 percent bail was set between $250 and $1,000; in the remaining 40 percent bail was set above $1,000.[4]

While the law asks the judge to consider a great many aspects of the crime and the defendant, in practice his bail decision is guided by the small amount of information available at the time bail is set. Normally, the bail judge has no more before him than the defendant's criminal record, if he has one; the crime with which he is charged; and whatever information the assistant district attorney, the defense counsel, and the defendant himself might bring to the court's attention, either on their own initiative or at the court's request.[5]

4. The bail information we were able to collect is incomplete since it does not record whether the bail was posted in cash or through bond. The omission was discovered only after we had received the criminal history information for the individual cases, which made it impossible to go back to the files since we had been obliged to remove the defendant's identification. The harm is small because the two types divide according to the bail amount set. We obtained the corresponding data (shown below) from the Brooklyn Pretrial Services Agency.

Bail and Cash Bond Amounts in Brooklyn Criminal Court in 1972–73

Amount ($)	Percent of Cases (No. = 1, 418)	Percent Unsecured Cash Bonds
1–250	20	98
251–500	28	13
501–1,000	17	5
1,001–2,500	17	2
2,501–5,000	10	1
5,000 or more	8	. . .
All cases	100	25

Bail amounts up to $250 were predominantly cash bonds; all higher bail amounts contained only a small fraction of cash bond.

5. This pattern has changed in recent years. The Pretrial Services Agency, pioneered by the Vera Institute of Justice originally in one of the boroughs, is now operating on a citywide basis as an independent organization under the guidance of the deputy mayor for criminal justice. One

Figure 52 shows how the bail decision is influenced by the severity of the arrest charge and the seriousness of the defendant's prior record. The defendants arraigned before the bail judge are grouped in the graph according to the crime class charged (across) and their criminal record (down). The graph indicates for each of the resulting twelve subgroups the proportion of defendants for whom bail was set at $250 or more; the complementary percentage (not listed) comprises the defendants for whom bail was set at less than $250 or who were released without bail.[6] The twelve bars that form the body of the graph show how the severity of crime and the defendant's record combine in determining the amount of bail. Throughout, the difference between defendants with major records and those with minor records is small, whereas that between those with any record and those with no record is great. Predictably, the highest proportion of no or low bail (81 percent) is found in the lower right-hand bar, the defendants with no record charged with the lowest felony. Since both the severity of the charge crime and the defendant's criminal record are also the prime determinants of the sentence that may eventually be imposed on the defendant, the bail decision is therefore also related to the expected sentence.

As figure 53 shows, there is also a relationship between the bail decision and the likelihood of eventual conviction, but it is not as strong as one might expect. The proportion of convicted defendants increases only by small increments from those released without bail (ROR) to those for whom high bail was set. Only the 3 percent of the de-

---

of the contributions of this innovative agency is to provide the arraignment judge with detailed information about the defendant.

6. If bail is set below $250, nine out of ten defendants are able to make it. And since only 8 percent of all defendants fall into this minimal bail category, we group them with the defendants who were released without bail. The number of cases included in this and the following graphs does not always reach the number of cases in fig. 54, because in some cases the additional information required for the more detailed statistic was not available.

Fig. 52
Bail Decision by
Class of Charged Crime and Defendant's Criminal Record

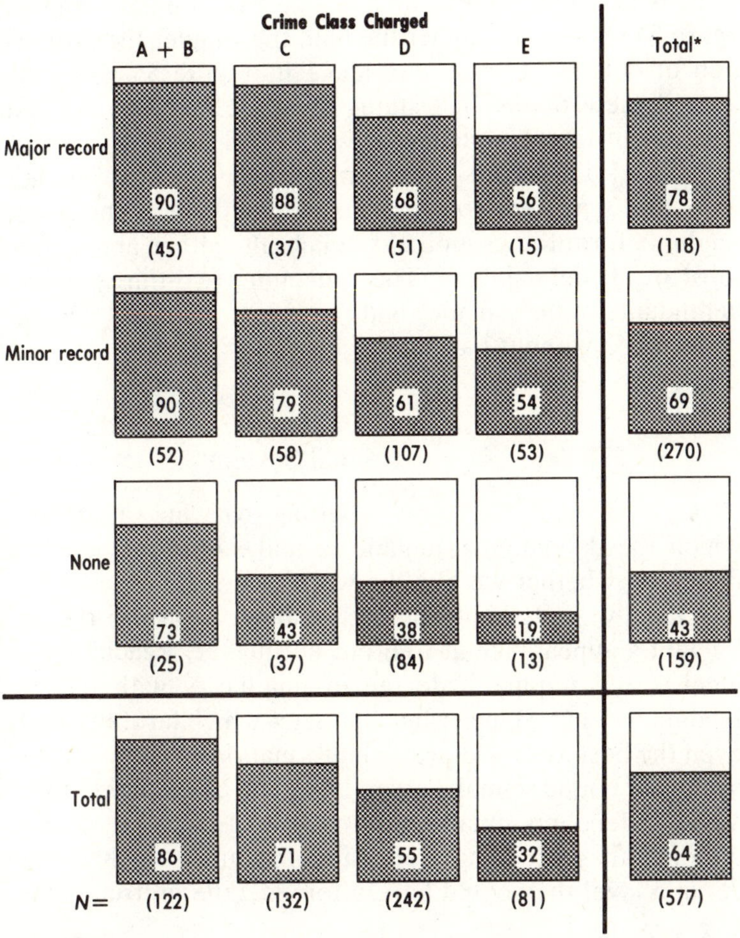

*The number of total cases exceeds the sum of the group numbers because the information on crime class charged and criminal record was not always available.
Source: 2000 Sample

fendants held without bail showed an above average conviction rate.

Once bail is set, the next move—to make bail if he can—is up to the defendant. As one would expect and as figure 54 shows, the higher the bail, the smaller the proportion of defendants who can make it. Figure 55 gives the overall view of the bail status of all defendants. Almost one-half of the defendants for whom bail was set—29 percent of all defendants—were unable to make it. Together with the 3 percent to whom bail was denied, these defendants form the group held in jail, altogether about one-third of all defendants.[7] The remaining two-thirds of the defendants either made bail or were released on recognizance without bail.

Potential Errors of the Bail System

Setting bail at an amount which the defendant is unable to make is in fact pretrial detention whether we like the word or not.

Ideally, bail should be high enough to insure the defendant's appearance at trial but not higher. Reaching this ideal would require a degree of familiarity with the defendant's circumstances and character which far transcends even the best available pretrial information. As a result, the system is bound to make errors. In some cases, it will force some defendants unable to make bail to stay in jail, although they would have appeared in court if bail had been set at a level they could have afforded;[8] the pretrial deten-

7. Some of these defendants (their number has not been determined) make bail at some later point, prior to the disposition of their case.

8. The situation is aggravated for the detained defendant who eventually is acquitted or whose case is dismissed. This, however, is a different problem, created by the higher standard of proof required for conviction than for the pretrial stage of prosecution. This unresolved problem has engendered the proposal to hold an evidentiary hearing prior to a defendant's pretrial detention (Jeff Thaler, "Punishing the Innocent: The Need for Due Process and the Presumption of Innocence Prior to Trial," *Wisconsin Law Review* [1978], p. 441).

Fig. 53
Bail Decision and Percent of Defendants
Subsequently Convicted

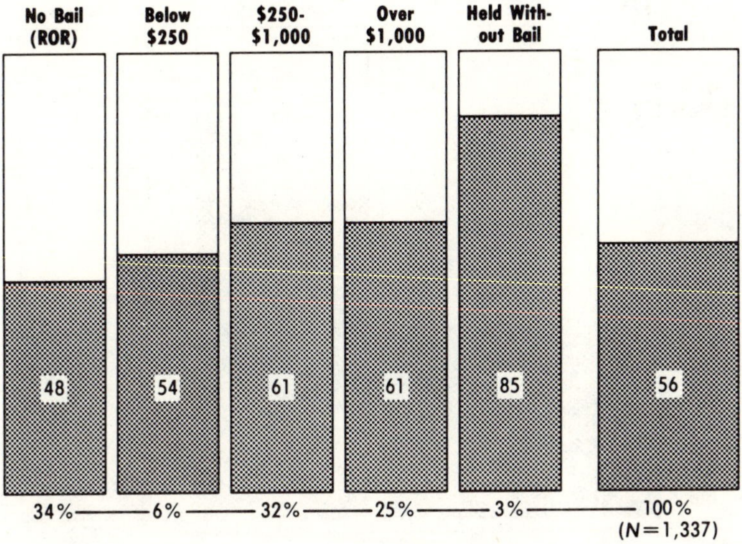

Source: 2000 Sample

Fig. 54
Percent of Defendants Making Bail by Size of Bail

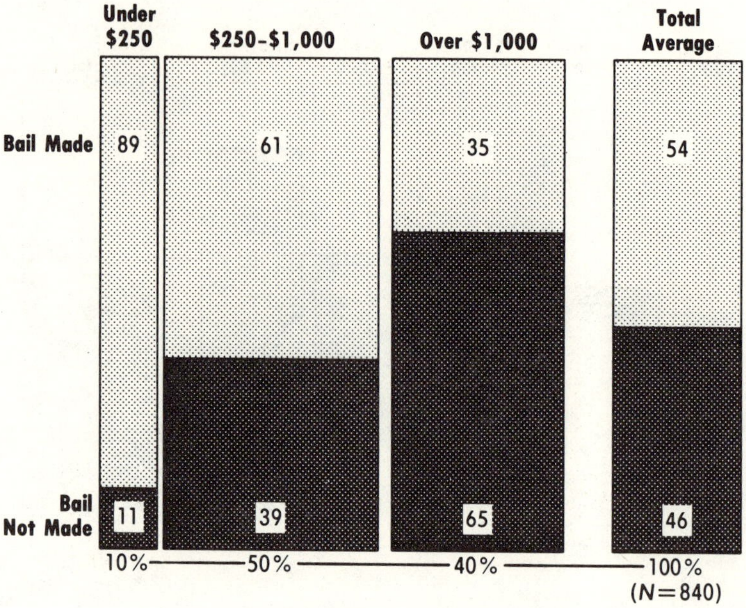

Source: 2000 Sample

Fig. 55
Bail Status of All Defendants

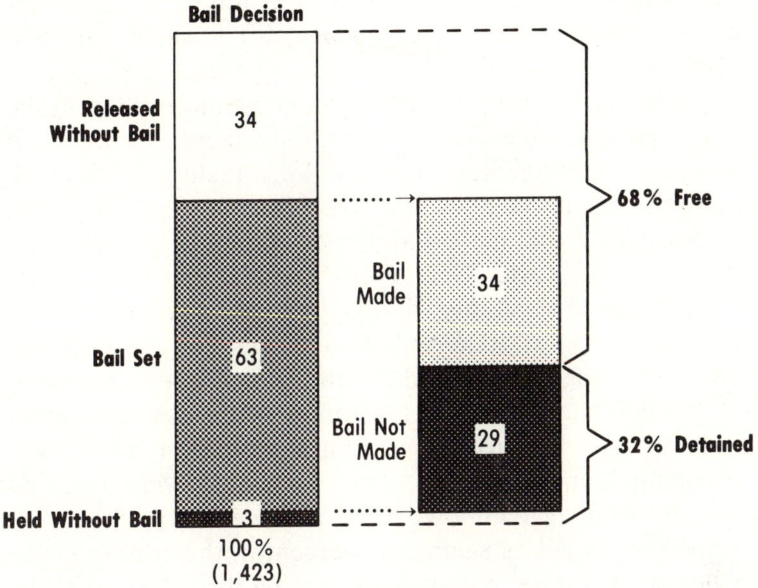

Source: 2000 Sample

tion of these defendants represents the system's most signal failure. In other cases, the system will make the error of releasing some defendants who then jump bail but conceivably would have appeared in court if higher bail had been set.

Traditionally, the courts have erred more often in the first direction. A massive reform movement, spearheaded by the Vera Foundation, now the Vera Institute of Justice, has done much to reduce that error. In 1961 Vera conducted a controlled experiment with important implications for the direction of reform. Defendants in the New York courts were assigned randomly, that is, by lot, to two groups: in a control group the judge set bail as usual; in an experimental group the judge was provided with background information on the defendant and with a recommendation as to whether or not it was safe to release him without bail. In this experimental group, many more defendants were released without bail on their own recognizance; only 40 percent were kept in jail as against 86 percent in the control group where bail was set as usual. Increasing the release rate did not result in an increase in the number of defendants who jumped bail; the proportion of bail jumpers did not exceed 1 percent in either group. Releasing more defendants without requiring bail turned out to be a cure without undesirable side effects.[9]

That pioneering experiment powerfully stimulated the growth of a nationwide reform movement to reduce the number of defendants held unnecessarily in pretrial detention, a reform achieved primarily through improving the quality and increasing the amount of information about the defendants arraigned before the bail judge.[10]

9. See Charles E. Ares, Anne Rankin, and Herbert Sturz (n. 34, Chap. 1).

10. For reasons I have never appreciated, Vera's recommendations have always been based on the defendant's demographic and background characteristics and not also on the seriousness of the offense or the expected severity of the sentence. It was left to the judge to base his judgment on the joint weight of all factors. This division makes it impossible to decide whether the judge followed the recommendation; it also makes it impossible to evaluate it.

We might note that knowledge of that first type of error—detaining defendants who need not be detained—can come only from a controlled experiment such as Vera conducted. There is no other way of estimating how many of the defendants who could not make bail would have appeared in court if they had been released. The data from the present study, since they were not derived from such an experiment, cannot illuminate that part of the issue; however, they do provide a measure of the second type of error, the proportion of released defendants who jump bail.[11]

Until recently the courts, for understandable reasons, have not been eager to publish bail-jumping figures.[12] Also, the reform-minded critics of the bail system have a tendency to minimize the importance of these figures, perhaps because in the original Vera experiment they formed indeed a negligible quantity. Thus we read in one recent major study, "The number of defendants who . . . are lost to the court system and thereby evade justice is quite small"; for eleven of the fourteen cities in that study the proportion of "fugitives" of defendants released after a felony charge was indeed less than 3 percent.[13]

Our data, in contrast, suggest that the bail-jumping rates have reached a level that demands attention. In New York, bail jumping is no longer a negligible event: among the 65 percent of all defendants "at risk" (those who made bail or were released without bail) the proportion of bail jumpers was 9.5 percent, which amounts to ($9.5 \times 0.65 =$) 6.5 percent of all defendants. To put that figure into per-

11. The term "jump bail" here includes also defendants released without bail (ROR) who failed to return to the court.

12. For some time now, however, the quarterly reports of the New York Criminal Justice Agency have been reporting bail-jumping figures.

13. See Wayne H. Thomas, *Bail Reform in America* (Berkeley: University of California Press, 1977), p. 104, table 36. The figure, however, is suspect. For the cities of San Diego, Philadelphia, and Hartford (these cities provide roughly three-fourths of all cases in the study) the cited statistics claim that zero percent fled the jurisdiction of the court. Allowing for the rounding-off effect, this means that less than ½ of 1 percent jumped bail. For Kansas City, which released only 37 percent of its felony defendants prior to trial, the bail-jumping rate is recorded as 18 percent. Such stark differences suggest error in the data compilation.

spective: in 1973 more defendants jumped bail (6.2 percent) than were eventually sent to prison for more than one year (5.4 percent).[14]

Figure 56 shows how little the bail-jumping rate varies with the amount of bail set and made; through all brackets, it hardly deviates from the 10 percent average. Since bail jumping is clearly an undesirable event, one would like to see its overall distribution. Figure 57 makes such an effort: it shows the jump rate for all defendants—whether at risk or not—for the twenty combinations of four criminal record and five arrest categories.

Only 3 percent of the bail jumpers had a prison record. Two-thirds of all bail jumpers had no record and were charged with the two lowest felony grades. From what we know from this study, these defendants had relatively little to fear from the court's disposition.

In the two categories that mark the potentially most dangerous offenders, there is hardly any bail jumping. Nobody charged with a class A crime jumped bail, and those defendants who had a jail or prison record form only 4 percent of all bail jumpers. This comes as a surprise. One would have expected the jump rate to increase among the defendants who faced the risk of a severe sentence rather than among these low-level defendants. The bulk of the bail jumpers clearly are the minor and less dangerous offenders.

At first glance one might see here the counterpart of the system's earlier error of releasing too few defendants and argue that it now releases too many. Our data suggest that this would be a poor answer. Unless one could pinpoint the future bail jumpers in advance—which one cannot—the error rate of unnecessary incarcerations would rise sub-

14. Determining the jump rate is a tricky business because nonappearances range in kind from the involuntary missing of a court appearance to the deliberate decision not to appear again. The issuance of a bench warrant seldom distinguishes the temporary from the permanent disappearance. The proper way of making the distinction is to define flight through the lapse of a sufficiently large time interval. As defined in this study, bail jumpers include all persons whose arrest warrant had not been returned by the time, at least several months later, when our data were collected and the case recorded as not disposed.

Fig. 56
Percent Defendants Jumping Bail by Amount of Bail
(All Defendants at Risk, i.e., Not in Jail)

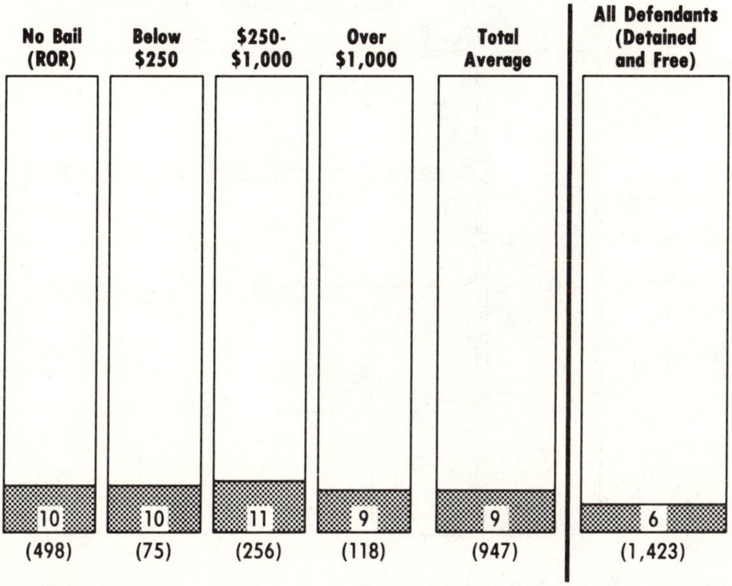

Source: 2000 Sample

Fig. 57
Distribution of Bail Jumpers (= 100 Percent) by Charged Crime Class and Defendant's Criminal Record

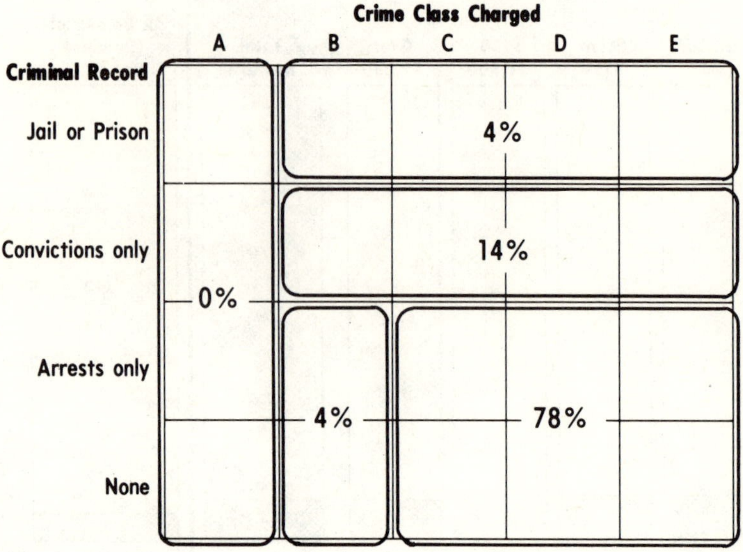

Source: 2000 Sample

stantially if one were to increase the number of pretrial detentions. For every foiled bail jumper one would have to keep ten defendants unnecessarily in jail because they would have appeared in court anyway. This follows from the finding that the average bail-jumping rate in all groups at risk is approximately 9 percent, about one out of every eleven cases.[15]

The data suggest a better remedy. The new bail jumpers, on the whole, face only minor charges and have either no record or only a minor one; they have, therefore, relatively little to fear from the law. The worst they face is a minor jail sentence. Bail jumping, therefore, is a decision to disappear not so much because the consequences of the pending criminal prosecution are too threatening but rather because the consequences of disappearing are negligible. The judge will issue a warrant for arrest, but to search out such defendants and execute the warrant could be time consuming, and the police probably assign a low priority to it. As a rule, these defendants reappear when they are arrested on another charge. A more thorough follow-up by the police of the court-issued warrants should bring some of the bail jumpers back.

Increasing the number of pretrial detentions seems to be the wrong solution because it invariably increases the number of unnecessary detentions, including defendants who eventually are not even convicted.

Congenital Defects of the Bail System

We now turn to the most serious congenital flaw of the system. A growing body of evidence suggests that some defendants unable to make bail are, for that reason alone, more likely to be convicted and, if convicted, more likely to be sentenced to jail. The discriminatory effect was observed for the first time serendipitously in the Vera experiment, designed to discover

15. See fig. 56, this chapter.

whether more defendants could be released without bail. The Vera findings were later buttressed by studies that formed the foundation of two major lawsuits attacking the constitutionality of the New York bail laws.[16] The data in the present study corroborate these earlier observations; in addition, they bring us closer to their explanation.

The first suggestion of the jail effect came from the raw comparison of the conviction and sentencing rates of defendants on bail and defendants in jail, as shown in figure 58. Many more of the defendants who could not make bail, and therefore remained in jail, were convicted than of the defendants who made bail. And of the convicted defendants, those in jail received a custody sentence more often than the defendants who made bail. Such raw comparison, however, does not prove discrimination because, in some cases, cause and effect may be reversed; for the defendants more likely to be severely sentenced if convicted, higher bail may have been set, which fewer of them could make.[17]

To separate cause from effect in this entangled situation is difficult. Perfect separation could come only from a controlled experiment in which for a group of defendants the decision to be released or detained would be made randomly (by lot) instead of on the basis of the defendant's ability to make bail. Selection by lot would insure that the two groups would be equal in every respect, except that one half, the experimental group, would be kept in jail, while the other half, the control group, would be out of jail. If under these controlled conditions the detained group would show a higher conviction and custody rate, the difference could be unambiguously ascribed to the fact of detention, because being detained or not being detained would be the only difference between the two groups.

Although such an experiment could not be permitted,

16. Bellamy v. Judges & Justices, 41 A.D.2d 196, *aff'd,* 32 N.Y.2d 866, 346 N.Y.S.2d 812, *remittur amended,* 33 N.Y.2d 632, 347 N.Y.S.2d 582 (1973); and Wallace v. Kern, 520 F.2d 400 (1975), *cert. denied,* 424 U.S. 1912 (1976).

17. The law indeed instructs the judge to do this. See point 8 of the statute reported in the section Setting and Making Bail above.

Fig. 58
Likelihood of Conviction, and Likelihood of Custody Sentence for Defendants on Bail and Defendants in Jail

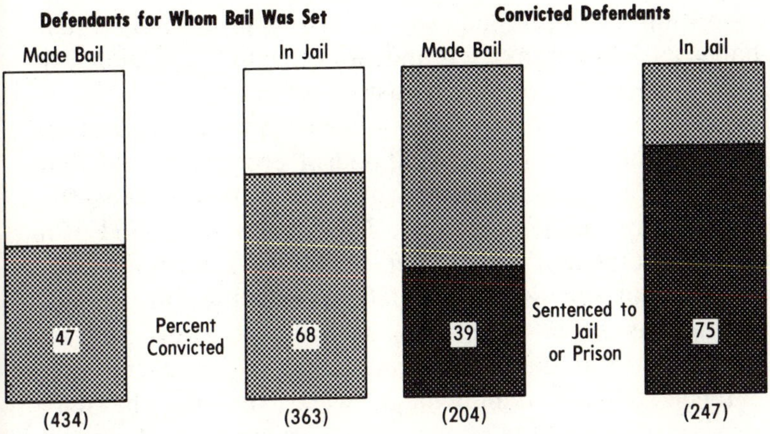

Source: 2000 Sample

at least not in the radical form outlined above, looking at its structure will aid in the analysis of the data available on this crucial issue. This analysis, modeled after that ideal, impossible experiment, proceeds by restricting comparison to more narrowly defined subgroups, that, except for the in-jail–out-of-jail difference, would have a reasonably equal chance of being convicted and, if convicted, a reasonably equal chance of receiving a custody sentence.

Of the two propositions—that defendants in pretrial detention have a higher likelihood of conviction and that they have a higher likelihood of a custody sentence—the latter is more understandable. The greater likelihood of a detained defendant's ending up with a jail sentence if convicted is not surprising. If a defendant at the time of sentencing has spent some time in jail, the court will be tempted to make the time served "legal" by imposing a jail sentence rather than allowing a "walk" sentence that may raise doubts about the merits of the earlier imposed pretrial detention.

We begin the analysis with a test of the second proposition. We present this effort in figure 59 by sorting the convicted defendants first by the seriousness of the crime they had been charged with and then by the seriousness of their criminal record. In each of these groups we then compare the frequency of a custody sentence among the defendants free on bail and among the defendants in jail. With the exception of the few defendants charged with a class A crime, the analysis reveals that in every class the defendants who could not make bail were worse off than their counterparts out of jail. The same is true for the four comparisons of defendants with similar criminal records.

We now turn to the analysis of the first, less understandable proposition that defendants in pretrial detention, for that reason alone, are more likely to be convicted than if they had been free on bail. Figure 60 shows the comparison of sixteen subgroups, the combinations of four crime classes and four types of criminal records. Compared with figure 59 this is a more elaborate analysis, made possible by the greater sample at our disposal; we can use all de-

Fig. 59
Different Likelihood of Custody Sentence (Percentage Points) for Defendants in Jail Compared to Defendants on Bail by Class of Charged Crime and Defendant's Record

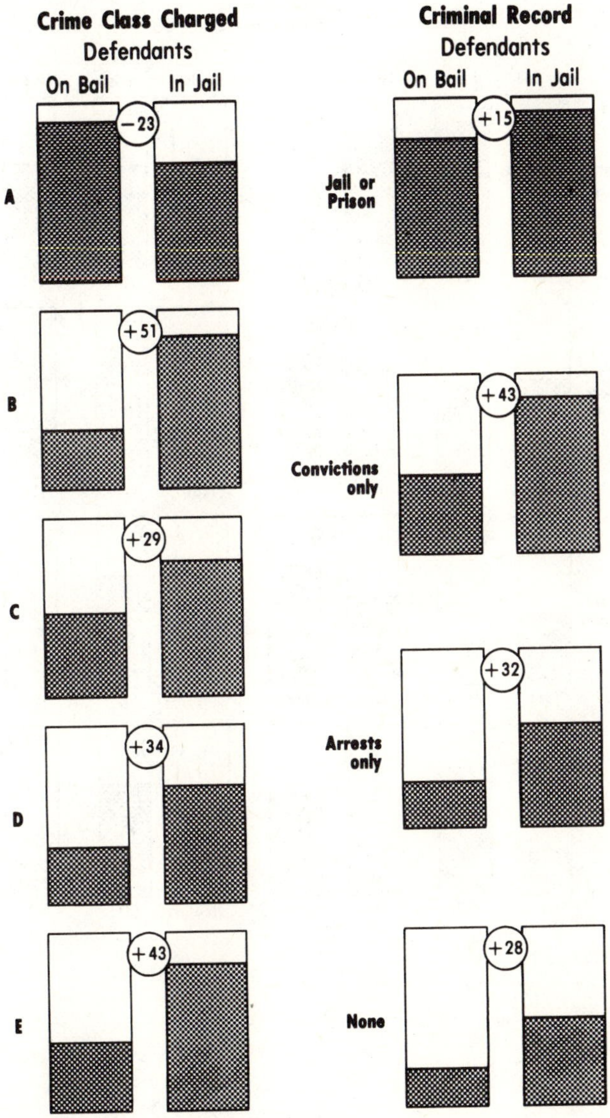

Source: 2000 Sample

Fig. 60
Different Likelihood of Conviction (Percentage Points) for Defendants in Jail Compared to Defendants on Bail by Class of Charged Crime and Defendant's Record

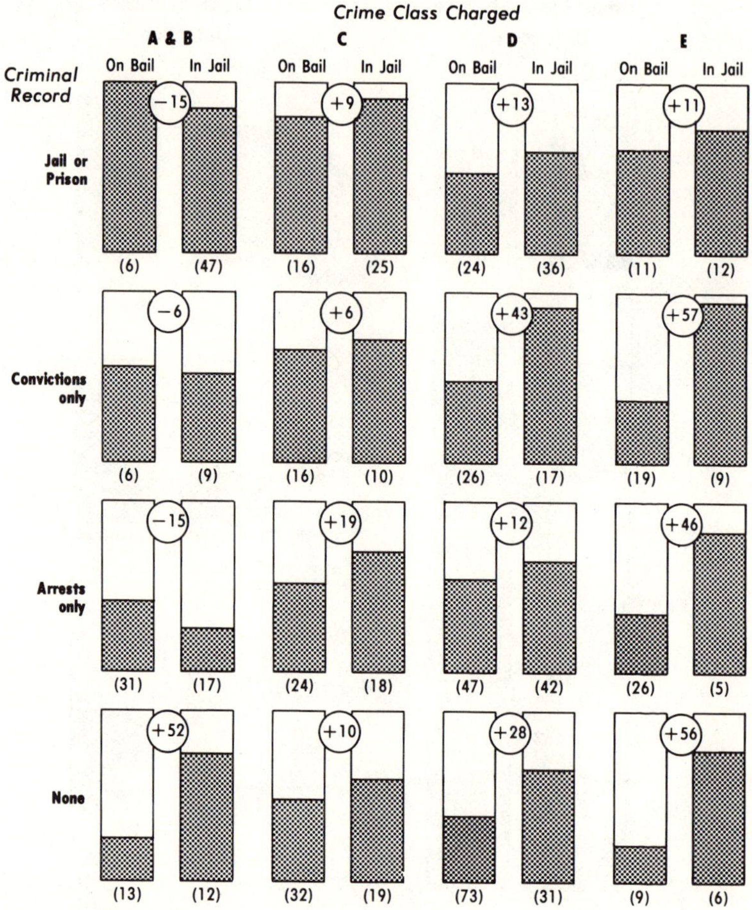

Source: 2000 Sample

fendants rather than only the convicted ones. In all but three of the sixteen cells of figure 60 comparison of defendants with the same record and charged with the same crime class shows that the defendants in custody have a higher conviction rate than the defendants who make bail. The three reversals occur again among defendants charged with the highest crime classes (A and B) who have at least a prior arrest record. The reversal, in spite of the small sample, makes sense; when the stakes are very high, being in jail will make little difference for the outcome.

There is, nevertheless, a loophole left in the evidence of figure 60. The judge may set higher bail for defendants against whom the evidence is strong. If he does that, we must not be surprised that defendants who stay in jail are more often convicted.

In response to this objection, figure 61 shows, in addition to the grouping by criminal record, the grouping by the dollar range within which bail was set. Again, in all but two groups the defendants who could not make bail have higher conviction rates than those who could. The puzzle is why this should be so. A 1971 study advanced the following hypothesis:

> One factor which might explain differences in guilty findings is that the incarcerated defendant cannot consult with his lawyer as freely or as often as the person not detained. Neither is he free to prepare his case fully, to gather witnesses, or to establish an alibi. . . .
>
> . . . Detainees also are less able to afford the service of paid investigators, or the expense of witnesses. Incarcerated defendants are also more readily available to law enforcement officials for involuntary participation in lineups and other police processes that may increase the likelihood of a finding of guilt. Finally, defendants who come into court in the custody of police officers, stripped of their self-confidence by detention, and wearing prison clothes or the clothes in which they were arrested, may be prejudiced in the eyes of the jury.[18]

18. Arthur R. Angel, Eric D. Green, Henry R. Kaufman, and Eric E. Van Loon, "Preventive Detention: An Empirical Analysis," *Harvard Civil Rights, Civil Liberties Law Review* 6 (1971): 289, 348–49.

Fig. 61
Different Likelihood of Conviction (Percentage Points) for Defendants in Jail Compared to Defendants on Bail by Amount of Bail and Defendant's Record

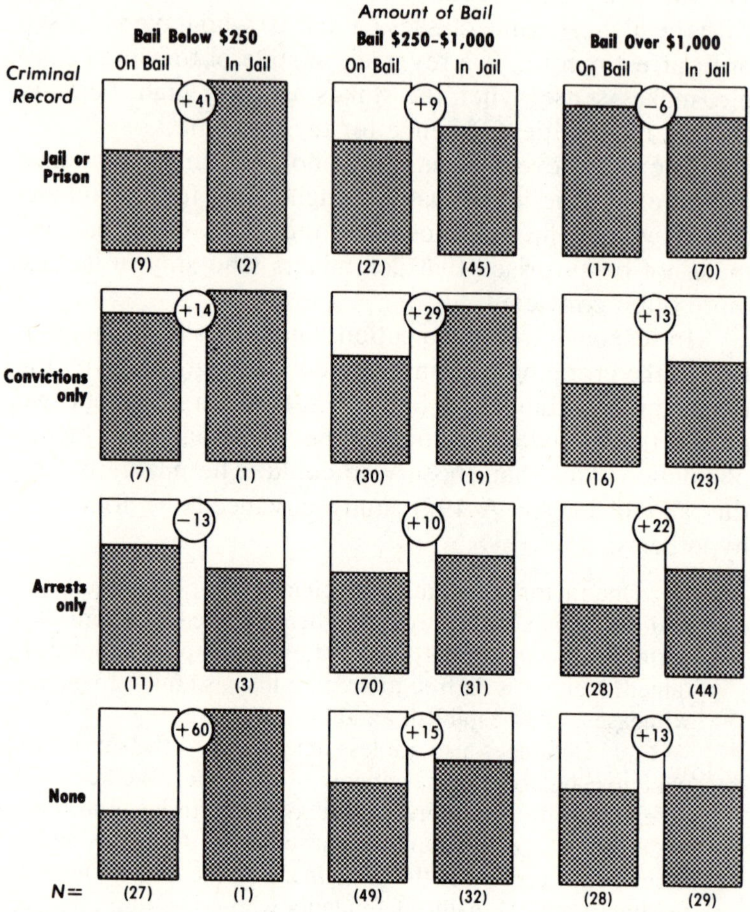

Source: 2000 Sample

The data in the present study suggest a different or at least a supplementary explanation: that the bargaining power of a defendant is reduced when he is in jail and, conversely, that the bargaining power of the prosecutor is reduced when the defendant is free on bail.

The issue comes up as follows. The defendant in jail is told one day by his lawyer: "The D.A. has agreed to a jail sentence of such and such length if you plead guilty," or words to that effect. Often that sentence will be equal to the time spent in pretrial detention so that the defendant would be freed immediately upon pleading guilty. Such a sentence is dubbed "time served." If the offered sentence were to exceed somewhat the time spent in pretrial detention, the guilty plea would secure at least an early release. This is an incentive to pleading guilty which the defendant who made bail does not have. As a result, every so often a guilty plea is given by a defendant in jail who would have refused such a plea had he not been in jail. In some cases this refusal will eventually be rewarded by the prosecutor's decision to dismiss the case rather than to try it: "If the defendant had not pleaded guilty to a B misdemeanor, the case would have been dismissed; the complaining witness, herself a junkie with a record, refused to come to court" (assistant district attorney in case 198). And every so often, the defendant free on bail, before pleading guilty, will be able to negotiate for a nonprison sentence, where under equal circumstances the defendant in custody will accept "time served."[19] The following cases illustrate the "time served" offer:

> When a transit policeman entered an IRT subway train, he saw two youths standing at the car door. They were the only passengers in the car. As he moved into the car, the

19. There is a hint in our data that being in jail may also affect the defendant's decision whether to go to trial or to plead guilty at all.

Percent of Defendants Going to Trial

Defendants	Percent	Approximate N
Free on bail	3.3	425
In jail	1.7	381

policeman saw a brown paper bag with a handgun; he said he could see the contents from where he stood. On the opposite seat, under some newspapers, he discovered a pistol. The gun was in operating condition. The two youths were charged with possession of a prohibited weapon. Bail was set, which the defendant (in our sample) could not make; the codefendant made bail and was eventually indicted on a different charge and separated from the case. Eventually, the defendant pleaded guilty against an offer of "time served." [Case 50]

The defendant and three unapprehended accomplices were charged with robbery at knife point. A knife had been found at the scene of the crime but it could not be linked up with the defendant. No blood had been found on the weapon, no property was found on the defendant, who had been apprehended near the scene of the crime, though the assistant district attorney did not know how close. Defendant and complainant had known one another and probably had been lovers. The case was a year old when it was evaluated for disposition. During all that time, the defendant had been in jail. The prosecutor thought the case weak; he interviewed the complainant prior to disposition and found that he had changed his testimony. There were also contradictions between complaint and indictment. On the basis of these facts, the prosecutor offered a plea to a D felony and a sentence of "time served," and the defendant accepted. [Case 96]

The complainant was the common-law wife of the defendant. There had been a fight the night before. When the woman complained to the police and the defendant was questioned, he went back to her and hit her over the head with a soda-water bottle. He was charged with assault and possession of a dangerous instrument. He could not make bail. After spending some time in jail, he pleaded guilty to assault in the third degree, an A misdemeanor. He received a five-month sentence because he had a record of some twenty convictions. Since the complaining witness had withdrawn, there is a good chance that the case would have been dismissed had the defendant not been in jail. [Case 281]

We should expect the effect of being in jail to be particularly large among defendants in the lower sentence brackets were a jail sentence, especially a time-served sentence, and a walk sentence are plausible alternatives. Looking back at figure 61, we find this to be the case. The differences are lowest (even negative) after arrests for the most serious crimes and the most serious prior record, and they are highest around the lower right-hand corner where the expected sentence will be modest.

The effect of pretrial detention is minimal where serious crimes are concerned; the effect is likely to grow where the crime is minor. The differential effect is aggravated if the prosecutor is less eager to go to trial. Since that eagerness is likely to decline with the seriousness of the defense, this is another reason why the effect of pretrial detention on conviction rates is likely to be greatest where the crime is least serious. For these reasons, an analogous study among defendants charged with a misdemeanor instead of a felony should reveal an even greater effect of pretrial detention on the likelihood of conviction.[20]

Statistical Concerns

It was one of the purposes of this book to put before the concerned reader some of the statistics the law enforcement system should have at its disposal anytime and everywhere.

The overall task consists of two distinct but overlapping parts. Counting and analyzing the incidence of crime is one core element of the endeavor; to perceive with clarity the operation of the enforcement process is the other one. No institution of such complexity can understand and manage itself unless it keeps lucid records of its transactions. Law enforcement keeps few such records and has managed its performance accordingly.

The statistics it produces, with some notable exceptions, far from illuminating the system's complexity, barely

20. The effect should be enlarged by a problem that has long plagued the New York court system: the notorious difficulty of obtaining a courtroom for misdemeanor trials.

circumscribes its outlines. Normally, law enforcement reports on its activities in four separate layers:

1. Crimes reported to (and by) the police.
2. Arrests made and reported by the police.
3. Prosecution, trials, convictions, sentences (occasionally) reported by the courts.
4. Prisoners held in correctional institutions, reported by these institutions.

In recent years, the count of crimes reported to the police has been supplemented through sample surveys of the general public:

5. Victimization surveys designed to obtain more detailed descriptions of the counted crimes as well as a count of the committed crimes not reported to the police.

All five data layers have engendered a long list of criticisms and suggestions for improvement. But their main shortcoming is that they allow only what one might call horizontal perspectives, and fail to link these layers by tracing the individual offender on his itinerary through the system and his possible return to it.

The first linkage problem concerns the count of crime as reported to and by the police (1), and the count of the unreported crime through the victimization surveys (5). The victimization surveys have presently been reduced to a holding level because of their great costs and an as yet insufficiently analyzed yield. By revealing a substantial amount of unreported crime, roughly again as large as the amount reported, and by allowing us to see the crime victims with clarity, they have made an important contribution to our knowledge. But the manner in which they have been collected and categorized has made it difficult to link the unreported crimes meaningfully to the reported ones. It might be possible to restructure the victimization surveys in a way that facilitates their linkage to the Uniform Crime Reports. Such linkage would make long-range statistical plans more effective by allowing them to consider the total crime count as being composed of two parts not only theoretically but operationally: the number of crimes reported to the police and the then no longer dark numbers of unreported crimes, expressed, if the data allow this, in more or less constant ratios of the reported crimes.

The next linkage problem awaiting solution is that between reported crimes (1) and arrests (2). The arrest rate and the closely related clearance rate are crucial parameters of the law enforcement system. If properly constructed they could measure both the efficiency of the police operations and the offender's risk of arrest. Their proper construction will have to consider not only the gross characteristics of the crime but, as we saw, also such important refinements as to whether the offender was a stranger or not. Many police departments have this and other relevant information readily available but have as yet to make full use of it.

For the task of linking arrests (2) with the disposition in the criminal courts of first instance (3), the statistics in this book may serve as a starting point. It will have to be extended to the appeals process and, of course, to the prison statistics (4). Ironically, the difference between the sentence imposed on an offender and the sentence he actually serves is well known to him and his fellow prisoners, but we know little about it. By counting the number of inmates on certain dates, the prison statistics, moreover, are unable to tell us whether an increase in their number reflects longer sentences for the same number of prisoners, or more prisoners for the same lengths of sentences.

The final linkage problem will be the unification of enforcement statistics within the state and ultimately its coordination with other states. It is a difficult task because law enforcement is entrusted to ten thousand different power centers, local police departments, elected prosecutors, state and federal courts and prisons, each with some degree of operational autonomy.

Generally, the statistics of law enforcement is in an unsatisfactory condition. A few states have started on the road toward an integrated longitudinal statistics. The State of California, often a leader in the field, is now publishing an admirably composed and illustrated report on its disposition of adult felony arrests. The main dimensions of that process are reassuringly close to the New York data.[21]

In addition to this traditional pattern is a system developed since our study began, by INSLAW, the Washington, D.C.–based Institute for Law and Social Research. It is called PROMIS, short for Prosecutor's Management Information System, and has been adopted by prosecutors in many major cities. That system records for each defendant the police action, the pertinent information on the defendant, the charged crime, the prosecutor's own decisions and those of the court. And if a defendant returns into the system through re-arrest, a cumulative record is developed. Until such time as the states have established an integrated offender-based recording system, PROMIS offers a valuable interim solution. Its data base, however broad it is, requires extension into the details of the crucial plea bargaining process. To record these sensitive details is a difficult assignment for the recorder of the PROMIS data, the prosecutor, who has a stake in defending the merits of his bargains.

The task of coordination continues to be urgent and should be pursued by a permanent task force in which representatives of the administrative power centers work jointly with the appropriate technicians and academicians.

The guiding principle of such a task force must be the potential usefulness of the developed statistics both for short-range operational insights and for basic criminological and operational studies with long-range returns. Since the main concern here is with administrative statistics, counterconsiderations of costs will play a major role. The task force, therefore, might begin its labors by suggesting a reform that would cost little and increase sharply the usefulness of the collected data: standardization that would facilitate linkage between the various statistical systems now in operation without substantially enlarging the re-

21. Adult Felony Arrest Dispositions, Sacramento Division of Law Enforcement, California Department of Justice.

cording job. Occasionally, however, minor additions in the collected information, such as whether the offender was a stranger, will substantially increase the total yield.

Most important, the task force should dispel the notion that all statistical operations are costly because once installed they must continue forever. The task force should develop the great potential of one-time or periodic sampling operations that will provide valuable insights at much reduced costs. Finally, the task force should make an effort to overcome the parochial character of law enforcement, which makes learning from experiences elsewhere a rare event.

In the end, there will be a limit to the data one can reasonably expect from the system. For the time being, however, that limit is not even in sight.

The streamlined record keeping of the law enforcement system is bound to affect its quality. Knowing with some precision where the system malfunctions and where it improves will encourage effective reform and discourage cosmetic change. Precise record keeping will then also invite the use of that most powerful and much too neglected instrument of reform, the controlled experiment.[22] Without it, one seldom knows what if anything has been accomplished by a reform. By insisting that all reforms are accompanied by a controlled experiment, we will learn to separate the wheat from the chaff.[23]

22. See, e.g., n. 54 in Chap. 1.

23. See H. Zeisel, "The New York Expert Testimony Project: Some Reflections on Legal Experiments," *Stanford Law Review* 8 (1956): 730. Also see chap. 21, "The Case for the Official Experiment," in H. Zeisel, H. Kalven, Jr., B. Buchholz, *Delay in the Court,* 2d ed. (Westport, Conn.: Greenwood Press, 1979; originally published 1959); H. Zeisel, "Reflections on Experimental Techniques in the Law," *Journal of Legal Studies* 2 (1973): 107. The Federal Judicial Center has published a very useful overview of the promises and problems of that important instrument; see *Experimentation in the Law* (Washington, D.C.: Government Printing Office, 1981).

Afterword

The Lapse of Time

When the data on which this book is based were collected in 1973 and 1974 in New York City, I wondered how typical New York's law enforcement system was of American law enforcement in general. And when this book was ready to go press there was the second concern: whether the data from the early seventies would still be pertinent to the law enforcement problems of our day.

Both concerns, as it turned out, were unwarranted. As we saw in Chapter 1, law enforcement in New York is not too different from law enforcement in other American cities, and in important respects not even too different from law enforcement patterns in other Western countries. And as the comparisons of some 1973 New York law enforcement data with corresponding 1979 data show, the intervening years have changed little.

The continuous concern about our inability to control crime has brought many reforms to the criminal court system of New York City since the time of our study. The prosecution staffs were greatly expanded; early screening of cases was instituted to assess their importance and strength shortly after their arrival in the system; at the formidable annual cost of some 34 million dollars, forty-five new trial parts were added to the Supreme Courts; and recently even efforts have begun to help strengthen the evidence in felony arrests by early cooperation between prosecution and police.

There was some cumulative effect of these measures,

but it was small. Moreover, in appraising its magnitude one must keep in mind that some of our disposition data for the years 1971 through 1973 still fell into a period in which the system was engaged in a radical effort to clear its backlog.

The basis for assessing the change between 1971–73 and 1979–80 is still a narrow one because the criminal court system has as yet no record system that would duplicate our data. The system has essentially two sets of data: first for the whole city, the dispositions of all felony indictments in the Supreme Court, second for New York County (Manhattan), the complete record of dispositions both for the Supreme Court and the lower Criminal Court. These data sets allow two comparisons.

Figure 62 compares the Supreme Court dispositions as proportions of all felony arrests for 1973 and 1979.

In both years, slightly over 20 percent of all felony arrests were disposed of in the Supreme Court, which alone can convict of a felony. The proportion of dismissals and acquittals has hardly changed; the structure of the guilty findings, however, has shifted. The proportion of cases going to trial in the Supreme Court has nearly doubled, and as a result the number of convictions after trial has increased. In both years, close to 80 percent of the defendants who reached the Supreme Court pleaded guilty. But the proportion of defendants allowed to plead guilty to a misdemeanor after the case had reached the Supreme Court declined from 4.6 to 1.3 percent. Since only the Supreme Court can convict for a felony, this means that the proportion of all defendants found guilty of a felony has increased from (12.4 + 0.8 =) 13.2 percent to (13.3 + 1.9 =) 15.2 percent, if we make the probably not completely correct assumption for both years that all convictions after trial in the Supreme Court resulted in felony convictions.

Figure 63 compares for the borough of Manhattan (New York County) the disposition of all felony arrests made in 1971 with the felony arrest dispositions made in 1978.

In Manhattan, the proportion of dismissals has de-

Fig. 62
Disposition of Felony Arrests in New York City: 1973 Compared to 1979

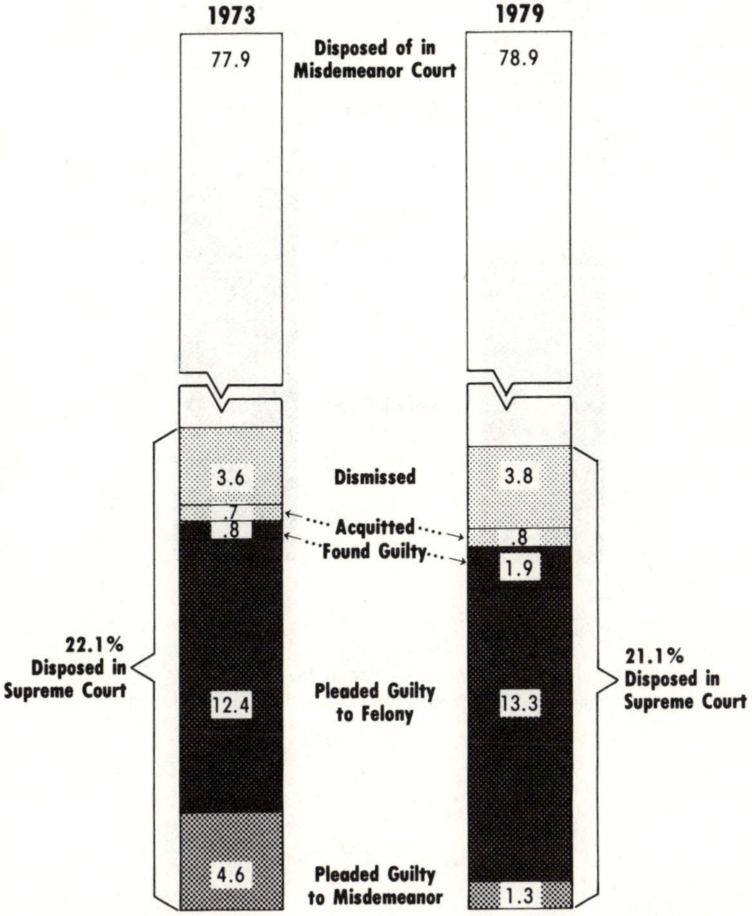

Source: N.Y. Criminal Court System

Fig. 63
Disposition of Felony Arrests in New York County:
1978 Compared to 1971–73

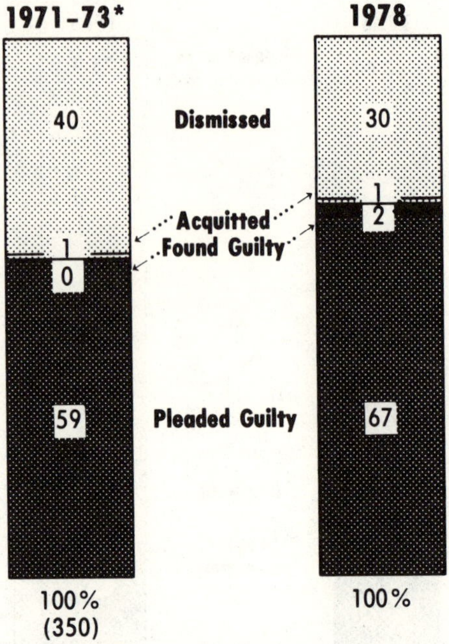

*of the Felony arrests made in 1971
Sources: 2000 Sample (1971–73), PROMIS tabulations (1978)

clined from 40 to 30 percent. The proportion of convictions has correspondingly grown from 59 to 69 percent. Also the proportion of felony arrests disposed of by trial in the Supreme Court has increased somewhat from roughly 1 percent to 3 percent of all dispositions.

It is, however, difficult to decide how much of this change is due to the reforms enacted during the intervening years and how much to the fact that during the years of our study the system had made a major effort to clear the accumulated backlog of cases.

As this book is about to go press, an episode is being reported that shows how slowly things change. The event that provided the first stimulus for the present book was an address by the police commissioner in which he blamed the courts for failing to convict the offenders brought to them, and the response of the courts which blamed the police for failing to provide sufficient proof of the charged offenses.[1] On page 1 of the *New York Times* of May 16, 1981, we read, " . . . city police officials and . . . the Manhattan District Attorney, have engaged in some public disputes, each side blaming the other for the gap between the number of felony arrests made by the police and the smaller number of felony complaints brought by the prosecutor's office."

The overall stability of the law enforcement system is the more remarkable since so many of its decisions appear to be discretionary. This suggests that the discretion is guided in turn by rules whose stability is insured by institutional constraints, primarily by the capacity limits of the various segments of the system—the prosecution staff, the defense lawyers available for the great majority of indigent defendants, the number of judges and courtrooms available for trying cases, and even the limits on the capacity of jails and prisons. These institutional constraints translate themselves into guide lines for the exercise of discretion which, in the prosecutor's office, occasionally attain explicit formulation.

In any event, we can be confident that most of the

1. See n. 3 in Introduction.

findings of the present study are valid for our day and in all likelihood for some days to come

Thanks

When I began this study, I was very much a novice in this field of criminology and law enforcement. Whatever wisdom I have since acquired I owe to the data in this book and to colleagues and friends, students in the field, who over the years have read drafts of the manuscript and in conversations and correspondence have offered criticism and reflections.

There is first of all my colleague and friend Frank Zimring, who has been an inexhaustible source of knowledge and encouragement. As directors of the Center for Criminal Justice Studies, moreover, he and Norval Morris have generously financed the last phase of this study. Others, not as close by, but always ready to help, have shared with me their experience and wisdom: Frank Allen of the University of Michigan, Albert Blumstein of the Carnegie Mellon University, Edith Flynn of North Eastern University, Brian Forst of the Washington Institute for Law and Social Research, Daniel Glaser of the University of Southern California, Peter Greenwood and Joe Chaiken of the Rand Corporation, Don McIntyre of the American Bar Foundation, Lloyd Ohlin of Harvard, Albert Reiss of Yale, Leslie Wilkins of State University of New York at Albany, and Marvin Wolfgang of the University of Pennsylvania. None of them, though, must be held responsible for the shortcomings of this book.

I am indebted to John McWillie for his critical reading of parts of the manuscript. He was a member of the VERA team when this study began and, in his present capacity as officer of the city's Criminal Justice Coordinating Council, has lived with New York City's law enforcement system ever since.

My particular thanks go to Darryl Beck, the best chart maker I have ever met, who helped me to put into perfect shape the vision of a book in which statistical tables are replaced by graphs. My colleague Spencer Kimball, the former director of the American Bar Foundation, was kind enough to prepublish earlier versions of sections of the book in the foundation's research journal; I am much indebted to him and to the journal's managing editor Bette Sikes.

My gratitude goes also to Helen Flint, the ever helpful secretary of the Center for Criminal Justice Studies, and to Mildred South, Harry Kalven's and my long-time secretary and friend, who with infinite skill and patience has typed and retyped this manuscript, as she had done for two earlier books, until it was ready.

This is also the proper place to recall my collaborators in the research department I founded at the Vera Institute of Justice. Lucy Friedman and Jessica deGrazia had the arduous task of organizing and supervising the data gathering for this study. Ilene Asner, Helen Breshinsky, Irene Finel, Barry Friedman, Lee Pollack, Carole Reynolds, Anthony Salzman, Lennie Schlossberg, Christie Schmidt, and Leonard Schrier did the actual field work. For many months they searched the often scattered files, pursued busy policemen, prosecuting attorneys, defense counsel, and judges. They gave generously of their time; their cooperation above all made this study possible. I also want to preserve the memory of my friend Paul Lazarsfeld's efforts to resolve some of the political difficulties the project faced at one time.

My special thanks to Sgt. McGuire of the New York City Police Department for sharing with me some of his statistical data; to Ellen Fredell, an alumna of our law school, who with circumspection and tolerant patience made the computer tapes obey every analytical whim.

Last but not least, I want to thank three good and wise friends for their counsel at various decision points of my labors: Robert Merton, Cuthbert Daniel, and Nathan Leites.

Index*

*The detailed Contents (pp. vii–viii) and the List of Figures (pp. ix–xiii) make an index of subject matters unnecessary.